Nancy Drew® and Company

Nancy Drew® and Company:

Culture, Gender, and Girls' Series

edited by

Sherrie A. Inness

Bowling Green State University Popular Press
Bowling Green, OH 43403

Nancy Drew is a registered trademark of Simon & Schuster, Inc. Its use
herein is by permission of the publishers.

Copyright © 1997 Bowling Green State University Popular Press

Library of Congress Cataloging-in-Publication Data
Nancy Drew and company : culture, gender, and girls' series / edited
   by Sherrie A. Inness.
       p.   cm.
   Includes bibliographical references and index.
   ISBN 0-87972-735-7 (clothbound). -- ISBN 0-87972-736-5 (pbk.)
   1. Children's stories, American--History and criticism. 2. Children's
literature in series--Bibliography. 3. Popular culture--United States--
History. 4. Girls--United States--Books and reading. 5. Drew, Nancy
(Fictitious character) 6. Sex role in literature. 7. Girls in literature.
I. Inness, Sherrie A.
PS374.G55N36   1996
813'.5099282--dc21   96-37500
                                                                   CIP

Cover design by Dumm Art

For my mother

Contents

Acknowledgments

I would like to thank a number of people who have read drafts of essays included in this collection, including Ruth Ebelke, Faye Parker Flavin, Michele Lloyd, and Annette Shook.

My thanks go to my friends, among them Alice Adams, Martina Barash, Nikki Barry, Cathy Ebelke, Valija Evalds, Julie Hucke, Kate Johnson, Debra Mandel, Gillian O'Driscoll, Cindy Reuther, Wendy Walters, and my colleagues at Miami University. I also wish to acknowledge the institutional support I received from a number of sources. An NEH Summer Seminar directed by Professor John Seelye offered financial and intellectual support for one summer when I was working on this project. The participants in this seminar, Stephen Cernek, Patricia Derby, Richard Flynn, Dona Helmer, Bruce Henderson, Winona Howe, Myra Jones, Elizabeth Keyser, Patricia Pace, Anne Phillips, and Jan Susina, provided a great many thoughtful insights into my own work in children's literature. Miami University generously allowed me a Summer Research Appointment and an Assigned Research Appointment for one semester, both of which allowed me time to develop this project.

It is impossible to name all the scholars who have influenced and enriched my own work in girls' reading and culture, but I would like to mention a few who have been important: Kathleen Chamberlain, Kirsten Drotner, Jerry Griswold, Peter Hunt, Deidre Johnson, Sally Mitchell, Claudia Nelson, Perry Nodelman, Penny Tinkler, and Lynne Vallone.

I would like to end by thanking my parents and my sister for their continuing support.

For permission to include revised versions of essays that have been published elsewhere, I wish to acknowledge the following journal and book:

Sherrie A. Inness. "Girl Scouts, Camp Fire Girls, and Woodcraft Girls: The Ideology of Girls' Scouting Novels, 1910-1935." *Continuities in Popular Culture: The Present in the Past and the Past in the Present and Future.* Ed. Ray B. Browne and Ronald J. Ambrosetti. Bowling Green: Bowling Green Popular Press, 1993. 229-40.

Nancy Tillman Romalov. "Mobile Heroines: Early Twentieth-Century Girls' Automobile Series." *Journal of Popular Culture* 28.4 (1995): 231-43.

Introduction

You can't escape them. They are everywhere. In bookstore after bookstore, girls' series books crowd the shelves, competing for space. Whether Sweet Valley High books, Outdoor Girl adventures, Nancy Drew mysteries, Cherry Ames nursing stories, or hundreds of other books, girls' series books have been a dominant presence in children's literature throughout this century, a trend that shows no sign of abating. The names of the heroines change; they drive different cars and pursue different adventures, but the plots are essentially formulaic. The leading character (with or without her pals) is remarkably capable, gorgeous, and far more intelligent than any adult. Because of her innate ability, this paragon is able to solve mysteries, fly planes, cure the ill, and perform many other exploits with incredible ease, not even breaking into a sweat. Although there are some variations to this dominant character, the heroines of girls' series are similar in many ways.

What explains the long-lasting allure of girls' series and their heroines? Why have these books been phenomenally popular throughout the century? What messages about societal values do the books contain? How do the books help socialize young women? These are a few of the questions that the essays in this collection try to answer, as we attempt to decipher clues that might baffle anyone (except Nancy Drew).

Despite their prevalence in the twentieth century, girls' series have been studied with less frequency than one might expect.[1] Girls' reading has long been considered unimportant when compared to adult reading. Girls' series books have been quadruple outcasts from critical circles because they are written for young readers, are targeted at girls, are popular reading, and, even worse, are series books, which often have been regarded with disdain by literary critics.[2] This situation is slowly changing as a greater number of scholars, many of them influenced by feminist philosophies, recognize that studying girls' reading is an important building block in understanding how girls are socialized. As critical theory plays an ever-increasing role in the study of children's literature, a greater number of scholars are scrutinizing how popular reading reinforces cultural ideologies.[3] Many of these critics also recognize that girls' interests have too long been marginalized as less significant than those of boys.[4] Despite the current 1990s upswing in studying girls' cul-

1

ture, series books have continued to languish as outsiders, little regarded except in passing: Few girls' series characters, except for Nancy Drew, have received extensive scholarly attention. This collection seeks to redress the paucity of research on girls' series. I hope that the essays in this collection will provide a starting point for future scholarship on girls' series and their importance in this century and beyond.

One of the reasons I have brought these essays together is that I believe it is important to recognize the cultural significance of girls' series and the importance of *all* children's literature, which has long been slighted, despite the attempts of some scholars to emphasize its continuing importance in American culture. As Jerry Griswold points out in his influential study *Audacious Kids: Coming of Age in America's Classic Children's Books* (1992): "[In the United States] Children's Literature is not marginal, but squarely within our central literary tradition" (241). Although Griswold is writing specifically about well-known children's books by authors such as Louisa May Alcott or Mark Twain, his words also apply to girls' series, which have had a central place in girls' reading experiences throughout the century. Any literary genre that can last over a century and continue to thrive deserves critical attention, I believe, because it is clearly accomplishing important cultural work.

At this point it is essential to clarify one important term: series book. The difficulties of defining this seemingly simple term are tremendous and have yet to be solved in a completely satisfactory manner. The biggest problem comes in differentiating between books in a series (the Little House books) and series books (Nancy Drew and her ilk). There are some typical stylistic differences between the two. Series books are more apt to take place in a timeless world where the characters never grow any older or only grow older in the most gradual fashion (think of Nancy Drew); in books in a series, the characters generally age as real people do. The plots of series books are likely to be more formulaic than those of books in a series. In series books, characters are typically less fully developed, less rounded, than characters in books in series. These are a few of the distinctions that may be drawn between series books and books in a series, though a hard and fast distinction between the two types should not be made, since books have a disturbing fashion of slipping over the lines. For instance, L. M. Montgomery's *Anne of Green Gables* is considered a classic of children's literature and might be considered a book in a series (which is typically more highly regarded from a critical standpoint than a series book). Yet the other Anne books are of significantly less literary value than *Anne of Green Gables* and were marketed as popular literature; one could call them series books. I would advise against insisting upon the distinct difference between books in a series and series books; instead, it is perhaps more reasonable to study the interplay and interweaving of the two styles.

Because of the extreme variability of the girls' series book throughout the century, it is not possible or even desirable to come up with a definition of a series book that encompasses *all* the works that have been published. It is more feasible to list the characteristics that some girls' series books share, with the caveat that my readers always will be able to find books that fail to adhere to these guidelines. Girls' series typically star a girl, usually but not always a teenager, who, with or without friends, has exciting adventure after exciting adventure in a series of books that focus on her experiences. Vicki Barr, Trixie Belden, Ruth Fielding, Nancy Drew, Judy Bolton, Cherry Ames, Marjorie Dean, Betty Wales, Beverly Gray, Ruth Darrow, Ann Bartlett, and Ann Sterling are only a few of the numerous heroines from series books whose exploits fill many volumes. Teams of girls are also popular, as is clear from the scads of books that chronicle the adventures of the Automobile Girls, the Adventure Girls, the Camp Fire Girls, the College Girls, the Moving Picture Girls, the Radio Girls, the Red Cross Girls, the Motor Maids, and many others. In book after book, girls' series recount the exploits of heroines who are often superior to any girl in real life, whether that might entail being stronger, more beautiful, or more intelligent. In depicting the lives of these superior beings, girls' series books typically create a world that is full of adventure and intrigue, but also a world that is reassuringly knowable: Nancy Drew is not going to get injured seriously in a car accident; Cherry Ames is not going to discover that she has cancer. The heroines of series books are as tough as Teflon; they endure throughout the decades, perhaps one of the reasons for their appeal, while mere mortals must succumb to the ravages of time.

The girls' series book did not spring into being in the twentieth century fully formed, like Athena from Zeus's brow. It had precursors throughout the 1800s, some of the earliest being the Rollo stories by Jacob Abbott, a Congregational minister, who began publishing the series in 1835. Although his books were popular, their content was fairly tame. Rollo might take a trip or have a mild adventure, but he was usually accompanied by adults who would give him long preachy lectures on the importance of growing up to be a good man. Yawn. The books were not targeted particularly at girls; the girls' series had yet to arise.

The Rollo series offered no glimpse of what was to come as children's books, particularly those targeted at boys, became increasingly more adventuresome, as in the hundred-plus books authored by William Taylor Adams (writing as "Oliver Optic"). In book after book, Adams told tales of danger and daring-do, featuring stalwart young white men as heroes, who were a match for anyone who confronted them. In a similar vein, Horatio Alger's rags-to-riches books featured a whole city full of noble, but ragged, young men, each eager to accomplish the good deed that would bring him his fortune when he was discovered to be a missing heir or perhaps the scion to a large industrial fortune. Anne Scott MacLeod describes some of the components that made up Optic's, Alger's, and other early boys' series books: "series books were long on action, if short on credibility, and offered a welcome change from the quiet domestic tales that otherwise dominated the children's market" (119-20). With this winning combination, both Adams and Alger dominated the series book field in the late nineteenth century and achieved great popularity, but their books were targeted at boys. When a girl or woman did dare to step into an Oliver Optic or Horatio Alger tale, she was likely to be someone's sister or mother, and never had a chance to do much, except, perhaps, to marry the hero.

Along with the boys' adventure series that flourished in the second part of the nineteenth century, another early precursor of the girls' series was the dime novel, which was one of the most popular forms of reading in this period. Produced by the thousands, dime novels were cheap, flimsy booklets published largely by the company Beadle and Adams. They were marketed originally to adults, but quickly became the province of boys, too. Chock-full of desperadoes, cowboys, Indians, and detectives, dime novels were the 1800s version of the comic book, and boys flocked to them. Girls, however, were only rarely depicted in dime novels and had far less adventuresome roles than the men and boys who filled the cheap novels. Girls were still being shunted to the side and told to read the religious or domestic novels that were prevalent in the nineteenth century and that featured far tamer exploits than the stirring adventures of the boys' stories.

But girl readers were not going to be left standing in the wings for long, as publishers began to recognize that girls could be a lucrative market for popular reading. One of the earliest series to be addressed to a young female audience was Martha Finley's saga of Elsie Dinsmore (1867-1909). Elsie Dinsmore is no Nancy Drew or Judy Bolton. Elsie is good, sweet, kind, considerate, and boring. Her adventures are mild, not wild, yet they managed to fill many volumes that sold well, showing the marketing possibilities of the series format for girls. But it took another book to truly display the potentially lucrative nature of girls' series books: Louisa May Alcott's *Little Women* (1868). Not only was the first book popular, but so were the volumes that continued to follow the exploits of Jo and her sisters. After the success of Elsie and the March girls, the series book for girls became a staple of the children's book business. Although girls' series books rarely sold in the same large numbers as boys' books (Nancy Drew being a rare exception), they still sold well, which encouraged numerous book companies to venture into publishing girls' series.

The early years of the twentieth century saw the sudden flowering of a specialized form of juvenile literature, the serial novels written for and about adolescent girls. From 1900 to 1917, literally dozens of new series emerged to chronicle the adventures of teenage heroines at school, at play, at work, and in what was invariably called "The Great Outdoors." (Smith 155)

In the first three decades of the twentieth century, both girls' and boys' series expanded tremendously and dozens of separate series were published, many of them by the Stratemeyer Syndicate, which produced a large number of series, including the Nancy Drew books.[5] With the aid of the Syndicate, the series was well on its way to becoming a rationalized commodity, written by a stable of ghost writers who would churn out books similar in content and style. Although these books were often the bane of librarians and educators who considered them "trash," girls and boys bought and read them by the score.

After the golden age of series books from 1900 to 1930, series books would never again be so prominent a force, as they had to share their audience's attention with an ever greater number of other popular media sources, including television and radio. But series books for girls have endured and even thrived up to the present with books such as the Sweet Valley High books and the Baby-Sitters' Club books. Such contemporary series books, which sell by the millions, are worthy of study, but they are beyond the scope of this anthology, which focuses chiefly on series books that originated from approximately the 1910s to the 1950s. Thus, this collection has its limitations. It is unable to cover the very broad range of girls' series books. Also, it is unable to do justice to the hundreds of girls' series books published from the 1900s to the 1950s. There are simply too many books and too many different issues to cover in one collection, or even ten collections, but this collection is at least a beginning to the scholarship that still needs to be done.

The essays in this anthology cover a broad spectrum of girls' series, from better-known publications, such as the Betsy-Tacy books or the Cherry Ames novels, to lesser-known works, such as the Isabel Carleton series or Josephine Lawrence's Linda Lane series. These essays provide an overview of some of the many ways that scholars are approaching girls' series today. The first study in the collection, K. L. Poe's "The

Whole of the Moon: L. M. Montgomery's Anne of Green Gables Series," analyzes one of the world's most famous series.[6] Poe argues that a matriarchal community is formed in Montgomery's books that is surprisingly radical, given that the books appear so conventional. This, Poe suggests, is one of the strengths of the Anne of Green Gables books; they are able to present a matriarchal society as entirely "normal" and acceptable. Moreover, the women's society is not only acceptable, but even something to be desired. In this fashion, the Montgomery books promote ideas that today would be called feminist. Poe shows the potential that girls' series have for promoting greater autonomy for their readers.

Poe points out some of the ways that girls' series can offer their readers greater independence and a sense of their power as young women. It is also important, however, to recognize that early series novels excluded as many readers as they included. Not all readers were equally "welcome" to these books, which tended to feature middle-class or upper-middle-class white heroines, and the books were engaged, often quite explicitly, in maintaining traditional class boundaries. Class relationships in girls' series are the focus of the next essay: Kathleen Chamberlain's "Gender, Class, and Domesticity in the Isabel Carleton Series." Chamberlain shows the ways that Margaret Eliza Ashmun's Isabel Carleton stories grappled with changing class and gender norms at the turn of the century, a time when society's values were changing rapidly. Chamberlain argues that the Carleton books served as a map for their readers, identifying desirable and undesirable behavior during a period of great cultural disruption.

Like Chamberlain, Deidre A. Johnson also examines class dynamics in her essay "Community and Character: A Comparison of Josephine Lawrence's Linda Lane Series and Classic Orphan Fiction." But Johnson's study casts a more positive light on the ability of girls' series to rescript society by presenting an image of independent, capable women. Johnson turns her attention to the Linda Lane series, which was published from 1925 to 1929 by Barse & Hopkins, because the series does not focus on the typical affluent characters prominent in many other series books. Instead, as Johnson argues, the Linda Lane books focus on outsiders: people marginalized by their age or economic standing. Johnson suggests that the Linda Lane books, rather than making such individuals look pathetic or needy of middle-class assistance, actually portray these outsiders as strong and capable women, who are quite able to take care of themselves. In this sense, Johnson's essay, like Poe's, seeks to show the ways that girls' series encourage the building of an all-female community and self-reliance. Johnson's work shows the tremendous difficulties of condemning or praising all girls' series; instead, it is important to study individual series and untangle the sometimes disparate messages that they contain.

While Chamberlain's and Johnson's essays address issues of social class, the next two essays explore how the social activities of girls were depicted and shaped in girls' series. In "Mobile and Modern Heroines: Early Twentieth-Century Girls' Automobile Series," Nancy Tillman Romalov analyzes the many automobile series for girls that appeared in the first decades of the 1900s. Whether it was the Automobile Girls, the Motor Girls, the Motor Maids, or the Outdoor Girls, series girls in ever-increasing numbers hopped into their automobiles and roared away to adventure. Romalov explores the messages sent to readers by these intrepid mobile heroines, arguing that such fictional characters helped to spread the Progressive Era notions of the New Woman, that bold turn-of-the-century woman who was no longer content to remain by her fireside. Instead, much like the heroines who flooded the pages of girls' series, the New Woman wished to set out on her own, whether that entailed working at a settlement house, attending college, or living in her own apartment. Romalov, however, does not perceive automobile series as offering their readers only freedom and autonomy. She also analyzes the often contradictory messages of such texts that espouse greater physical freedom for their girl readers but still restrict them where behavior is concerned, insisting that they always act like "ladies."

The next chapter, "Girl Scouts, Camp Fire Girls, and Woodcraft Girls: The Ideology of Girls' Scouting Novels, 1910-1935," is also concerned with the contradictory messages sent to readers by girls' series. Examining a number of the many scouting novels that appeared in the first third of this century, I study how these books, much like automobile series, gave girl readers conflicting messages about their role in the world.[7] Scouting novels insisted upon the importance of physical activities for girls and encouraged all girls to become scouts, affording them the opportunity to explore the natural world. At the same time, these novels also helped to perpetuate conservative ideology that suggested scouting was best thought of as physical and mental training to ensure healthy mothers for the next generation. By studying scouting novels in conjunction with the scouting rhetoric that flourished in the early years of the century, I demonstrate the complex ways that the ideology of scouting pervaded both fact and fiction.

Chapters 1 through 5 are in one way or another concerned with issues of historical understanding of texts. The next two essays, by Maureen E. Reed and Sally E. Parry, address questions of historicity in more depth, exploring how girls' series complicate our understanding of history. Each writer is rightly skeptical about considering such works of fiction "real" versions of history. Reed and Parry are interested in how series books alter and influence history, both negatively and positively. Reed begins her exploration of the connections between girls' series books and history in the essay "A Companion to History: Maud Hart Lovelace's Betsy-Tacy Books." Reed explores how Maud Hart Lovelace's series provides a beginning to historical understanding for its readers. Even though Lovelace's history is altered and changed in some ways, Reed argues, the Betsy-Tacy books still present a plausible account of history for middle-class women, as long as readers are careful to recognize the many voices of women from other cultures, racial backgrounds, and social classes that Lovelace does not acknowledge. Although Lovelace's account of history might not be comprehensive, it still offers, as Reed points out, a more personal, less formal introduction to history, which might make it more accessible than other more formal sources. For these reasons, Reed suggests the importance of studying popular fiction, such as the Betsy-Tacy books, from the perspective of the historian or material cultures specialist.

Like Reed, Sally E. Parry is concerned with how our historical understanding can be enriched through studying girls' series books, even those that are no longer commonly read and that can be located only with difficulty through a book dealer or in an antique store or archives with a strong children's literature collection. By analyzing one such overlooked series, the Cherry Ames books, the author shows how the dozens of nursing books that were published during or shortly after World War II helped readers to gain both an understanding of real nurses' lives and of how those lives were also altered in fiction in order to serve the ideological purposes of a country at war. In " 'You are needed, desperately needed!': Cherry Ames in World War II," Parry examines the cultural context that Cherry fits into, presenting the series as one example of the many ways that popular culture was used to try to convince more women to join the nurses who were contributing to the War effort. Through a variety of means, including posters, films, and girls' series books, the nurse's career was made to look glamorous and alluring. At the same time this campaign resulted in attracting new recruits to nursing, it also operated to assure the audience that wartime nurses were in no way losing their femininity. Using biographical material from nurses who actually served in the war, Parry builds a multifaceted discussion of the connections between fiction and fact, and explains how series books help to perpetuate ideological messages about patriotism and women's roles.

While the first seven essays in this book examine a broad variety of girls' series, chapters 8 and 9 are more narrowly focused. Both address

Nancy Drew specifically and seek to explore her tremendous appeal. Beginning our search for the "real" Nancy Drew, Sally E. Parry compares Nancy to lesser-known Judy Bolton in "The Secret of the Feminist Heroine: The Search for Values in Nancy Drew and Judy Bolton." Parry argues that Judy, not Nancy, is actually the feminist sleuth because of Bolton's emphasis on human relationships, a value typically associated with women. Parry's argument is particularly intriguing because she, like Kathleen Chamberlain, is intent on addressing class issues and showing some of the many ways that girls' series books help to maintain the status quo by representing the "normal" girl as upper-middle class. But Parry also suggests that it is important not merely to dismiss series books as hopelessly bourgeois; instead, she demonstrates the ways that readers can still receive positive messages from texts that might be problematic from a class standpoint. Along with Chamberlain, Parry depicts the ways that girls' series books offer a barometer of class values in different decades.

Deborah L. Siegel also addresses class issues in the final essay of the collection, "Nancy Drew As New Girl Wonder: Solving It All for the 1930s," in which she explores why Nancy Drew was such a popular character during the Depression, a time when the girl detective's elite upper-middle-class values, one might assume, would be grossly out of place. Siegel argues that Nancy Drew was so successful during the Depression years because her character served as a bridge between the Victorian and the modern age. Much like the New Woman of turn-of-the-century fame, Nancy was a New Girl, as Siegel points out, with some old-fashioned values. Because of the duality of Nancy's character, Siegel argues, she was able to help her girl readers sort out the sometimes contradictory messages in 1930s society about what it meant to be a woman. By focusing on the 1930s, Siegel shows the importance of considering how girls' series have been interpreted differently in varying periods of the twentieth century, taking into account how the readership has changed dramatically. I find Siegel's approach to Nancy Drew particularly informative because Siegel acknowledges that Nancy is not a timeless essence who is always interpreted in the same fashion; instead, she is constructed and reconstructed by readers from different decades, with each generation bringing new considerations to bear on the girl detective's career. Siegel's essay is only a beginning to the more extensive scholarly work that needs to be undertaken on how readers from different periods have understood girls' series.

From issues of the historical development of Nancy Drew, to questions of class in the Isabel Carleton Series, to concerns about technology in the Automobile Girls, I hope that the essays in this book will open readers' minds to the wide variety of ways that scholars are studying girls' series and the cultural work that they have accomplished and continue to accomplish. The scholars included in this collection have shown that the examination of girls' series, due to their enduring popularity, is one particularly intriguing way to explore how girls' culture is constituted. While the messages such books send can offer their readers new freedom, the books can also help to perpetuate traditional gender relationships and class stereotypes. Obviously, there is no one right way to read a series book. Instead, these essays suggest the importance of understanding the books in their historical context and of recognizing that individual readers interpret the works differently.

Due to the ever-changing nature of girls' series books throughout this century and the differing societal messages that they contain, these books are a fruitful source for examining our cultural past. Studying the proliferation of contemporary girls' series books in the 1980s and 1990s, analyzing the connections between series books and their film and television counterparts, interpreting the changing messages of girls' series in times of war and peace, or studying the connections between society's changing notions of acceptable careers for women and their depiction in girls' series—the possibilities for scholarship on girls' series books are endless, and the essays in this collection are only the beginning of the work that should be done to understand better how girls' series have shaped our culture. I hope that other scholars use this collection as a steppingstone for further exploration of girls' series and other forms of girls' popular reading. This early reading material has a tremendous amount to say not only about girls but also about the women they become.

Finally, I hope this collection illustrates the ongoing importance of studying popular literature in order to understand the culture around us. It is too simple to disregard such reading materials as "frivolous" and "lacking literary merit." Although we as adult critics might scorn such books (doubly so if they were intended for young readers, particularly female ones), such popular reading does constitute one of the most prevalent and important forces that shapes both young minds and old. Thus, if we wish to understand how we are constituted as subjects, popular literature is a vitally important source that deserves our closest scrutiny, as this collection has demonstrated. For it is in such popular books that we shall discover the ideological messages that mold and shape us into the individuals that we are. Read a Nancy Drew or Hardy Boys mystery or another American series book; it will tell you much about our culture's values, mores, and biases.

Notes

1. Some notable earlier critical studies of girls' series should be mentioned, such as Bobbie Ann Mason's groundbreaking book, *The Girl Sleuth: A Feminist Guide*, and Jane S. Smith's carefully researched essay "Plucky Little Ladies and Stout-Hearted Chums: Serial Novels for Girls, 1900-1920." Mary Cadogan and Patricia Craig's influential book, *You're a Brick, Angela!; A New Look at Girls' Fiction from 1839-1975*, is not solely about series books, but does discuss British girls' series at some length. Anyone interested in girls' series also must read Carolyn Stewart Dyer and Nancy Tillman Romalov's edited collection, *Rediscovering Nancy Drew*, which offers a fine group of essays that focus on Carolyn Keene's famous detective. The entire June 1994 issue of the children's literature journal *The Lion and the Unicorn* likewise concentrates exclusively on Nancy Drew. Also of interest is Kathleen Chamberlain's essay "Careers in Girls' Series Fiction, 1940-1970" and my essay "The Feminine En-gendering of Film Consumption and Film Technology in Popular Girls' Serial Novels, 1914-1931." Two other pieces that I wrote—*Intimate Communities: Representation and Social Transformation in Women's College Fiction, 1895-1910* and "It Is Pluck, but Is It Sense?': Athletic Student Culture in Women's College Novels, 1895-1910"—discuss girls' series novels extensively, but not exclusively.

For more information about the specific girls' books that exist, one invaluable source is *Girls Series Books: A Checklist of Hardback Books Published 1900-1975*.

2. Typical of the scholarly reaction to series books is the comment in Peter Hunt's *Children's Literature: An Illustrated History*. In this book, Stratemeyer series books are called "series fodder" (250) and are contrasted with "serious books" (250). My point is not to claim that series books are always shining examples of literary art, but to show that such attitudes have resulted in series books being infrequently studied, when, despite their sometimes limited literary merit, they are still engaged in important cultural work.

3. Works that discuss the meeting place of critical theory and children's literature are increasingly prominent. See, for instance, Peter Hunt, *Criticism, Theory, and Children's Literature*; Jill P. May, *Children's Literature and Critical Theory: Reading and Writing for Understanding*; Lissa Paul, "Enigma Variations: What Feminist Theory Knows about Children's Literature"; and John Stephens, *Language and Ideology in Children's Fiction*.

4. Some of the new work on girls' reading and girls' culture includes Shirley Foster and Judy Simons, *What Katy Read: Feminist Re-Readings of 'Classic' Stories for Girls*; Sally Mitchell, *The New Girl: Girls' Culture in England, 1880-1915*; Claudia Nelson and Lynne Vallone, eds., *The Girls' Own: Cultural Histories of the Anglo-American Girl, 1830-1915*; Kimberley Reynolds,

Girls Only? Gender and Popular Children's Fiction in Britain, 1880-1910; Penny Tinkler, *Constructing Girlhood: Popular Magazines for Girls Growing Up in England, 1920-1950*; and Lynne Vallone, *Disciplines of Virtue: Girls' Culture in the Eighteenth and Nineteenth Centuries*.

5. For further information on the Stratemeyer Syndicate, see Carol Billman, *The Secret of the Stratemeyer Syndicate: Nancy Drew, the Hardy Boys, and the Million Dollar Fiction Factory*; Deidre Johnson, *Edward Stratemeyer and the Stratemeyer Syndicate*; Peter A. Soderbergh, "The Stratemeyer Strain: Educators and the Juvenile Series Book, 1900-1973"; and Bruce Watson, "Tom Swift, Nancy Drew and Pals All Had the Same Dad." Many of the essays in this current collection also discuss the Syndicate in greater depth.

6. Although Montgomery's saga is Canadian, I have included Poe's study in this collection because Anne of Green Gables has been thoroughly integrated into U.S. culture, so much so that she is an integral part of many girls' childhoods in the United States.

7. For the sake of convenience, I use the term "scouting" to refer to stories that contain Girl Scouts, Camp Fire Girls, or Woodcraft Girls.

Works Cited

Billman, Carol. *The Secret of the Stratemeyer Syndicate: Nancy Drew, the Hardy Boys, and the Million Dollar Fiction Factory*. New York: Ungar, 1986.

Cadogan, Mary, and Patricia Craig. *You're a Brick, Angela!; A New Look at Girls' Fiction from 1839-1975*. London: Gollancz, 1976.

Chamberlain, Kathleen. "Careers in Girls' Series Fiction, 1940-1970." *Dime Novel Roundup* Dec. 1991: 106-11.

Dyer, Carolyn Stewart, and Nancy Tillman Romalov, eds. *Rediscovering Nancy Drew*. Iowa City: U of Iowa P, 1995.

Engelhardt, Tom. "Reading May Be Harmful to Your Kids: In the Nadirland of Today's Children's Books." *Harper's* June 1991: 55-62.

Foster, Shirley, and Judy Simons. *What Katy Read: Feminist Re-Readings of "Classic" Stories for Girls*. Iowa City: U of Iowa P, 1995.

Girls Series Books: A Checklist of Hardback Books Published 1900-1975. Minneapolis: U of Minnesota, Children's Literature Research Collections, 1978.

Griswold, Jerry. *Audacious Kids: Coming of Age in America's Classic Children's Books*. New York: Oxford UP, 1992.

Hunt, Peter. *Criticism, Theory, and Children's Literature*. Oxford: Basil Blackwell, 1991.

——, ed. *Children's Literature: An Illustrated History*. Oxford: Oxford UP, 1995.

Inness, Sherrie A. "The Feminine En-gendering of Film Consumption and Film Technology in Popular Girls' Serial Novels, 1914-1931." *Journal of Popular Culture* 29.3 (1995): 173-86.

——. *Intimate Communities: Representation and Social Transformation in Women's College Fiction, 1895-1910*. Bowling Green: Bowling Green Popular Press, 1995.

——. "'It Is Pluck, but Is It Sense?': Athletic Student Culture in Women's College Novels, 1895-1910." *Journal of Popular Culture* 27.1 (1993): 85-108.

Johnson, Deidre. *Edward Stratemeyer and the Stratemeyer Syndicate*. New York: Twayne, 1993.

MacLeod, Anne Scott. "Children's Literature in America from the Puritan Beginnings to 1870." *Children's Literature: An Illustrated History*. Ed. Peter Hunt. Oxford: Oxford UP, 1995. 102-29.

Mason, Bobbie Ann. *The Girl Sleuth: A Feminist Guide*. Old Westbury: Feminist Press, 1975.

May, Jill P. *Children's Literature and Critical Theory: Reading and Writing for Understanding*. New York: Oxford UP, 1995.

Mitchell, Sally. *The New Girl: Girls' Culture in England, 1880-1915*. New York: Columbia UP, 1995.

Nancy Drew Issue. *The Lion and the Unicorn* 18.1 (June 1994).

Nelson, Claudia, and Lynne Vallone, eds. *The Girl's Own: Cultural Histories of the Anglo-American Girl, 1830-1915*. Athens: U of Georgia P, 1994.

Paul, Lissa. "Enigma Variations: What Feminist Theory Knows about Children's Literature." *Signal* 54 (Sept. 1987): 186-202.

Reynolds, Kimberley. *Girls Only? Gender and Popular Children's Fiction in Britain, 1880-1910*. Philadelphia: Temple UP, 1990.

Smith, Jane S. "Plucky Little Ladies and Stout-Hearted Chums: Serial Novels for Girls, 1900-1920." *Prospects* 3 (1977): 155-74.

Soderbergh, Peter A. "The Stratemeyer Strain: Educators and the Juvenile Series Book, 1900-1973." *Journal of Popular Culture* 7.4 (1974): 864-72.

Stephens, John. *Language and Ideology in Children's Fiction*. New York: Longman, 1992.

Tinkler, Penny. *Constructing Girlhood: Popular Magazines for Girls Growing up in England, 1920-1950*. London: Taylor & Francis, 1995.

Vallone, Lynne. *Disciplines of Virtue: Girls' Culture in the Eighteenth and Nineteenth Centuries*. New Haven: Yale UP, 1995.

Watson, Bruce. "Tom Swift, Nancy Drew and Pals All Had the Same Dad." *Smithsonian* 22 Oct. 1991: 52+.

1

The Whole of the Moon:
L. M. Montgomery's Anne of Green Gables Series

K. L. Poe

> I saw the rain-dirty valley
> You saw Brigadoon
> I saw the crescent
> You saw the whole of the moon . . .
> —Mike Scott

When one considers feminist writings, children's literature is not often the first application that springs to mind; in spite of the recent increase in critical readings of children's literature, it might be suggested that feminism is the concern of adult women alone, and children should be neither seen nor heard. This unfortunate attitude neglects to consider the valuable feminist educational aspect of children's literature, and dismisses a genre that can and does influence generations of young girls. The influence can be particularly felt in the Anne of Green Gables series by L. M. Montgomery. Again, often dismissed as "sentimental" or "pretty" fiction (Montgomery herself felt her books were destined only for the Sunday School shelf), this series offers, on closer inspection, a societal view in which patriarchy is a façade that masks a truly matriarchal structure. This structure, which Nina Auerbach refers to as the "subtle, unexpected power" of a community of women (3), is seen in the series as a rare portrait of such a community. Additionally, as this series extends from Anne's arrival at Green Gables at the age of eleven to the end of World War I as she waits for the return of her sons from the front, the reader is able to see the growth of a true feminist spirit from girlhood through womanhood, and even into a second and third generation.

The ways in which Montgomery constructs this matriarchal view are cleverly masked in the telling of the tale; it would appear, in fact, to be one of the least-radical feminist depictions in literature, and therein lies its strength: matriarchy is viewed as a normal, natural way of life, rather than the "corporate and contradictory vision of a unit that is simul-

15

taneously defective and transcendent" (Auerbach 5). For modern readers, this depiction may even appear to be contrary to contemporary ideas of feminism, which it is, particularly if that contemporary view insists on but one type of feminism. Feminism, in this series and, indeed, most of Montgomery's work, does not fall easily into a modern definition; it is, more precisely, "womanism": the females in this series are separate from the male world and recognize this as a positive advantage, rather than a negative confinement. Realizing that their roles in society might be circumscribed superficially, they realize as well that these roles have more latitude, more power, even, than appears on the surface. Certainly the protagonist, Anne Shirley, sees her role as unlimited in spite of the conventions that bind her. She does not waste time fighting against the societal boundaries that she cannot change, but, with a rich and independent spirit, makes her life worth living.

In this essay, I hope to show the ways in which the subversive matriarchal order is played out in this series, providing a feminist road map for its young readers then and now. The world-wide popularity of this series, particularly of the initial installment, has allowed Montgomery's theme of "womanism" to enrich the lives of girls and women in many diverse cultures. Although Montgomery wrote eloquently of life on Prince Edward Island, Canada, her brand of nationalism and love of home and hearth, particularly in the shadow of war, shows that the heart of a nation, no matter where or when, is truly found in its women. Mavis Reimer, in her introduction to a collection of essays on *Anne of Green Gables* (*Such a Simple Little Tale: Critical Responses to L. M. Montgomery's Anne of Green Gables*), indicates that "explicated in terms of its appeal to audiences widely separated in time and place, *Anne* loses its circumscribed national and historical personality" (5). Gillian Avery, in her discussion of the differences between American and English children's literature, states:

Homely details were never so prominent in English books; indeed the great advantage that Americans had when it came to writing family stories was their passionate feeling for home and domesticity. . . . For Americans, the household community was a microcosm of the ideal republic they saw themselves to have created. (44)

Although many of the residents of Avonlea speak disparagingly of the "Yankees," they actually have more in common with them than with their own English and Scottish forebears. Hence, the series has less to do with the English tradition of girls' fiction and is often accepted as part of the American canon of children's literature, in spite of its Canadian origin.

It is interesting to note as well the extreme popularity of *Anne* in Japan, a country not particularly known for its empowerment of women. Douglas Baldwin writes that the similarities between life in Anne's Avonlea and Japan, the common love of nature and the adherence to propriety, strikes a chord with Japanese readers:

the emphasis on education, politeness, self-sacrifice, love of nature, hard work, frugality, and community spirit parallel the current situation in Japan. So too does the restrictive nature of this society [Anne's Avonlea], particularly for women, and the struggle for young people to break free. (131)

Baldwin also notes that Prince Edward Island is still a major travel destination for Japanese tourists, who throng to the fictional Avonlea in Cavendish, where Montgomery was raised (124).

These "traditional" values, which are part of mythical American heritage as well, are portrayed with such loving detail that the reader is easily transported through a nostalgia for a time that probably did not exist for anyone at any point in history, regardless of locale. But as Elaine Showalter has noted, "rather than contesting the myth of the American spirit, American women saw their own writing as its true incarnation" (11); Montgomery's creation of a protagonist that embodied that spirit helped to create a new, feminine version of that myth.

The universal appeal of Montgomery's heroine and her story is evidence of the strength of Montgomery's craft and the sincerity of her message, in spite of her frequent claims to the contrary. After the success of the original installment of the series, Montgomery was disinterested in continuing Anne's saga, and was contractually bound to do so by her American publisher, L. C. Page. The strong personal code Montgomery adhered to throughout her life, her dedication to duty and personal morality, would not allow her to shirk her obligation, however, and the series continued (Gillen 78-80). What makes the series interesting still for the reader of today is not Montgomery's adherence to "formula" as much as her ability to conform the "formula" to suit her own needs. By taking the story of Anne from childhood to womanhood, Montgomery shows that even through one person, the world can be examined and, in effect, directed to show a myriad of connected stories and themes. Fred Inglis indicates that the realm of children's literature allows the author "the chance to bring culture and individual spirit into one focus" (36). The journey through Anne's life in a series of novels allowed Montgomery the luxury of sharpening that focus in a way that a single novel would never have allowed. While several novels in the series can stand on their own, disconnected from the series, the reader would miss out on the larger portrait that Montgomery so carefully constructed, particularly in the creation of parallel characters such as Matthew and Captain Jim, Marilla and Susan, Katherine Brooke and Leslie Moore, Mrs. Lynde and Miss Cornelia. These characters are not identical, but carry an echo of remembrance that helps Anne (and, consequently, the reader) understand and appreciate them individually as she encounters them in different times in her life. Additionally, Montgomery tests the theory that the spirit of childhood ends with the onset of adulthood; is the spirited child lost in the sedate matron? Montgomery is able to show the redefinition of that spirit as a natural transition, rather than a loss, and creates not an immature child trapped in the body of an adult, but the transformed spirit of the child in the woman.

It is important to note here the first of two important misconceptions regarding the Anne of Green Gables series and its creator. Although much of the writing done on Anne is firmly attached to the "fact" that Anne Shirley is the autobiographical creation of L. M. Montgomery, this assumption is not true. Montgomery discusses this at length in her personal journal and in her "autobiographical" tome, *The Alpine Path.* "*Anne* is as real to me as if I had given her birth—as real and as dear," she wrote in her journal (I: 332), and, in a later entry, examined the "confusion" between herself and her most famous creation:

I have *never* drawn any of the characters in my books "from life," although I may have taken a quality here and an incident there. I have used real places and speeches freely but I have never put any person I knew into my books . . . when I am asked if *Anne* herself is a "real person" I always answer "no" with an odd reluctance and an uncomfortable feeling of not telling the truth. (II: 38-39)

Montgomery's use of "speeches" in particular serves to solidify this false composite, since many in the series were drawn, sometimes word for word, from her personal journals; Hilary Thompson notes that the reading of Montgomery's journals offers a "glimpse into the process of weaving fiction from life" (206). This is a familiar situation for writers who keep journals, yet it is also used as justification for making the conflation of author and protagonist. As several girls' series *are* based closely on the life of the author, and can be documented as such (the *Little House* series by Laura Ingalls Wilder and the *Betsy-Tacy* series by Maud Hart Lovelace are two well-known cases), a character speaking words from the author's journal and having similar life experiences can lead to the conclusion that the author is writing autobiographically, and there is no harm in making such an assumption casually or fancifully. When it is used as a basis for a critical argument, however, the assumption and the arguments that follow it cannot be sufficiently supported. It is essential to the understanding of the series that the personages of L. M. Montgomery and Anne Shirley be separate, in accordance with Montgomery's stated assertions.

Seen as a separate entity from Montgomery, Anne Shirley and her "life book" can be more clearly examined for their "womanism." It is a credit to Montgomery's literary skill that Anne is so distinct a personage in the first volume of the series; by the end of that first and most well-read installment of the series, the reader knows Anne well enough that although she fades from view in later volumes and is less scrutinized psychologically past this point in the series, one seems to know almost instinctively what Anne would say, do or think about a situation without being told. The reader has, in effect, grown with Anne from her arrival at Green Gables to her decision to give up the Avery Scholarship and stay home with Marilla; the orphaned waif who waited at the Bright River station is still inside, but greatly expanded in terms of her relationship with herself and others. Had Montgomery not been contractually obligated to continue the series and ended Anne's story with *Anne of Green Gables*, Anne Shirley would still probably be considered a popular children's heroine, but the expansion of Anne's story into the seven succeeding volumes of the series offered Montgomery the opportunity to sustain both theme and character through to adulthood.

Although read by more current generations as a straight chronology of Anne's life from *Anne of Green Gables* to *Rilla of Ingleside*, the series was, in fact, written in the following order: *Anne of Green Gables* (1908), *Anne of Avonlea* (1909), *Anne of the Island* (1915), *Anne's House of Dreams* (1917), *Rainbow Valley* (1919), *Rilla of Ingleside* (1920), *Anne of Windy Poplars* (1936), and *Anne of Ingleside* (1939). While reading the books in the order in which they were written offers an interesting literary perspective and explains placement of some characters, it should be noted that after their initial publication, and in their paperback re-release in the 1980s, most readers would have had no knowledge of the original publishing chronology. Does this place a different emphasis on the stories themselves? Possibly, because writing backward to cover Anne's years after her graduation from Redmond and before her marriage, and in the early years of her children's upbringing (in *Anne of Windy Poplars* and *Anne of Ingleside*), Montgomery had to carefully construct a past for Anne that fit comfortably and believably into the existing framework. While this works well in *Anne of Ingleside*, it is less successful in *Anne of Windy Poplars*, which, although enjoyable, seems oddly fragmented and out of place with the rest of the books in the series. Elizabeth Rollins Epperly notes with irony that Kevin Sullivan's Canadian television production of the sequel to his popular *Anne of Green Gables* focuses on *Windy Poplars* and suffers, production-wise, from its fragmented text and thus is forced to gloss Montgomery's text so completely that the end result was barely recognizable to her readers (132). Sullivan's insistence on the refiguring of Anne as a "sentimental" heroine creates an image of Anne that is completely contrary to Montgomery's depiction of Anne as a more realistic character shaped by feminism, not sentimental fiction.[1]

The "sentimental" or "domestic" fiction inherited by Montgomery and channeled through Anne, was, as Showalter notes, "permeated by the artifacts, spaces, and images of nineteenth-century American domestic culture: the kitchen . . . the Edenic mother's garden . . . the caged songbird, which represents the creative woman in her domestic sphere" (14). Ann Douglas describes a typical sentimental heroine that Anne Shirley not only recognized, but attempted to emulate:

The typical heroine of such stories was, of course, beautiful. Her beauty was less a matter of looks, however, than a privilege of protection . . . [she] could afford to be modest; . . . Her fictive fate might be harsh, but the person on whom she was ultimately dependent, her reader, would never reject her. She was a narcissist freed of the obsession of self-involvement. . . . Special treatment was her destiny. (63)

Montgomery's brand of "domestic" fiction, however, turns a world of seeming confinement into a world from which all other worlds are created and supported. Anne comes to Green Gables full of daydreams torn from the pages of "sentimental" fiction, yet, as she finds her new residence becoming her longed-for home, she is able to put aside the daydreams for the more satisfying reality. As the series continues, her adjustment from the world of daydreams to the reality of everyday life is seen as a natural progression; Anne does not regret their loss because she has found the ability to envision romance in her daily life. Where the standard for late nineteenth-century society was for young girls to have the minimum education, then to marry young and begin producing a family, Avonlea society offers something more, though within what appear to be the same societal constraints. The difference, Montgomery shows, is how the woman approaches marriage, her reasons for wanting to be married, and a realization of the choices around her. The world young Anne Shirley enters upon her arrival on Prince Edward Island offers, for the late nineteenth century, a relatively significant variety of choices; by the end of the series, the reader has seen successful, happy unmarried women, female scholars, content matrons, and tender, caring mothers along with the traditional shrewish spinsters and unhappy, vindictive mothers. As Anne matures, she finds that the romantic idea of "happy ever after" she so favored from her voracious reading is less fairy tale than a matter of attitude and a knowledge of self. Although Mrs. Rachel Lynde might call a feminist reading of Anne's life "the world turned upside down," it is really closer to "the world turned inside out": in an examination of Anne's life and times, the reader, in effect, sees how the "inside" or domestic side of life has a direct effect on the "outside."

Anne Shirley, at the beginning of the series, is about as far removed from society as one could get in the late nineteenth century: as an orphan, her origins were suspect; as a girl, she was useless for hard farm work and hard to marry off because of those same suspicious origins, and even more so because of her uncommon red hair and spindly frame. Not exactly the typical heroine of sentimental fiction, Montgomery needed to create a character that would stand out from that bland fictional land-scape. What makes Anne stand out to Matthew Cuthbert, who lives in dread fear of all females and little girls in particular, is her spirit; he is, quite simply, fascinated with her in spite of himself. Montgomery was often accused of having patterned Matthew after a neighbor, but she asserted quite firmly that he was created precisely because he was very different from Anne and to contrast with Anne's loquaciousness (*Journals* II: 38).

Similarly, Green Gables is about as far removed from Avonlea society as it could be and still be considered part of the community (Drain 123). Managed under the competent control of Marilla Cuthbert, a middle-aged spinster, Green Gables is so neatly clean and efficient that it seems even less a home than a shrine to the cult of no-nonsense. Matthew, Marilla's brother, is a silent, gentle soul, dedicated to his farm work and not much else; it is revealed after Anne's arrival that he has barely been beyond the sphere of farmyard, his room, and the kitchen for several years. He is the first of the many semi-silent male characters introduced in the series; his more verbal counterpart, Captain Jim of *House of Dreams*, seems to speak for most of the men in Anne's realm. Matthew's treatment of Anne is far more maternal than Marilla's, which, in turn, takes on a distant, paternal nature (Foster and Simons 163).[2] Matthew is the nurturer of Anne's spirit; Marilla is the word of law and society. This reversal mirrors the community of Avonlea itself. In a society based, as Muriel A. Whitaker argues, on "the twin pillars of church and work" (12), the Cuthberts fit in quite nicely, thank you. Since Matthew, again, is semi-silent, it is Marilla who makes most of the verbal contacts between Green Gables and the outside world; with characteristic efficiency, she wastes no words and is distrustful of glibness.

They are industrious, thrifty, church-going participants of a community that is without a doubt completely in the control of women.

Where Marilla is the spokesperson for the Cuthbert family, Mrs. Rachel Lynde, their nearest neighbor and the first character introduced in the series, speaks for the rest of the village. She is involved in politics, the church, Ladies' Aid, and the lives of all her neighbors. Mary Rubio points out that the first image in the book is of Mrs. Lynde at her window, surveying her "world," and the last image is of Anne at hers, surveying not only her world, but also her future. Where Mrs. Lynde's view suggests a type of containment, Anne's suggests a broader view of subject and spirit (80).

This growth of view is typical of the traditional *Bildungsroman*, or coming of age story, though the term is usually reserved for stories about boys. Eve Kornfeld and Susan Jackson argue that authors constructing a female *Bildungsroman* set in the nineteenth century "create a matriarchal society—a feminine utopia" in which the young protagonist must assimilate the "proper values" (141-42). Perry Nodelman suggests that *Anne of Green Gables* is an excellent example of this utopia, in that its island setting creates a sense of otherworldliness that underscores the illusion of paradise (33). Kornfeld and Jackson assert that the authors avoid the male influence on this utopia, utilizing men only when absolutely necessary, to "perform a useful function" that the women would have managed themselves had society or "circumstances" not "conspired against them" (143-44). This view underscores the second-class role of women in nineteenth-century society, and renders their "utopia" just that: a fantasy, not a reality. The female *Bildungsroman* becomes, then, a sort of fantastical "wish-fulfillment" that could not occur in real life; Kornfeld and Jackson's argument indicates that since the female protagonist cannot, because of societal constraints that exist in spite of the female utopia, enter completely into the male world, fantasy is the most that can be hoped for (151). This, they explain, accounts for the collapse of the *Bildungsroman* once the female protagonist emerges from adolescence; the female utopia becomes "oppressive" because the heroine realizes its futility (150). Janet Weiss-Townsend argues that this collapse must occur because it indicates the lack of validity in the "premise that eternal childhood is a valid, desired, feminine state" (114). If Anne's story had ended with *Anne of Green Gables*, the idea of an "eternal childhood" would have left Anne with little hope of a satisfying adult life. Montgomery's development of Anne's character in the remaining volumes of the series shows that Anne's passing into adulthood is not what Showalter calls the "capitulation to the dominant culture's image of feminine propriety" (43) but the adjustment of her childhood self into the realities of adult life.

As *Anne of Green Gables* draws to a close, Anne makes a decision that might seem, to a modern reader, to be the destruction of her future: giving up her college scholarship, Anne decides to stay in Avonlea and teach, a move that will enable Marilla, whose eyesight is endangered, to remain at Green Gables. Although Anne's strong sense of duty (a major theme for Montgomery) would probably have made this decision for her, it is more that Anne has realized that though she came to Green Gables an orphan, she has become a part of it and "converted" Marilla to her point of view. As Marilla confesses to Anne after Matthew's death: "I love you as dear as if you were my own flesh and blood" (297-98); the bond between them is so strong that Anne does not see giving up her chance to go to college as a sacrifice, or an end of her future, but, instead, a "bend in the road" (305). The loss of Matthew's nurturing maternal influence causes an adjustment for both women as they assume a more maternal role to each other. When her childhood chum, Gilbert Blythe, who has to become a teacher himself to earn the money for college, gives up the Avonlea school to Anne so that she can be closer to Marilla, it is a sacrifice that Anne can truly appreciate. They both accept the "bend in the road" and decide to keep up their studies together, moving from the intense intellectual competition of their childhood in the Avonlea school to a mature, supportive alliance. Temma F. Berg points out this episode as an example of the way in which the "dialectic" between Anne and Gilbert "works itself out in each individual, not between individuals" (162). Although Anne eventually marries Gilbert, it is at this point, and until the end of the third book, *Anne of the Island*, merely a close friendship between two "kindred spirits" looking outward at the same goal. What Gilbert's romantic motives are is not known; the reader can only speculate. At this point in her history, Anne has learned that although the constraints of society have told her that she is inferior, her experience has told her that she is not (Papashvily 11).

Epperly calls the next installment in the series, *Anne of Avonlea*, a book "about doing and reacting," whereas its precursor dealt more with "being and seeing" (40). She continues that *Anne of Avonlea* is a successful sequel in its continuance of "good times" but, "as an exploration of Anne's development and thinking, the book is a qualified failure" (41). The bustle of activity in the story, which moves, as the title might suggest, beyond Green Gables and into the larger community of Avonlea itself, takes the reader away from the closeness with Anne felt in the first book. It also conveys the feeling one gets after a busy period in one's life: when do I get to *me*? Anne has little time to get to be herself in this second book, and it does mirror, in some respects, the pressures felt by Montgomery herself during the writing of it; Epperly notes that the pressures of life became so intense for Montgomery at this point in her life that she suffered a nervous breakdown when the book was completed (39). Further, Epperly considers the book as being "bent on teaching, though not necessarily learning" (42). It is true that everyone seems engaged in inculcating some sort of moral lesson, just as Marilla did in the first installment, and the multiplicity of voices provides what Auerbach calls a "plurality of perspectives" that forms the basis of a strong community (12). It is this multiplicity of voices that helps Anne in terms of emotional development; Anne's movement out into the community as an adult, rather than a child, indicates a step, though tentative, to the development of a personal identity. As Shirley Foster and Judy Simons have noted, "Anne's pragmatic and humanitarian ethics, meaningful because they are unsullied by the justifications and codification of adult creeds, are not only sympathetically presented . . . but actually become the means of converting others" (159). While Anne herself admits that she has "quieted down" from her verbose arrival at Green Gables, there is still the conflict of identity to be resolved. Anne Shirley the orphan became Anne of Green Gables, that is, part of a family, and in this second book of the series, she must adjust that dreamy-eyed child to the responsibilities of employment and community. There is no doubt that this time of work, both external and internal, often seems lackluster in comparison to the wonder and beauty in *Anne of Green Gables*, but within the confines of "formula," Montgomery manages, nevertheless, to inject a healthy dose of reality into Anne's life, and, rather than bringing the series to a screeching halt, actually moves it forward, however slowly. She has not lost her romantic idealism, Epperly asserts, but rather adjusted the viewfinder to accommodate reality (46).

The second common misconception about Anne Shirley begins to take shape in *Anne of Avonlea*, namely, that Anne had a career as a writer. In the first book, Anne writes stories with her "Story Club" that are enlivened by her energetic imagination; here, she puts together (while stuck in the roof of the duckhouse belonging to the "Copp girls") a "string of fancies" about a dialogue between the flowers, birds and "the spirit of the garden." Her "bosom friend," Diana Barry, is as enthralled as she was with Anne's Story Club tales, and urges her to send it to *Canadian Woman*. Anne negates the idea, because "there is no plot in it, you see . . . I like writing such things, but of course nothing of the sort would ever do for publication, for editors insist on plots. . ." (158). While the "plotless" fancy does eventually get published later in the series, and Anne continues to write "things for children," this seems more a sly commentary by Montgomery on the valuation of children's literature than on Anne having a "career" in writing. Montgomery was a full-fledged author, having published her first poem ("On Cape LeForce") in the Charlottetown, P.E.I. newspaper, *The Daily Patriot*, days before her sixteenth birthday (Bolger 28), and continuing to publish with relative frequency throughout her career. Anne, so far as the series indicates, has had only a few of her "fancies" published; the townspeople of Summerside, where she is later principal of the high school, and of Avonlea worry that she might just put them in a story, but her writing does not constitute a career. Unlike Montgomery's *Emily*, who is more likely an autobiographical creation and does pursue a writing career, Anne does not represent, as T. D. MacLulich indicates, a "failure on Montgomery's part of both the literary and social imagination" (91); she doesn't fully pursue a literary career because she is not necessarily a writer beyond her "fancies."

This conception of "Anne the Author" can be traced to the character of Jo March, who, like her creator, Louisa May Alcott, actually did pursue a literary career. Elaine Showalter's examination of Jo brings out the "literary daughter's dilemma: the tension between feminine identity and artistic freedom, and even more important, between patriarchal models of the literary career and those more relevant to women's lives" (43). While this "tension" exists in the character of Anne Shirley, the comparison ends there; Jo's literary career is a far cry from Anne's "fancies" and it is not possible to connect the two characters beyond that point.

Anne of the Island, the third book in the series, finds Anne going around the "bend in the road" to a new world, away from her beloved island home. Although infused with the excitement of college life, new friends, and romance, it is also a book about homesickness for the community of Avonlea and Green Gables and the further creation of an adult identity in a new community of women. While vacations are spent on the Island, the balance of the book deals with Anne's relationships with those of her "set" and other adult women. The contrast between the "coeds" and the other women encountered reinforces both the need for independence and a sense of belonging. From jolly Aunt Jamesina, whose common sense tells her that she need not chaperone Anne and her friends ("I know you expect me to look out for you and to keep you proper, but I'm not going to do it. You're old enough to know how to behave if you're ever going to be. So as far as I'm concerned," concluded Aunt Jamesina with a twinkle in her young eyes, "You can all go to destruction in your own way." [125]) to the globe-trotting Miss Spofford ("I'm seventy years old, but I'm not tired of living yet. I daresay I'd have gone to Europe before if the idea had occurred to me." [73]), Anne sees that womanhood can be different from the Avonlea brand of matron. Sharp-tongued Aunt Atossa, a foreshadowing of the dreadful Aunt Mary

Maria of *Ingleside*, sees no hope in life, whereas vivacious Philippa Gordon turns away from her mother's plans to marry her off so that she can pursue her education. This new community of women shows Anne (and the reader) that the roles afforded them in society are not as circumscribed as they may appear to be.

Anne's romanticism is sorely tested in this novel by a series of comic proposals of marriage and the rejection of the story she had hoped to sell to a respected women's magazine, which was instead reconfigured into an advertisement and submitted by Diana for a contest. Whenever she tries to recapture the romance of her Island life, the "cold water" thrown on her by her friends and acquaintances in Avonlea shows her instead that the true romance of the Island is that which she holds in herself and in her point of view. As Marilyn Solt notes, it is Montgomery's use of setting that affects Anne's point of view, and, consequently, that of the reader as well (61). In spite of her homesickness for the beauty of the Island, Anne is able to see the romance of Kingsport, and, later, Bolingbroke, where she visits the house she was born in. By removing Anne from the "safety" of the Island, Montgomery risks losing the most attractive element of the first two novels of the series. She succeeds because Anne is not the Island, but *of* the Island: no matter where Anne goes, the connection to her home remains strong and enriching.

Anne's romanticism is most sorely tested with the entrance of "Prince Charming"—Roy Gardner—the suitor of her dreams. Having turned down Gilbert's proposal as a betrayal of friendship, Anne is swept off her feet by Roy's melancholic charms. When he proposes, however, she realizes that dreams may be fine in their place, but if they don't fit into reality, they are useless. At convocation, Anne puts aside Roy's violets for Gilbert's lilies of the valley, partially as a commemoration of the accomplishment of a shared dream, but also as a foreshadowing of her true feelings and readiness to step into another sort of community.

After graduation and the unsatisfying outcome of her relationship with Prince Charming, Anne feels Avonlea life has left her behind. Diana has married and given birth to her first child, Jane Andrews (who had unsuccessfully proposed to Anne for her brother Billy) has found a millionaire, and Ruby Gillis has died without ever knowing "womanhood joys." It is only after Gilbert's brush with death that Anne realizes Philippa was right: she did not know love when she refused Gilbert, but, realizing it now, she hopes that it is not too late. The happy ending is achieved with a second, more successful proposal from Gilbert, but it is spared from over-sentimentality by the knowledge that many years of work must be completed before they can marry. Looking outward again at the same goal, the kinship between Anne and Gilbert underscores the importance of mutual respect; their love is not the fairy-tale romance of Anne's daydreams, but the reality of an adult relationship.

Before they can marry, Gilbert must finish medical school, so Anne accepts the principalship of the Summerside High School in *Anne of Windy Poplars*. The epistolary style ("love letters" to Gilbert) is dropped after a few chapters, followed by more *Avonlea*-like episodes, set this time under the matriarchal eye of the Pringle clan. Unaccepted for the first time, Anne is forced to make her own inroad in the community. Her self-confidence is shaken, but her spirit is unbroken as she works to find her place in Summerside. The most interesting personage in the book, save the humorous Rebecca Dew, is Katherine Brooke, a disagreeable teacher at the high school. While an excellent teacher, Katherine's caustic personality repels everyone, even Anne, until, perhaps remembering the lonely, unloved child she was herself (or maybe even the unloved Aunt Atossa), Anne invites Katherine to spend Christmas at Green Gables. The barriers between Anne and Katherine are broken down in a scene Epperly describes as "excellent drama" while noting that the Sullivan production could not capture the poignancy of Montgomery's prose (136-37). Katherine declares that there is no way that Anne, living "in a little enchanted circle of beauty and romance," could ever understand the heartbreak of Katherine's childhood.

"You seem to have everything I hadn't . . . charm . . . friendship . . . youth. Youth! I never had anything but starved youth. You know nothing about it. You don't know . . . you haven't the least idea what it is like not to be wanted by anyone . . . anyone!"

"Oh, haven't I?" cried Anne. In a few poignant sentences she sketched her childhood before coming to Green Gables. (142-43)

The "conversion" of Katherine Brooke seems to echo the conversion of Green Gables, but this time, Green Gables itself takes part in the conversion. This is one of the rare moments in *Windy Poplars* that captures the spirit of the earlier books, reminding the reader that although Anne has left Green Gables, the magic is still there and still with her.

Anne's House of Dreams offers another sort of female bonding ritual, this time in the true friendship that grows between Anne and the tragic Leslie Moore. Leslie, one of the most striking of Montgomery's characters, survives, but barely, in the prison of her marriage; in contrast to Anne's loving, companionable marriage to Gilbert, Leslie's life is heartbreakingly cruel. As this novel was written during wartime, Epperly suggests that Montgomery's depiction of the friendship between Anne and Leslie is a metaphor for the restorative powers of love for the ravaged world (79). Perhaps because in this book Anne experiences the extreme joy and tragedy of womanhood (love in marriage, motherhood, the death of a child), the Anne of *House of Dreams* is more real than any of her incarnations since the original volume. These experiences, along with the friendships of other "kindred spirits," are portrayed against the seas of Four Winds Harbour, where the power of nature seems to illuminate the realities of adult life.

Along with her friendship with Leslie, Anne's other important relationship is with Captain Jim, keeper of the Four Winds lighthouse. Like Matthew, Captain Jim is an earthy, common man of uncommon insight; unlike Matthew, Captain Jim is a vocal, outgoing man. It is interesting to note that of all the men depicted in the series, these two are the most memorable; even Gilbert seems a mere boy in their presence. Montgomery underscores the importance of these two men in Anne's life by having each of them speak the words of blessing. Shortly before his death in *Green Gables*, Anne wistfully wishes aloud to Matthew that she had been the boy he and Marilla had hoped to get from the orphan asylum, and Matthew is vocal at last in his reply:

"Well, now, I'd rather have you than a dozen boys, Anne," said Matthew, patting her hand. "Just mind you that—rather than a dozen boys. Well, now, I guess it wasn't a boy that took the Avery scholarship, was it? It was a girl—my girl—my girl that I'm proud of." (294)

Captain Jim, also near death, offers a further benediction:

"I don't need the fire to read your futures," he said. "I see happiness for all of you—all of you—for Leslie and Mr. Ford—and the Doctor here and Mistress Blythe—and little Jem—and all the children that ain't been born yet but will be. Happiness for you all—though, mind you, I reckon, you'll have your troubles and worries and sorrows, too. They're bound to come—and no house, whether it's a palace or a little house of dreams, can bar 'em out. But they won't get the better of you if you face them *together* with love and trust. You can weather any storm with them two for compass and pilot."

The old man rose suddenly and placed one hand on Leslie's head and one on Anne's.

"Two good, sweet women," he said. "True and faithful and to be depended upon. Your husbands will have honour in the gates because of you—your children will rise up and call you blessed in the years to come." (216)

This double blessing underscores several of Montgomery's favorite themes: the sense of belonging, the virtue of motherhood, the duty of life and identity, chivalry and the love of home and family. Given the war-torn times in which this book, and the three that followed (both in publishing and Anne-chronology) were written, these themes show that during times of strife, the constancy of home is worth fighting for.

These themes are used in various ways in the last three books of the series. While *Anne of Ingleside* is, on the surface, merely the chronicling of the "baby days" of Anne and Gilbert's five children, it is also the only novel in the series that explores the adult relationship between Anne and Gilbert in the reality beyond the House of Dreams romance. It is crucial that Montgomery show that marriage, even a happy one, is not always rosy romance; just as Anne's childhood daydreams had to be adapted to accommodate reality, so do the reader's expectations of "happily ever after." It is what Helen Waite Papashvily calls a "true partnership that makes the fullest use of each individual and his particular gifts to complement and sustain and fulfill and advance the entity" (212). Anne at this point is in the opposite position from which she entered the Avonlea community; Four Winds is, as Avonlea, a matriarchal community, but Anne as an adult woman in the community assumes a different vantage point than the scrawny orphan had.

Otherwise mostly comic in nature, *Ingleside* is a celebration of the halcyon days before World War I. Written in the shadow of World War II, the book hearkens back to a time when war was unthinkable, although the fog of war was once again approaching the coast of Montgomery's beloved Island. The most notable characters in the book are not to be Anne and Gilbert, however (aside from the few marital scenes in which they appear), but Susan Baker, the housekeeper from the House of Dreams, and Walter, the Blythe's second son and echo of the dreamy, sensitive Anne of Green Gables, though with less outward expression of spirit. Where Anne, as a child, expressed her feelings, Walter is more inwardly based; he is sensitive and introspective. Susan, on the other hand, is the talkative bulwark of the household, and a surrogate mother to the Ingleside "fry." Susan's pithy comments are based on the strong sense of duty admired so by Montgomery, but without the deeper intellect of Anne; this refreshing viewpoint admires beauty no less than the enraptured mistress of Ingleside, but she finds instead as much or more beauty in her daily chores of house- and child-keeping. Although a "spinster" by village standards, Susan has the advantage of her spirit and attitude over the more "fortunate" females of the community.

The feeling of halcyon days is maintained in the seventh installment of the series, *Rainbow Valley*, though, in this instance, it serves as a reminder that the children of today are the soldiers of tomorrow. Written during World War I, *Rainbow Valley* follows the tradition of chivalry and honor through the children of Ingleside and the children of the Reverend John Meredith, widowed pastor of the Glen church. Anne is mostly absent in the last two books of the series, but her spirit is clearly there in the community of her children and their playmates. Montgomery uses Walter as a sort of Galahad in embryo, with Una Meredith as his female counterpart; oldest son Jem is the future general, anxious for the battle, but not thinking of the moral consequences, and Faith Meredith is his counterpart. These pairings reinforce the central themes in Montgomery's war-connected novels (*Anne's House of Dreams, Anne of Ingleside, Rainbow Valley,* and *Rilla of Ingleside*), showing that war is fought not only on the battlefield, but on the home front as well. Epperly calls this a vision of "heroism's childhood"—a noble courage rarely seen in children's literature, and even rarer in its inclusion of females into the scenario (98-99).

The girls in this story, including the orphaned Mary Vance, reflect the women they will and must become in the years that follow, which offers the reader, particularly if she is a young girl herself, the tools with which adversity can be faced. Under Aunt Martha's haphazard care, Faith and Una try, nevertheless, to "bring themselves up"; while their brothers are interested, the bulk of this "bringing up" falls to the girls. As daughters of a minister, they realize that their position in the community requires more responsibility than is usually settled on other girls. Through trial and error, Faith and Una (with Mary Vance following their lead) not only try to raise themselves properly but also attempt to put their faith into action. That the girls' attempts are often far from successful seems not as important as their courageous and earnest desire to do their best. Unlike the moralistic Elsie Dinsmore or the simpering Ellen Montgomery, these girls are complex, *involved* women-in-training; the foundation Montgomery prepared so carefully in the earlier books of the series supports these characters as the "iconography of the ideal child" is debunked in favor of more realistic heroines (Foster and Simons 7).

This foundation also supports the final book in the series, *Rilla of Ingleside,* which leads the reader through the World War I home front not with Anne particularly, but through the eyes of two characters: the aforementioned Susan Baker, and Rilla, the youngest of Anne's children, who grows from a selfish adolescent to a caring, responsible woman as she, in the words of her brother Walter, "keeps the faith." Marie C. Campbell notes that though this book was originally "considered a lesser light in the Montgomery canon, [it] is now recognized as a valuable fictional account of the Canadian experience on the World War I home front, one of very few such records" (466).

Drawing largely, again, from her own journals, Montgomery paints a heart-wrenching picture of the realities of life on the home front, hearing news of war and seeing the boys of the village become soldiers. Montgomery was thus able to access the public voice denied women during World War I by channeling her private voice through literature (Bicker 99). Rilla, with little ambition beyond getting to the next dance, is forced from her frivolous world as the distant idea of war becomes a reality when her brothers are shipped out. She dives into war work with the "Junior Reds" (following Susan, her sisters' and her mother's example with the Red Cross), which leads her to the adoption of a war baby. This adoption is neatly paralleled with Anne's adoption in the first book; Nancy Huse draws out this comparison by focusing on the journeys of Marilla and Rilla (her namesake) with their "foundlings." Marilla is fully convinced that Anne will not stay at Green Gables until they go to visit Mrs. Spencer to uncover how the mistake (of sending a girl, rather than a boy) occurred. Marilla is offered the opportunity to rid herself of her charge by the shrewish Mrs. Blewett, but comes to the sudden realization that she could not, in good conscience, hand over a sensitive, innocent child like Anne to that woman's cruel hand. Similarly, Rilla is faced with the option of not taking home the orphaned baby boy, but knows that she could never leave a helpless infant to the drunken hag tending it; she takes the baby home in a soup tureen, his only inheritance. The drives home that both women take with their charges are strikingly similar (130-37).

A third "mother" is, of course, Susan; her dedication to the children of Ingleside is as strong as if they were her biological children. Contrasted with the fourth "mother," Miss Cornelia, who adopts the orphan Mary Vance (in *Rainbow Valley*), Susan is even more "motherly." Miss Cornelia loves Mary, and is obviously devoted to her, but she lacks the depth of feeling that Susan has, suggesting perhaps that Susan's life before the House of Dreams and Ingleside was not the nurturing, comfortable childhood enjoyed by Miss Cornelia.

If Rilla is Montgomery's "tribute to the girlhood of Canada" (Gillen 79), then Susan is the home light of a nation:

[S]he went out and ran up the flag, for the first time since the fall of Jerusalem. As it caught the breeze and swelled gallantly out above her, Susan lifted her hand and saluted it, as she had seen Shirley do. "We've all given something to keep you flying," she said. "Four hundred thousand of our boys gone overseas—fifty thousand of them killed. But—you are worth it!" . . . She was one of the women—courageous, unquailing, patient, heroic—who had made victory possible. (255)

Susan's "homely" sacrifice, and Rilla's sacrifice of youth, capture Montgomery's themes of hearth and home in a strong and poignant way.

Carol Gay indicates that the success of the Anne of Green Gables series has been largely ignored because its readership has been almost exclusively girls and women (101). In her essay "'Kindred Spirits' All: Green Gables Revisited," Gay looks at the work of Gerda Lerner, who provided an alternative view of history with her book *The Majority Finds Its Past: Placing Women in History*, using Montgomery's *Anne* series to show the ways in which the series gives "place" to women. Gay states:

However Montgomery may not have realized, or wanted to accept, that you cannot substitute imagination for reality, her books show that life lived without imagination is not worth living. She created through her Avonlea series a world where the traditional women's values of love, warmth, sensitivity, imagination and endurance survive and overcome, a world where kindred spirits are intuitively identified and cherished. It is a world that has enough reality for women and girls of the past seventy-five years to respond to with deep recognition, and thus, it serves as an important document in "the development of feminist consciousness." (107)

In this series, the reader is given the option to view life in a different way: being a mother is not just a biological function; being a spouse is not subservience to the will of another; being a part of a community is not just living in one, but connecting with those around you. This combined appeal to adult and adolescent readers is cited by Shirley Foster and Judy Simons as a partial explanation for the series' extensive popularity (150). When the reader is a young girl, however, she is offered even more: a chance to guide her own life within societal constraints, to create the woman inside herself. This is perhaps Montgomery's greatest legacy; by giving young girls a road map for seeing more to life, she does not advocate entrance into or usurpation of the "man's world"—there is enough to be done in the world of women without, as Miss Cornelia would say, "cleaning up after the men." This is not what Papashvily calls a "handbook for another kind of feminine revolt" (xvii), but about making the most of what life can offer you as a woman, and as a part of society. Montgomery achieves what Inglis called the ability to "brace . . . values against both the family and the big world in the creative effort of all writers to transcend division and find a new unity of culture and being" (117). Some of Montgomery's female characters seize the opportunity to see beyond the crescent; others do not. As Foster and Simons suggest, the Anne of Green Gables series is a "revisionary" text: it allows for a revisioning of one's role on a personal and societal level, and allowed Montgomery the opportunity to direct both her personal and her literary vision by "suggesting new and more open attitudes toward girlhood" (164). There are new generations that have yet to read these books, yet to form their own vision of themselves and the world around them. For them, and for all of us, the whole of the moon is still there, shining on the land of dreams.

Notes

1. It should be noted that Kevin Sullivan has also published his own versions of Anne's story, based on his teleplays for the PBS productions of *Anne of Green Gables* and *Anne of Green Gables—The Sequel*. While not sold in the United States, these books are sold alongside those of Montgomery in Canada.

2. I am indebted as well to Mary Dockray-Miller for introducing this theory to me.

Works Cited

Auerbach, Nina. *Communities of Women: An Idea in Fiction*. Cambridge: Harvard UP, 1978.

Avery, Gillian. "Home and Family: English and American Ideals in the Nineteenth Century." *Stories and Society: Children's Literature in Its Social Context*. Ed. Dennis Butts. New York: St. Martin's, 1992.

Baldwin, Douglas. "L. M. Montgomery's *Anne of Green Gables*: The Japanese Connection." *Journal of Canadian Studies* 28 (Fall 1993): 3, 123-33.

Berg, Temma F. "*Anne of Green Gables*: A Girl's Reading." *Such a Simple Little Tale*. Ed. Mavis Reimer. Metuchen: Children's Literature Association, 1992. 153-64.

Bicker, Lyn. "Public and Private Choices: Public and Private Voices." *Women and World War I: The Written Response*. Ed. Dorothy Goldman. New York: St. Martin's, 1993. 92-112.

Bolger, Francis W. P. *The Years Before "Anne": The Early Career of Lucy Maud Montgomery*. Halifax: Nimbus, 1991.

Butts, Dennis. *Stories and Society: Children's Literature in Its Social Context*. New York: St. Martin's, 1992.

Campbell, Marie C. "Lucy Maud Montgomery." *Children's Books and Their Creators*. Ed. Anita Silvey. New York: Houghton, 1995. 466.

Douglas, Ann. *The Feminization of American Culture*. New York: Knopf, 1977.

Drain, Susan. "Community and the Individual in *Anne of Green Gables*: The Meaning of Belonging." *Such a Simple Little Tale*. Ed. Mavis Reimer. Metuchen: Children's Literature Association, 1992. 119-30.

Epperly, Elizabeth Rollins. *The Fragrance of Sweet-Grass: L. M. Montgomery's Heroines and the Pursuit of Romance*. Toronto: U of Toronto P, 1992.

Foster, Shirley, and Judy Simons. *What Katy Read: Feminist Re-Readings of "Classic" Stories for Girls*. Iowa City: U of Iowa P, 1995.

Gay, Carol. "'Kindred Spirits' All: Green Gables Revisited." *Such a Simple Little Tale*. Ed. Mavis Reimer. Metuchen: Children's Literature Association, 1992. 101-08.

Gillen, Mollie. *The Wheel of Things: A Biography of L. M. Montgomery*. Don Mills: Fitzhenry & Whiteside, 1975.

Huse, Nancy. "Journeys of the Mother in the World of Green Gables." *Such a Simple Little Tale*. Ed. Mavis Reimer. Metuchen: Children's Literature Association, 1992. 131-38.

Inglis, Fred. *The Promise of Happiness: Value and Meaning in Children's Fiction*. Cambridge: Cambridge UP, 1981.

Kornfeld, Eve, and Susan Jackson. "The Female *Bildungsroman* in Nineteenth-Century America: Parameters of a Vision." *Such a Simple Little Tale*. Ed. Mavis Reimer. Metuchen: Children's Literature Association, 1992. 139-52.

MacLulich, T. D. "L. M. Montgomery's Portraits of the Artist: Realism, Idealism, and the Domestic Imagination." *Such a Simple Little Tale*. Ed. Mavis Reimer. Metuchen: Children's Literature Association, 1992. 83-100.

Montgomery, L. M. *The Alpine Path: The Story of My Career*. Don Mills: Fitzhenry and Whiteside, 1975.

——. *Anne of Avonlea*. 1909. Toronto: Ryerson, 1942.

——. *Anne of Green Gables*. 1908. Toronto: Ryerson, 1942.

——. *Anne of Ingleside*. New York: Grosset and Dunlap, 1939.

——. *Anne of the Island*. New York: Grosset and Dunlap, 1915.

——. *Anne of Windy Poplars*. New York: Grosset and Dunlap, 1936.

——. *Anne's House of Dreams*. 1917. Toronto: McClelland and Stewart, 1922.

——. *Rainbow Valley*. 1919. Toronto: McClelland and Stewart, 1923.

——. *Rilla of Ingleside*. 1920. Toronto: McClelland and Stewart, 1921.

——. *The Selected Journals of L. M. Montgomery*. Volume I: 1889-1910. Ed. Mary Rubio and Elizabeth Waterston. Toronto: Oxford UP, 1985.

——. *The Selected Journals of L. M. Montgomery*. Volume II: 1910-1921. Ed. Mary Rubio and Elizabeth Waterston. Toronto: Oxford UP, 1987.

Nodelman, Perry. "Progressive Utopia: Or, How to Grow up Without Growing Up." *Such a Simple Little Tale*. Ed. Mavis Reimer. Metuchen: Children's Literature Association, 1992. 29-38.

Papashvily, Helen Waite. *All the Happy Endings: A Study of the Domestic Novel in America, the Women who Wrote It, the Women Who Read It, in the Nineteenth Century*. New York: Harper, 1956.

Reimer, Mavis. *Such a Simple Little Tale: Critical Responses to L. M. Montgomery's Anne of Green Gables*. Metuchen: Children's Literature Association, 1992.

Rubio, Mary. "*Anne of Green Gables*: The Architect of Adolescence." *Such a Simple Little Tale*. Ed. Mavis Reimer. Metuchen: Children's Literature Association, 1992. 65-82.

Scott, Mike. "The Whole of the Moon." Dizzy Heights Music Pub., Ltd./ Chrysalis Music (ASCAP), 1985.

Showalter, Elaine. *Sister's Choice: Tradition and Change in American Women's Writing*. New York: Oxford UP, 1991.

Solt, Marilyn. "The Uses of Setting in *Anne of Green Gables*." *Such a Simple Little Tale*. Ed. Mavis Reimer. Metuchen: Children's Literature Association, 1992. 57-64.

Thompson, Hilary. "Role Maker." *Canadian Literature* 111 (1986): 205-06.

Weiss-Townsend, Janet. "Sexism Down on the Farm?: *Anne of Green Gables*." *Such a Simple Little Tale*. Ed. Mavis Reimer. Metuchen: Children's Literature Association, 1992. 109-18.

Whitaker, Muriel A. " 'Queer Children': L. M. Montgomery's Heroines." *Such a Simple Little Tale*. Ed. Mavis Reimer. Metuchen: Children's Literature Association, 1992. 11-22.

2

Gender, Class, and Domesticity
in the Isabel Carleton Series

Kathleen Chamberlain

"Well, anything that keeps us from being too lower-middle-class won't hurt us any," says Isabel Carleton to her mother in *The Heart of Isabel Carleton* (212). The story of Isabel's efforts to negotiate the territories of class and gender in the American Midwest of the 1910s is told in a five-volume series written between 1916 and 1920 by Margaret Eliza Ashmun. Set in the years 1913 to 1916, the Isabel Carleton books reposition definitions of class and gender within narratives of domesticity at a time when such redefinition had become vital to anyone who looked to avoid being "too lower-middle-class." By the 1910s, many of the middle-class and gender constructs of the nineteenth century could no longer fully delineate effective cultural boundaries, yet many of the strategies that would provide such boundaries in the twentieth century, such as consumerism and professionalism, had not yet reached their peak. In the decade in which the novels were written, earlier definitions of class were being undermined and revised by such important economic and social developments as the struggle to establish national labor unions, the growth of the power of the federal government, the rapid increase in the nation's industrial base, and the concomitant decrease in agricultural occupations. To maintain its status in the face of such sweeping changes, the middle class needed to assert a definition of itself that incorporated the new developments without completely rewriting its former identity.

Such a process is discernible in Ashmun's Isabel Carleton series. In these domestic narratives, produced at a period when previous encodings of the class had eroded, one can read what Elizabeth Langland has called "the semiotics of middle-class life" (9). At the same time that it offers acceptably redefined signs, however, Ashmun's discourse reveals the instability of these codes. Her method is one of accommodation; she seeks to create new constructions of class and gender that are nonetheless based on older domestic paradigms. In doing so, she cannot avoid the tensions inherent in a culture that needs to combine concepts of class and gender inequity with the concept of democratic egalitarianism.

To make sense of Ashmun's ideologies, we must go beyond a conception of class based solely on income. In identifying class, mainstream sociologists usually consider three other measures in addition to the yardstick of income: education, occupational prestige, and family background (composed of the family's history in the first three categories). An understanding of the semiotics of class will include other material indicators as well: the location, size, type, and cost of housing; clothing; the type and number of such goods as household appliances, furnishings, and "luxuries"; the type of food eaten, and so on. Added to material goods are intangible indicators such as "taste," speech, behavior, habits of consumption, social relationships and the boundaries of allowable acquaintance, and access to and conceptions of "culture."

To stop at the preceding list would be to limit our concept of class to essentially static categories. It is equally important to conceive of class as a continuing historical process. E. P. Thompson (and others) posit class formation and definition as responses to a specific set of historical and cultural events. In his analysis of Victorian families, Steven Mintz argues in favor of this historical model, writing that such an approach "views the emergence of the term [class] at once as an index of broader social transformations and as a perceptual lens through which individuals sought to make sense of social change" (204). Finally, we should note the degree to which a given class is aware of itself as a discrete group, for such a consciousness will in turn affect the way that a group creates and redefines itself. This view of class as a dynamic process is crucial if we are to understand how popular literature such as the Isabel Carleton series helped shape, as well as reflect, contemporary urban middle-class attitudes.

If defining "class" in general is complex, then defining the "middle class" is in some ways even more difficult. While most writers on the topic go beyond a strictly economic conception, some define the "middle class" simply in terms of what it is not. Writing in 1935, Lewis Corey characterized the middle class as "all those people who are not big capitalists, wage earners, or farmers" (20). As Steven Mintz writes, "the problem with this omnibus approach . . . is that the category that emerges is not meaningful in either economic or social terms" (204). Scholarship has suggested that the American middle class evolved as a distinct historical construction during the nineteenth century. In his study of "the emergence of the middle class" in nineteenth-century America, Stuart Blumin argues that the class was not "fully formed" until after the

Civil War; that is, though "middling folk" had existed in America since colonial times, the development of a distinct middle-class ideology and "way of life" was part of the process of industrialization and urban growth that characterized the nineteenth century (9-13).

For Blumin, the main line dividing the middle and working classes in nineteenth-century America is that between manual and non-manual labor (13), a criterion that applies primarily to males. In her excellent study of the impact of household technology on housewives' lives, Ruth Schwartz Cowan chooses to "abjure the usual socioeconomic class terms" when creating her hypothetical illustrative families because "those terms refer either to the work done, or to the income achieved, by the male head of a household" (152). But using a broader, more histori- cal concept of class allows us to recognize that such male-oriented cate- gories as Cowan describes achieve meaning only in context of women's participation in creating an entire middle-class ethos. Women enter the American middle-class construct through the concurrent development of the domestic ideal, which in the nineteenth century evolved into a com- plex encoding of class, gender, and racial-ethnic standards. Blumin shows that the nineteenth-century formation of the middle class "went beyond the realignment of work, workplace relations, incomes, and opportunities" (191) to incorporate the roles of women as domestic con- sumers and producers, as (ideally) constructors of moral values, and as keepers and creators of many of the signs and codes of the class. The home, as the space most easily controlled by individuals, became the locus for demarcating the lines of class (179). "The 'separate sphere' of domestic womanhood," writes Blumin, was "influential, perhaps even crucial, in generating new social identities. To this extent, middle-class formation is women's work" (191).[1]

Other studies suggest that Blumin is too cautious when he writes that domestic ideals were "perhaps" crucial in forming the middle class. In fact, domestic negotiations are essential if one views class, as Blumin does, as being "formed through the convergence of relevant experience" (11), that is, through the coalescing of people's experiences of daily life and communal relations into a recognizable ideology. The centrality of the home to such "relevant experience" seems clear. Thus, it is not sur- prising that the construction of the concept of "home" should be equally central to the content of the emerging class ideology. As Nancy Cott writes, "[T]he canon of domesticity expressed the dominance of what may be designated a middle-class ideal, a cultural preference for domes- tic retirement and conjugal family intimacy over both the 'vain' and fashionable sociability of the rich and the promiscuous sociability of the poor" (92). Elizabeth Langland argues that women's domestic responsibility for inculcating class lessons can even account for the "non-narratability" of certain plots in fiction (9).[2] Langland stresses what she calls the

close imbrication of economic conditions with cultural constructions, where financial resources cannot position individuals more irrevocably than do the networks of representations through which they negotiate their daily lives. In this dimension of cultural currency as opposed to economic capital, women dominated Victorian society. (7)

This dominance extended to class formation. Langland asserts that "women controlled representations of the middle class" (2) because their place in the home required them to "perform the ideological work of managing the class questions and displaying the signs of middle class status" (9).

American domestic fiction suggests that much of what was true of the British middle-class household could also be true of the American. While many elements of the domestic ideal, notably the evangelical fervor of the antebellum years, had been modified by the time that Margaret Ashmun wrote the Isabel Carleton series, her books show that women remained as managers of the signs and questions and continued redefinitions of class. Though the particular picture of mostly urban middle-class domesticity presented in such instructive young adult fiction represents an ideal rather than a reality, Ashmun's vision might for that very reason be a more direct indicator of class ideology in the Progressive Era than a more "factual" account.

The depiction of the middle class in the Isabel Carleton series is essentially conservative, based on long-standing codes of gentility and on patterns established as far back as the early nineteenth century, when, as Mary Ryan argues in *Cradle of the Middle Class*, "the American middle class molded its distinctive identity around domestic values and family practices" (15). Thus Ashmun could draw on a strong heritage of the home as a shaper of what historian Joan Shelley Rubin sums up as internal moral "character," as opposed to the more modern (and more superficial, external, and secular) "personality" (3-5; 23-25). In keeping with this older ideal and with revised twentieth-century versions of it, Ashmun posits the home, complete with an idealized mother, as the main source, to use Nancy Theriot's term, of "scripts" by which middle-class women defined themselves and their culture (2). Onto this fairly traditional domestic ideal, Ashmun grafts many of the Progressive Era issues that were reshaping American narratives of class and gender: suffrage and women's rights, immigration, the growth of an industrial labor force, the growth of a consumer culture, increasing secularization, changes in household technology, and the development of standards of professional-ism, even in housework and mothering. The result is in some ways a "new" narrative, yet one that reveals, in what Langland calls textual "ruptures" (4), the inability of such narratives fully to contain the materi-als of cultural and class dominance.

Though her outlook is primarily conservative, Margaret Ashmun herself was not a typical product of middle-class domesticity. Born in 1875,[3] she received a master's degree and served as an instructor of Eng-lish at the University of Wisconsin during the early years of the twenti-eth century, a time when fewer than 3,000 of the nation's 500,000 female teachers taught in institutions of higher education (Filene 31). Like many of her contemporaries among the early generations of American women to flock in great numbers to higher education, Ashmun did not marry, but supported herself though teaching and writing.[4] In addition to the Isabel Carleton series and other novels, she wrote books on composition and edited educational anthologies of prose and short stories. Her first text-book, *Composition in High School*, appeared in 1908. *Modern Short Stories*, published in 1914, was still in print in the 1940s and had by then gone through numerous editions.

Ashmun's college composition text, *The Study and Practice of Writing English* (co-written with Gerhard Lomer, "Ph.D.," in 1914 and revised in 1917) offers interesting insights into her semiotics of class. To Ashmun, language is one of the signs that separates the middle from the working class. Though she and Lomer caution instructors that "formal-ism and the memorization of rules have little place in the modern study and practice of writing English," Ashmun is clearly a prescriptive gram-marian who uses the vocabularies of education, taste, and gentility to show that "correct" speech is one of the barometers of middle-class status (iv). She applies such terms as "crude" (169), "vulgar" (118), "illiterate" (170), "commonplace" (147), "inelegant" (182) and "in bad taste" (184) to grammatical situations ranging from inadequate transi-tions to the overuse of compound sentences to usage "errors" such as saying "real" for "really" and "raise" instead of "rear" or "bring up" (180). Ashmun and Lomer tend to equate education with intelligence and mental development, comparing "illiterate writers" to children, both of whom use compound sentences because they do not "weigh values and note relations" (75). The book's list of "vulgarisms" shows a clear rhetoric of class, since many of the terms seem to be so designated either because they are used by servants and workers ("gent"; "gentleman friend") or because they blur class boundaries by linguistically linking the designations of the upper classes with working-class occupations: "scrublady," "washlady," and "saleslady" (184).[5] Even the tone of one's voice is a class marker: Ashmun and Lomer urge readers to correct their "mispronunciations" by "consciously noticing the pronunciation of cultured people and by realizing that correct pronunciation involves the cultivation of a pleasant speaking voice and a refined intonation" (118).

Ashmun brought similar lessons in class to her own fiction. The initial Isabel Carleton volume, *Isabel Carleton's Year*, appeared in 1916, though portions of the book had been published earlier in the venerable *Youth's Companion* magazine. *Isabel Carleton's Year* was followed by *The Heart of Isabel Carleton* in 1917, *Isabel Carleton's Friends* in 1918, and *Isabel Carleton in the West* in 1919. The series ended in 1920 with *Isabel Carleton at Home.* Unlike many other juvenile series books, especially those of the Stratemeyer Syndicate, the Isabel Carleton series was treated seriously by reviewers and educators, a reflection, perhaps, of the books' generally high literary quality. According to advertising blurbs that follow the text of *Isabel Carleton's Friends*, the *San Francisco Chronicle* said that the books were "considerably out of the rut of young-life fiction." *Shorthand Writer* stated that "fathers and mothers cannot give to maturing sons and daughters more wholesome stories than those of Isabel Carleton." Both *The Christian Advocate* and *The Christian Register* found the books "realistic," an interesting designation considering that the stories, despite their surface verisimilitude, present what today seem to be highly idealized portraits of domestic felicity, girlhood, and motherhood.

The series tells of Isabel Carleton's struggle to define herself and her place in her world as she grows from a high-school senior to a college junior who becomes engaged at the series' end to her childhood sweetheart, Rodney Fox. Each volume spends a great deal of space on Isabel's reflections about her future as an adult, a woman, and a mother. Ashmun only occasionally offers overt judgments of Isabel's conduct; readers must draw conclusions for themselves. For instance, not until volume 2 does Isabel (and presumably a young reader) recognize that in volume 1 she has been too preoccupied with jewelry and other material goods.

The stories are set mostly in the midwestern town of Jefferson, home to a large state university, both thinly disguised portrayals of Madison and the University of Wisconsin circa 1915. The Carleton family consists of father Arthur, who is a professor of classics at the university; mother Laura; eldest daughter Isabel; middle sister Fanny; and youngest sister Celia. Other continuing characters are Rodney Fox, an engineering student; Grandmother and Grandfather Stuart, who live nearby on a farm; and two servants, first Swedish immigrant Olga and later "American" Melissy.

Isabel Carleton's Year begins in January of 1913, when seventeen-year-old Isabel is a senior in high school. Fanny is thirteen, and little sister Celia is seven. The plot is fairly tame by the standards of the more sensationalistic juvenile series of the time: there are no mysteries, no sinister strangers, no long-lost relatives, no missing wills. Instead, Isabel must come to terms with the facts and mysteries of everyday life. When she has to choose between a ring she craves and donations and gifts she wants to make, she learns to establish class-related financial priorities; when a jealous friend tells spiteful lies about her, Isabel learns that her life, which she sees as one of sacrifice and self-denial, looks quite different from someone else's perspective. She comes to regret moments of hardheartedness with her sister Fanny, and she faces and overcomes her fear of giving the commencement address. The story's most dramatic event, and one that in its seriousness might help account for critical assessments of the series' "realism," occurs in the summer of 1913, only weeks before Isabel is to enter college. During a canoe ride on the lake, Isabel, Rodney Fox, Isabel's best female friend, Molly Ramsey, and Molly's escort, Eric Thomas, are overturned during a freak thunderstorm. Molly and Eric drown; though Rodney and Isabel survive, Rodney suffers for days from an unnamed, life-threatening illness, and Isabel endures what today might be labeled clinical depression. Ashmun spends a portion of each of the next four books describing how Isabel comes to terms with her loss. At the end of *Isabel Carleton's Year*, rich, widowed cousin Eunice Everard plans to take Isabel abroad for a year to help her cope with Molly's death.

The Heart of Isabel Carleton opens in the summer of 1914, at the end of Isabel's year in Europe, when she and cousin Eunice are in London waiting for passage back to America from the now war-torn continent. Amid sightseeing and much war-talk, Isabel meets Herbert Barry, a fraternity brother of Rodney's. Between them, Isabel and Herbert aid a rich but helpless Hindu woman whose French husband has been sent into battle. While visiting an expatriate American woman who makes hand-crafted jewelry, Isabel decides that to be a craftsperson is her vocational calling.

The second half of the book takes place in Jefferson as Isabel prepares for and begins her delayed first year of college. During the year's work and socializing, Herbert Barry grows more and more attached to Isabel, finally offering her a sort of oblique marriage proposal. When Isabel asks if they cannot just be friends, Herbert says no. "I'm not a boy; I'm a man. I know what I want. And I know when I can't have it," he asserts (266). After this disappointment, Herbert abandons college to go to France as an ambulance driver.

Isabel Carleton's Friends begins in April 1915, toward the end of Isabel's freshman/sophomore year. (Though this year is actually her first at college, she earns enough credits because of the languages she learned in Europe to qualify as a sophomore.) This volume details Isabel's friendship with Meta Houston, a rich girl from Montana, whom Isabel at first dislikes for being rather bold, loud, and interested in Rodney. After determining that what Meta most needs is the moral influence of home and mother, Mrs. Carleton and Isabel encourage her to spend a great deal of time in the Carleton family circle. In the course of the story, the girls' friendship is tested when Meta decides to shower Isabel with gifts of clothing since she knows that Isabel loves but cannot afford too many expensive items. Because the gifts leave Isabel feeling robbed of her independence, she and Meta must eventually agree to a friendship based on equality. Another tense episode concerns Fanny, who has developed into something of a violin prodigy. After Isabel complains when Fanny practices dozens of repetitions of one bar in a minor key, Fanny takes to her bed in a burst of artistic temperament and refuses to continue her violin lessons. Only the intervention of the servant Melissy, who shames the girls into realizing their pettiness, restores harmony.

The final major event of volume 3 explores the family relationships of the Houstons. When Meta's widowed father decides to marry the headmistress of a girls' school, Meta refuses to accept her new stepmother, even when that stepmother turns out to be loving, understanding, elegant, educated, and progressive in her views on women. Finally, in an emotional scene, the new Mrs. Houston wins Meta's allegiance. In celebration, the Houstons invite Isabel to spend the summer with them in Montana while Rodney Fox and Meta's beau, George Burnham, undertake summer engineering jobs.

This development leads to *Isabel Carleton in the West*, which opens in June of 1915 as Isabel and Meta arrive in Helena, Montana. The group sets up a fairly luxurious camp in the semiwilderness. The women rest, cook, and improve themselves while the young men work on building a dam. During their leisure time, the group discusses serious topics such as war, duty, family, and women's rights. At one point, they engage in a long and surprisingly mean-spirited diatribe against immigration. Each person's mettle is tested in various ways: the young men must face the consequences of bad planning when their dam washes away, Meta must accept that being a woman means learning such domestic arts as cooking, Isabel faces her fear of horses, and even Mr. Houston grapples with the idea that middle-class women need not give up employment after marriage. Toward the end of the novel, the group becomes acquainted with young Stephen Clark, the adopted son of rancher Emery

Clark and his genteel but lonely wife Sarah. The book concludes with Meta and George becoming engaged.

The final volume, *Isabel Carleton at Home*, begins back in Jefferson in October of 1915. At nearly twenty, Isabel is a college junior; Meta and Rodney are seniors. Stephen Clark of Montana has enrolled at the university in the agricultural program. During the year, Isabel becomes attracted to a glib graduate student from the English Department named Bertram Dodge. When Meta and Rodney object to Bertram (Rodney says, "I just don't think he's square" [102]), Isabel pursues Dodge and his poetic pretensions even further. All friendship stops, however, when Dodge publishes as his own a poem that Isabel wrote. She puts this episode behind her while Stephen's rancher mother, Mrs. Clark, comes to visit. When she sees how much Mrs. Clark appreciates the cultural opportunities of Jefferson, Isabel realizes how much she has taken for granted. The story concludes in June of 1916 with Rodney's and Meta's graduation and with Meta's wedding to George. On the evening of the wedding, Rodney proposes to Isabel. The book—and the series—end with the two characters standing on the Carletons' porch facing the beginning of their "real" lives.

In plot terms, then, the Isabel Carleton series draws heavily on the traditional domestic narratives of home, family, love, and marriage that are at the same time narratives of class and gender. In the occupational prestige of Mr. Carleton's job as a professor of classics; in the income level that enables the Carletons to support a roomy house, five family members, and a maid; in the acceptance of college as an educational given for women and men; and in the family history, which incorporates such class signifiers as the possession of heirlooms, trips to Europe, and college educations for both Mr. and Mrs. Carleton, Ashmun has satisfied the traditional sociological categories for defining class status. The semiotics of the family's material possessions, social activities, leisure time, dress, charity, language, taste, patterns of consumption, and concepts of culture also reveal the series' middle-class locus.

Money provides a useful starting point for an explication of class in the Isabel Carleton books. Though financial explanations cannot fully define class, they are still crucial. Most middle-class people face some financial restrictions, yet to demonstrate even the minimum standards of middle-class gentility, such people require at least some disposable income. Also, members of middle class need to draw more than one set of class boundaries. Unlike the upper class, which must set itself off only from those below, the middle class must distinguish itself from both the upper and lower classes. And as the quotation that opens this essay shows, Ashmun was conscious of further categories within the middle class itself. Money, or the relative lack of it, provides an effective means of making these necessary class divisions. For Ashmun and others who depict and define the middle class, the task is to encode the sign of money into narratives that assert its importance at the same time that they assert its limitations as a measure of middle-class status. In these constructions, class membership must depend to some extent on signs, such as heritage, that are not obtainable through money, *and* on signs, such as financial charity, that reveal the power of money.

In the Isabel Carleton stories, Ashmun accomplishes this tricky double inscription. She emphasizes the family's limited financial resources from the first page of the first volume, when the reader is introduced to Mrs. Carleton "turning sheets to make them wear longer" (*Year* 1). Throughout, the series emphasizes "making do" and "making over." The girls are often "saving" for desired ornaments. Mrs. Carleton is constantly mending, embroidering, crocheting, or remaking dresses that are "getting out of date" (*Friends* 193). In fact, the category of dress represents one of Ashmun's strategies for encoding money into her class narratives. She uses dress as one way to contain the threat posed by material items that are desirable but are so expensive that they threaten to disrupt middle-class boundaries.[6] Her method is to present such an item as something that can damage one's identity. After Meta Houston buys Isabel an embroidered silk dress, velvet hat, and stylishly heeled shoes, Isabel appreciates their distinctiveness while also sensing the erosion of her sense of self as defined through "independence." When Rodney sees her wearing the finery, he can scarcely talk to her. "You look like a princess or something," he says. "I don't know that I dare walk on the same side of the street with you" (*Friends* 132-33). Though she recognizes that the dress meets other middle-class standards by being "stylish" yet "reserved," Mrs. Carleton tellingly comments that the gown, in materials and trimming, is "almost too rich for a schoolgirl" (*Friends* 128).

By defining "too rich" as a danger to social community and even to selfhood, Ashmun inscribes middle-class financial limitation as a moral value and also implies, in this episode and elsewhere, that the upper classes, when they emphasize cost and appearance alone, represent a certain degree of moral degeneracy. Such an inscription locates moral guardianship within the middle class while simultaneously preserving the status quo by suggesting the possible dangers of crossing class boundaries. The standard of "too rich" also works in the other direction to ward off incursions from the working class into the middle class. When "too rich" becomes a class code to be avoided, "simplicity," whether in dress, housing, or behavior, gains corresponding moral status.

To continue with dress as an example, we see that characters frequently voice an aesthetic that emphasizes "excellent lines," "clean" colors, and "good" fabrics, elements that can be separated from ornaments and accessories. Since it is exactly such trimmings that might be fairly easily and inexpensively imitated by working-class members using middle- and upper-class models, one class-preservation strategy is to identify an excess of trimming as "vulgar," as an indication that its wearers do not understand the code.

Household furnishings offer a similar pattern of class containment and definition based on money.[7] Since furnishings, too, are class markers that might be imitated inexpensively by the working class, such items can be returned firmly to the middle class if one recasts their value in terms other than simple possession. Ashmun's other terms are family history and individual workmanship. Throughout the series, she emphasizes that many of the Carletons' household items are heirlooms: "thin old teaspoons," Great-grandmother's linens, family portraits, a Spode cup that "had been 'in the family' for ever so long" (*Year* 169). Outsiders might attain similar items, but they will be forever shut out of the history. By connecting value with wear and use in her descriptions of "thin teaspoons" and "faded" Axminster carpets, Ashmun not only defends the middle class against the extravagance often associated with the upper class, but she also allows herself a way to incorporate the growing consumer culture of the Progressive Era in her narrative of class without sacrificing her conservative, preservationist orientation. By replacing mere "things" with heirlooms, which represent family history and pedigree, Ashmun allows her middle-class characters to own commodities without the risk of becoming crass materialists, who desire objects merely for status or for pride of possession.

Ashmun's second means of reinscribing the value of household commodities concerns the superiority of hand-made over mass-produced articles, a focus that has implications for both her class and gender narratives. Throughout all five volumes of the series, characters never waver in their preference for the hand-made and hand-sewn. Isabel decides early that her vocation lies in creating attractive hand-crafted jewelry. Though she usually sets semiprecious stones into gold or silver, she is equally willing to work with "pebbles and beads" if the result is aesthetically pleasing. Miss Brookert, the woman who introduces Isabel to the idea of handicrafts, explains the allure of hand-made goods by saying, "it's the thought, the intelligence, that has gone into their making; every stitch and every nail has represented real thought on the part of the person making the article" (*Heart* 70). Isabel replies,

There is something a lot more intelligent about a house with hand-made rugs and furniture than with machine-made ones, no matter how expensive the department-store things may be. I've often noticed the difference in the houses of the people we know in Jefferson. (*Heart* 70)

This speech encapsulates the ways that hand-made goods enable the middle class to maintain its identity in relation to the upper and working classes. First, such articles establish an ethical and intellectual foundation of value that is independent of price, thus allowing the middle-class to turn the potential liability of insufficient funds (which can represent a threat to middle-class status) into a moral asset that can be set against the tradition of upper-class indulgence. Second, the creation of such items demands planning and thought, both of which require a type of currency—that of time and leisure—of which the working class has little.

Ashmun's emphasis on the value of hand-crafted goods links to other areas significant to the class and gender narratives of the Progressive Era, namely patterns of consumption and the growth of professionalization. As Jean Gordon and Jan McArthur note, "[B]y the 1880s and 90s, domestic consumption had become the norm for most Americans" (216). Most of these domestic consumers were women. Thus, consumption offered another arena in which definitions of class and gender could be contested and forged and in which members of the middle class could separate themselves from other classes. Gordon and McArthur identify four categories of female consumption: "traditional consumption, consumption based on upper-class European models, rational consumption, and consumption for personal gratification" (218). They also distinguish between consumption designed to promote social mobility and that designed to "[preserve] a stable way of life" (218), the latter goal being the one toward which Ashmun strives. Though the four categories can exist simultaneously, different periods privilege different patterns.

"Rational consumption," which was most prevalent at the time Ashmun wrote, connected the morality of the home directly to newly professionalized and scientifically established standards of housekeeping in which the woman, in keeping with the reconstruction of gender roles that characterized the period, could be seen, write Gordon and McArthur, as "the domestic counterpart of the professional man . . . knowledgeable in all branches of her job" (231-32). At the same time, such standards were being institutionalized through university departments of, and high school curricula in, Home Economics, Household Arts, and Domestic Science. As a result, Gordon and McArthur continue, "women writers and scientists, with the help of advertisers, were able to instill in the popular mind the concept of home-making as an activity suitable for an educated, upper-class woman as distinct from housework that was arduous, repetitious, and low in status" (231).

Keeping in mind that these words apply equally well to middle-class women, we can see that the Isabel Carleton series "instills" precisely the concepts that Gordon and McArthur describe. Isabel's aesthetic commitment to making and selling hand-crafted jewelry, tasks she pursues, significantly, in the Household Arts Department of her university, is but one instance of how Ashmun adapts the consumerism and professionalism of her age to her need to redefine class and gender in the face of just such social changes. "Domestic Science" is another example. Throughout the five books of the series, Ashmun mentions Isabel's and Fanny's training in high school "Domestic Science" no fewer than a dozen times. "I've had a lot of Domestic Science and Household Arts in high school and in college, too," Isabel explains to a poor but genteel acquaintance who expresses surprise that a college girl would have housekeeping skills (*West* 238). With such training, Ashmun indicates, household chores lose much of their drudgery. When Fanny and Isabel decide to surprise the maid, Melissy, by washing the lunch dishes, the narrator notes that the work went quickly when done by "nimble fingers trained in domestic science courses" (*Friends* 192). This statement also incorporates another tenet of the "professional" doctrine, namely that "knowing" easily translates into "doing." Rich Meta Houston's inability to "do" such tasks as cooking and cleaning is seen by her cultured, progressive stepmother not only as a practical deficiency, but also as an obstacle in Meta's development as a woman.

Though Glenna Matthews[8] and others have shown that the professionalization of housework and mothering also had the negative effects of increasing women's anxieties and of "devaluing" the earlier domestic tradition in which women played more tangible role in the family economy, Ashmun focuses on the progressive implications of standardization: Mrs. Carleton tells Isabel that the home that Isabel will create for her own children will be even better than the one in which she grew up because Isabel "will have a more modern attitude and training" (*Home* 166). Ironically, this "more modern attitude" undermines the focus on "doing" that is central to the Domestic Arts movement in particular and to the development of professionalism in general, since one important component of Isabel's "training" is that she learns to be more of a manager than a worker or "doer." The very fact that Melissy will be "surprised" when the girls do the dishes suggests that the function of the middle-class woman in Ashmun's "modern" depiction is to supervise the work of lower-class women (such as maids), rather than to do the work herself. In such a way, Ashmun is able to retain a middle-class identity in the face of Progressive-Era challenges to class definitions.

Despite her attachment to "modern" developments, Ashmun nonetheless presents fairly traditional concepts of domesticity and motherhood even while she revises these models. As she inscribes them, "modern" developments did not challenge older ideals so much as they provided new impetus for the view that the home should be the focus of women's intellectual and moral energies. Such an approach was actually more in step with the times, or at least with one direction of the times, than the more widely known contemporary issues of the "New Woman" and the agitation for suffrage and for female emancipation might seem to indicate. Since the early days of the Republic, the concept of the moral sanctity of home and motherhood helped define American cultural ideologies.[9] This concept remained viable even when restructured by changes in the technological makeup of the home, the movement away from the centrality of doctrines of Protestant evangelicalism, and the pressures of industrial and economic expansion. Paeans to the home continued to be printed well into the twentieth century. In 1904, Margaret Sangster published an elaborately decorated volume called *The Little Kingdom of Home* that designated the home as the source not only of familial morality but also of the strength of the entire nation. "On the integrity of the family, and the conservatism of the home, depend the stability of our republic," she claimed (vii). "A home is so sacred a thing," she wrote in a chapter on in-laws, "that no pettiness of motive, no meanness, no selfishness, should be allowed to creep in and spoil it" (42). Though Sangster's tone is far more syrupy than Ashmun's, Isabel Carleton and her mother frequently voice views that differ from Sangster's only in their degree of effusive sentiment. During one harmonious evening, Isabel watches the "happy home faces" and stores up memories of "dear home doings" that "would carry with her, far into her later life" (*Friends* 83). Mrs. Carleton, at one point, says strongly that "a home must be a *home*, and not a place where people snatch their food, and neglect their appearance, and air their grievances. I want my children, when they get out into the world, to remember their home as a refuge, as nearly perfect as love and care can make it" (*Heart* 209-10; emphasis Ashmun's).

Much of the rhetoric of home in the early twentieth century was more secular and often less personally fervent than in earlier decades, and professionalization was in many ways redefining homemaking. Yet the home itself, and the centrality of women in that home, were no less important than they had been previously. As middle-class married women continued to withdraw from the labor force as the twentieth century progressed, the image of the woman as shaper of the home became so powerful that, in her book *The House in Good Taste* (1913), actress and interior decorator Elsie De Wolfe could write in all seriousness that "it is the personality of the mistress that our home expresses. Men are forever guests in our homes, no matter how much happiness they may find there" (5). Such hyperbole aside, technological developments over the course of decades did mean that, by the 1910s, many middle-class women such as Mrs. Carleton, who had a sewing machine, telephone, ice box, carpet sweeper, and electric iron (not to mention a maid) to reduce her physical labor, now had more incentive and time to devote themselves to the spiritual, philosophical, and aesthetic aspects of womanhood and mothering and of life in general.

Of course, as Ruth Cowan demonstrates in *More Work for Mother*, new technologies often created higher expectations for women's homemaking, meaning that, despite significant reductions in actual drudgery, middle-class women in the early twentieth century ironically found themselves with less leisure time than before, a fact that did not escape Margaret Ashmun. At one point, when Mrs. Carleton is interrupted by the telephone, she smilingly remarks, "If it weren't for the telephone, one might get some work done. Progress is exchanging one nuisance for another" (*Friends* 44). Still, as Margaret Gibbons Wilson argues, "[F]or many women, the early twentieth century brought a revitalized emphasis upon the value and virtue of home and motherhood and a glorification of the many wonderful and important tasks that could fill the day of the 'home woman'" (85). When physical housework decreased or was reshaped, the culture could redefine the home and its work to emphasize women's social and emotional duties, among them, as Phyllis Palmer writes, "seeing to her husband's comfort, developing the moral and intellectual capacities of her children, and organizing charities" (5).

In just such terms does Margaret Ashmun cast the "home-people" and the "home-doings" that she portrays in the Isabel Carleton series, a depiction that encodes middle-class material attainments, moral attitudes, and social structures. Over the course of five volumes, Ashmun constructs the Carleton home as an insular space defined by cleanliness; leisurely, multi-course meals; and "refined" touches of fresh flowers, afternoon tea, and Spode china. The prevailing impression on the reader is one of quiet, spaciousness, and privacy. Ashmun reinforces these signs with a rhetoric of gentility based on the repetition of such key terms as "dignity," "taste," "simplicity," "harmony," "refinement," "distinctive," "cultivated," "gracious," and "courteous." At the heart of this oasis sits Mrs. Carleton, the perfect mother, who only rarely acknowledges fatigue or indicates that she feels the pressures of her physical and moral work. It is Mrs. Carleton who establishes and then validates the mechanisms by which the family plays out its class script. Thus, when Isabel, after her return from Europe, campaigns to have the family dress semiformally for dinner, Mrs. Carleton supports such a strategy both as an emblem of middle-class status and as a means of developing it. Though she moderates Isabel's initial enthusiasm by warning her that "you mustn't expect your father to get into his evening clothes every night," she also directly articulates the need "to keep up a cultivated standard of living" (*Heart* 211). In the final volume of the series, Mrs. Carleton leaves no doubt that she embraces the domestic priorities demanded of her sex and class. When Isabel asks her if she regrets not adopting a profession in which she could "earn [her] own way, gain some sort of glory, and achieve independence," Mrs. Carleton responds, "No, dear. I'm not sorry; and I don't regret a thing. It's been hard in some ways—but the reward is worth the sacrifice. I've always had more than I've given" (*Home* 21-22).

At the same time that the Isabel Carleton series iterates seemingly stable codes of class and gender, "ruptures" within the text deconstruct those codes to reveal their essential instability. A fairly obvious rift is created by the fact that many of Ashmun's assertions of female and male equality are juxtaposed with examples of gender differences that cast women as frail or dependent. At several points during the series, Isabel, Meta, and Mrs. Houston speak strongly about the need for middle-class women to support themselves financially, even after marriage. Female characters comment about the inevitability and justice of suffrage. Yet in almost every case of physical threat, the women have to be rescued by men. Isabel is saved from drowning only by Rodney's physical and psychological support. When a landslide buries two children in Montana, Isabel can only scream for Rodney and George and then wait to comfort the children when they are unearthed. After a drenching rainstorm, Isabel must be carried across a turbulent creek by Rodney and an old man and must rest once she returns home. Isabel's common assertion that she "is no fragile flower" (*Friends* 87) in terms of physical labor is undercut by Rodney's more common questions about her physical strength and stamina even in situations in which such worries seem unwarranted. In *Isabel Carleton in the West*, for instance, he says with concern after proposing a walk, "I don't want you to get so tired that you won't enjoy it" (148). A similar pattern occurs with many of the characters' discussions in favor of "women's rights." Though these views seem powerful by virtue of being strongly and directly voiced, they are, if not silenced, at least muted by the unquestioned, more pervasive rhetoric of female frailty and special needs. In keeping with Ashmun's practice of tempering potentially disruptive new ideas with more acceptable older ones, this rhetoric helps reassure readers that "progressive" women pose no real threat to traditional gender roles.

Ashmun's class narratives are even more thoroughly destabilized. The inescapable evidence in nearly every chapter that the Carletons live in a style of considerable comfort and even luxury creates a fissure into which Ashmun's more overt discourse of thrift and sacrifice disappears. Food provides just one example. Meals are served in courses by a maid on a table bedecked with candles and fresh flowers. Though the Carletons once eat a "poor man's dinner" of beef stew, rice, and apples in order to afford a desired treat (*Year* 74), page after page of descriptions of cream of celery soup, pancakes, ham, roasts, chicken, biscuits, gravy, fresh vegetables, creamed potatoes, scalloped potatoes, pink ice cream, blancmange, jelly roll, cake, bacon, eggs, oatmeal, oranges, coconut, and fresh grapefruit tell a different, more powerful story of privilege and ease.

A more complex example of rupture in the class narrative can be found in Ashmun's stories of dependence and independence. Middle-class morality in the series is often cast in terms of financial charity and other benevolence, especially toward the less fortunate. In the first volume, even when Isabel is the least self-aware, she sacrifices the money she was saving for a ring so that she can buy concert tickets for her parents and fresh flowers for the funeral of the family washer-woman's daughter. She arranges an impromptu picnic for two elderly residents of the local poor house. Later, Isabel organizes and helps administer, in her friend Molly's memory, a fund that advances expenses to women working their way through college. Her family members and friends are no less generous. Such actions are presented without question as essential to the continuance of a moral society and a moral personhood.

Yet Ashmun also offers a competing narrative in the story of Isabel's reaction to Meta Houston's gifts of clothes and trinkets. Though overjoyed by the pretty "fripperies," Isabel feels oddly uncomfortable accepting them. When Meta insists that she merely wants to give herself and Isabel pleasure by providing the presents, Isabel can at first think of no obvious objection. But finally she articulates the problem: "[Meta] almost acts as if I belonged to her; it seems as if she wants to dominate me," Isabel thinks (*Friends* 131). To Rodney she confesses, "[N]ow I begin to feel inferior and dependent, and at the same time I hate myself for ingratitude. It's destroying the freedom between us" (*Friends* 135). Once Ashmun introduces such terms as "inferior," "dependent," "dominate," "belonged to," and "destroying the freedom" as the consequences of charity, even when that "charity" is bestowed by an ostensible equal, her original encoding of financial benevolence as a middle-class virtue can no longer fully function. In the textual rupture exists the potential for class strife and human alienation that Ashmun's discourse seems initially to disallow.

Perhaps nowhere are Ashmun's class narratives disrupted as radically as in her rhetorics of democracy and ethnicity. The concept of class has never fit smoothly into a society that professes democratic egalitarianism. That tension is felt strongly in the middle class, which, as Stuart Blumin notes, often manifests its awareness of class by denying that class exists (10). The mental comfort of people in America's middle class depends upon perpetuating the myth that most other people are either like themselves or somehow do not deserve to be. For the most part, Ashmun does not disturb this myth in the Isabel Carleton series. Isabel might speculate occasionally about the unequal distribution of wealth among the equally deserving, but she never goes beyond concluding simply that "it's queer" (*Home* 221). Though the characters frequently assert the value of social democracy, these sentiments often manifest themselves as a form of tolerant patronage, as when the Carletons take an affectionate interest in the servant Melissy's romance with the iceman.

However, Ashmun clearly expects the democratic ideals of Americans to be universally recognized. Only the Americans, says an Englishwoman to Isabel in London, "are democratic enough to be really kind" to the Hindu woman in their hotel whose French husband has been called to war (*Heart* 35). But though Isabel and her cousin Eunice do befriend Madame Doret, they treat her as a pet or a child, a role she readily accepts by being weepy, helpless, and dependent. Usually, Ashmun extends democratic tolerance only to native-born Americans and, during war-time, to the brave (and white and western European) English and French. Her normally placid style erupts in a xenophobic frenzy, immediately deconstructing her rhetoric of democracy, when she writes of the "beetle-browed, sullen, uncouth" Hungarian who substitutes for Melissy's friendly "Yankee" iceman (*Home* 128), or when she describes the superstitious, murderous "dagos" and "greasers" whom Rodney must supervise while working in Montana (*West* 105). She interrupts the narrative of *Isabel Carleton in the West* for a long section against immigration in which, contrary to her usual practice, she allows no speaker fully to represent an alternative opinion. In this section, every character, regardless of his or her usual mode of speech, uses an intense, overwrought diction filled with extremes. Meta is "enraged" by foreign "anarchists" who want to "snatch" what they can get and then "destroy" the government. Isabel is "furious," and her words "burst out." George rants, "They're always howling about sweatshops. [But] who runs their blooming sweatshops? It's their own kind [who] grinds them down." He concludes, "[T]he place for anyone who doesn't like our government is back where he came from." Rodney "explodes" that "you couldn't pry them out of here with a crowbar . . . and then they want to stab you in the back." When Mrs. Houston hints that "we" might be exploiting "them" for "manual labor" because a native-born American thinks he is above such work, Rodney responds, "Well, he is, too." Mrs. Houston ultimately agrees that "the place for traitors and aliens is not in America" (*West* 131-33).

This violent textual disruption reveals how deeply the schisms of class, ethnicity, and democracy run in American thought. The Isabel Carleton series as a whole shows that Margaret Ashmun recognizes and acknowledges the existence of class in America. Yet when she tries to combine this recognition with a corresponding discourse of egalitarianism, her narratives break down. Since stories of class, gender, and democracy provided Ashmun with her version of what Mintz calls "the perceptual lens through which individuals [seek] to make sense of social change" (204), she needed to create an alternative narrative that would allow her to relieve some of the tensions threatening to fracture her initial model without completely recasting that model. Her "solution" was one common in her time: she added a new "lowest" level, the level of ethnicity, to her hierarchy of class. Only in this way could she maintain the coherence of the model that shaped her text.

The totality of this text was presented to young readers, in the words of *The Christian Advocate*, as "sweet and wholesome" tales that would "appeal to normal, eager girls everywhere" (qtd. in *Friends*, post-text advertisement, n.p.). Since works such as the Isabel Carleton series helped construct as well as reflect definitions of "normal" white, middle-class girlhood, readers who followed the story of Isabel's triumphs and trials also inherited scripts that they could act out to determine their own gender, class, and ethnic roles. The Isabel Carleton books themselves are ultimately a commodity through which their owners learn the cultural lessons that can keep them, in Isabel's words, "from being too lower-middle-class."[10]

Notes

1. For an analysis of the trope of "spheres" so commonly used in discussions of nineteenth-century domesticity, see Linda Kerber, "Separate Spheres, Female Worlds, Woman's Place: The Rhetoric of Women's History." Though

Kerber makes a compelling case for the limitations of this trope, the concept provides a convenient shorthand and so seems, at present at least, inescapable.

2. Langland concentrates on British fiction and the "non-narratable" plot of the servant girl marrying above her station, but her insights about the power of domesticity to shape class apply equally well to the American experience.

3. She died in 1940.

4. For some statistics on the marriage rates of female college graduates, see Shirley Marchalonis 156, and Peter Filene 27.

5. As is inevitable with a living language, others of the so-called "vulgarisms"—such as "phone," "pants" used as a noun, and "humans"—have, in the eighty years since the book's publication, become accepted parts of standard English.

6. Ashmun uses a similar strategy of containment to justify Isabel's trip to Europe in *The Heart of Isabel Carleton*. She clearly viewed European culture as essential to a full education, but the cost of such a trip, even in the 1910s, was beyond the resources of many middle-class families. Ashmun solves the dilemma by having wealthy cousin Eunice Everard pay for Isabel to accompany her as a companion and as a way of restoring Isabel's health after her near-drowning. Isabel avoids temptations to adopt "spoiled" upper-class habits by keeping constantly in her mind the image of the middle-class domestic pleasures represented by her mother and of "Jefferson-in-the-Middle-West" in general.

7. A similar argument might be made about patterns of speech. If, as Ashmun and Lomer suggest, "correct" speech is a matter not just of grammar but of "refined intonation," then mere grammatical accuracy cannot disguise class origin nor ensure class status.

8. See Matthews, Chapter 6, "The Housewife and the Home Economist," 145-71. Though useful, Matthews' work sometimes seems ahistorical in its idealization of domesticity.

9. The history and literature of nineteenth-century American domesticity has been treated at length by such historians and literary scholars as Nina Baym (*Novels, Readers, and Reviewers: Literary Domesticity in Nineteenth-Century America*), Nancy Cott (*The Bonds of Womanhood*), Carl Degler (*At Odds*), Barbara Leslie Epstein (*The Politics of Domesticity*), Lori Ginsberg (*Women and the Work of Benevolence*), Carroll Smith-Rosenberg (*Disorderly Conduct*), Mary P. Ryan (*Cradle of the Middle Class* and *The Empire of Mother*), Jane Tompkins (*Sensational Designs*), and others.

10. The author wishes to thank Dr. Daniel Quinlan of the Sociology Department at Emory & Henry College for his helpful suggestions, and Dr. Robert Chamberlain of CBM Technologies for his assistance with computers.

Works Cited

Ashmun, Margaret. *The Heart of Isabel Carleton*. New York: Macmillan, 1917.

——. *Isabel Carleton at Home*. New York: Macmillan, 1920.

——. *Isabel Carleton in the West*. New York: Macmillan, 1919.

——. *Isabel Carleton's Friends*. New York: Macmillan, 1918.

——. *Isabel Carleton's Year*. New York: Macmillan, 1916.

Blumin, Stuart. *The Emergence of the Middle Class: Social Experience in the American City, 1760-1900*. Cambridge: Cambridge UP, 1989.

Corey, Lewis. *The Crisis of the Middle Class*. New York: Covici, 1935.

Cott, Nancy. *The Bonds of Womanhood: "Woman's Sphere" in New England, 1780-1835*. New Haven: Yale UP, 1977.

——, ed. "Domestic Ideology and Domestic Work, Part 1." Vol. 4 of *History of Women in the United States*. New York: Saur, 1992.

Cowan, Ruth Schwartz. *More Work for Mother: The Ironies of Household Technology from the Open Hearth to the Microwave*. New York: Basic, 1983.

De Wolfe, Elsie. *The House in Good Taste*. New York: Century, 1913.

Filene, Peter. *Him/Her Self: Sex Roles in Modern America*. New York: Harcourt, 1975.

Gordon, Jean, and Jan McArthur. "American Women and Domestic Consumption, 1800-1920: Four Interpretive Themes." Cott, "Domestic Ideology" 215-43.

Kerber, Linda. "Separate Spheres, Female Worlds, Woman's Place: The Rhetoric of Women's History." Cott, "Domestic Ideology" 173-203.

Langland, Elizabeth. *Nobody's Angels: The Middle-Class Woman and Domestic Ideology in Victorian Culture*. Ithaca: Cornell UP, 1995.

Lomer, Gerhard, and Margaret Ashmun. *The Study and Practice of Writing English*. New York: Houghton, 1917.

Marchalonis, Shirley. *College Girls: A Century in Fiction*. New Brunswick: Rutgers UP, 1995.

Matthews, Glenna. *"Just a Housewife": The Rise and Fall of Domesticity in America*. New York: Oxford UP, 1987.

Mintz, Steven. *A Prison of Expectations: The Family in Victorian Culture*. New York: New York UP, 1983.

Palmer, Phyllis. *Domesticity and Dirt: Housewives and Domestic Servants in the United States, 1920-1945*. Philadelphia: Temple UP, 1989.

Rubin, Joan Shelley. *The Making of Middle-Brow Culture*. Chapel Hill: U of North Carolina P, 1992.

Ryan, Mary P. *Cradle of the Middle Class: The Family in Oneida Country, New York, 1790-1865*. Cambridge: Cambridge UP, 1981.

Sangster, Margaret. *The Little Kingdom of Home*. New York: J. F. Taylor 1904.

Theriot, Nancy M. *The Biosocial Construction of Femininity: Mothers and Daughters in Nineteenth-Century America.* Westport: Greenwood, 1988.

Thompson, E. P. *The Making of the English Working Class.* New York: Vintage, 1966.

Wilson, Margaret Gibbons. *The American Woman in Transition: The Urban Influence, 1870-1920.* Westport: Greenwood, 1979.

3

Community and Character:
A Comparison of Josephine Lawrence's
Linda Lane Series and Classic Orphan Fiction

Deidre A. Johnson

From 1925-1929, Barse & Hopkins (later Barse & Co.) published the six-volume Linda Lane series, a girls' series that is as unusual for what it does *not* do as for what it does. As *Girls' Series Companion* notes, Linda Lane does *not* contain "mystery, exotic locales, or daring adventures" (Society of Phantom Friends 155), nor does it chronicle the adventures of well-to-do schoolgirls, successful career girls, or dashing young aviatrices. Rather, it compiles a cast in which—as the *Companion* points out—"virtually every character is poor, elderly, an invalid, an orphan, or all of the above" (Society of Phantom Friends 155)—and where most of these characters are women. The result is a series that shows marginalized females networking and employing various strategies to create communities and survive within the limitations of existing social frameworks. Drawing on formulas from popular orphan fiction, Lawrence reworks them to develop a low-key series about an optimistic, assertive foster child, a series peopled with females who are not dependent on men, and one that modifies certain character traits found in classic orphan fiction, presenting a community of capable females who help themselves and others. The Linda Lane series thus merits examination from a dual perspective: first, for its relationship to other works, most notably orphan fiction, and second, for the messages it purveyed to female readers about women's social relationships and potential.

Josephine Lawrence and Her Fiction
Linda Lane's creator was Josephine Lawrence, an author who, like her fiction, seems to have been overlooked in recent years. This is unfortunate, for one of the more intriguing aspects of Lawrence's work is its interconnectedness, and Linda Lane touches on a number of Lawrence's

favorite topics—among them, family relationships, financial security, self-sufficiency, and personal responsibility. Lawrence's own life exhibited many of the attributes found in the Linda Lane series; it also provided her with the opportunity to learn about the problems and concerns of women first-hand. Born in Newark, New Jersey in either 1890 or 1897,[1] Lawrence began work at the *Newark Sunday Call* in 1915 as editor of the children's page; three years later she also became editor of the women's page. Part of the latter responsibility included managing a question-and-answer column, where readers—mostly female—wrote short letters in response to weekly questions posed by Lawrence. These touched on a variety of topics: "Why I Am Glad I Am a Woman," "Spending Money in the Name of Thrift" (or "My Most Extravagant Economy"), "Every Woman Her Own Budget Plumber . . . Quietly Find[ing] the Best Way to Stop Those Annoying Little Leaks That Drain the Family Purse," "Every Woman Has Her Ideas of Luxury," and even "Are Our Public Manners Better or Worse than They Used to Be?"[2]

Lawrence entered the field of children's fiction around 1920, when she began ghostwriting for the Stratemeyer Syndicate. She contributed to several series, among them a girls' series, Betty Gordon (her first work using an assertive female orphan, albeit one who enjoyed the benefits of having a wealthy male guardian), and several tots' series, including Sunny Boy, the Four Little Blossoms, Honey Bunch, and the Riddle Club. In 1921, she also started writing series under her own name, and ultimately authored fifty-one children's books outside of her Syndicate fiction. Forty-nine of these were issued in seven series intended for girls or young children: Brother and Sister (6 vols., 1921-27), Josephine Lawrence Stories for Girls (8 vols., 1922-31),[3] Elizabeth Ann (8 vols., 1923-1929), Linda Lane (6 vols., 1925-1929), Kiddie Wonder (7 vols., ca. 1926-ca. 1928), Two Little Fellows (5 vols., 1927-1929), and Toyland (9 vols., 1928).[4]

In 1932, Lawrence published her first adult novel, *Head of the Family*, and never returned to children's fiction. Her early adult novels, addressing the social and financial problems of everyday people, earned critical acclaim, including praise from Sinclair Lewis. One analysis of her work noted that Lawrence "made herself the chronicler of the commonplace . . . [filling her stories] with details of daily living, the little . . . problems of little people" (Guilfoil 365). Although her later works were not praised as highly as her first five books, she published a total of thirty-two adult novels between 1932 and 1975. Lawrence did not marry until 1940, and, after her marriage, continued in her two careers. Her life embodied the work ethic found in some of her books, including the Linda Lane series. In 1950, an article in *Newsweek* noted that "[Lawrence] lives in an immaculate apartment . . . crosses the Hudson each day to her office, edits a good deal of copy, handles budgets, does a column of book reviews and returns to New York at night to write from 7 until 10 o'clock on her novels," adding that "she has kept up this schedule ever since she began to write" ("Miss Lawrence" 78).

Overview of the Series

Because the Linda Lane series is somewhat obscure, it is best to begin with a brief summary of the stories. In the first book, *Linda Lane*, an independent, assertive thirteen-year-old orphan, comes to live with Miss Gilly, a kind and timid dressmaker, in the small town of Morrisville. A born manager (some would call her "headstrong" or "bossy"), Linda takes an active part in running Miss Gilly's house and chicken yard and in planning activities for a girls' club, which, at her instigation, has become a walking club. Linda's time is also occupied by the two children next door, for she possesses a knack for managing children; this is fortunate since Mrs. Hampton, their widowed mother, regards Linda as a convenient (and free) baby-sitter. In subsequent volumes, Linda helps care for the four wealthy but spoiled children of Morrisville's newest residents, Mr. and Mrs. Pine, while staying at the Pines' summer home. Upon returning to Morrisville, she gradually assembles an extended foster family at Miss Gilly's, beginning with an impoverished widow as resident grandmother and David, a destitute child, as little brother. An unexpected inheritance following the death of Miss Gilly's affluent Cousin Dorothea allows Miss Gilly to support Linda's plans for a family, and the household expands to include a four-year-old girl and a two-year-old girl, both orphans, plus a sixteen-year-old farm girl named Mary Rice—not an orphan—who needs a place to stay while completing high school. Linda keeps busy helping to care for the children, taking part in school activities—including managing the eighth-grade play— and helping Mary Rice and her family through several problems. The series ends while Linda is a freshman in high school and Mary, having discovered a talent for interior design, is anticipating an opportunity to begin an apprenticeship in the field.

Classic Orphan Fiction and Attitudes toward Women

In creating Linda Lane, Lawrence drew upon the formula of the transplanted orphan: a young girl with a distinctive personality is placed within a new environment to which she adapts while sharing her philosophy of life with those about her and thus, by extension, the reader. This formula forms the basis of four of the five "most influential books read by American girls in the early twentieth century" (Romalov 14):

Rebecca of Sunnybrook Farm (1903), *Anne of Green Gables* (1908), *Daddy Long-legs* (1912), and *Pollyanna* (1913).[5] What distinguishes the Linda Lane series from these predecessors, however, is its treatment of and attitudes toward women. In order to appreciate Lawrence's reworking of key images, it is necessary first to examine the depiction of females' relationships to men in these four books.

Ironically, although all four classics were written by women for a predominantly female audience and feature moderately strong females as protagonists, all four works frequently suggest that women need men for guidance and fulfillment. This usually occurs in two or more ways: through the depiction of female guardians, the inclusion of male mentors, and/or the resolution of the protagonist's future. In the first instance, the depiction of female guardians, three of the books place the protagonists with unmarried women who are initially unresponsive to the child and her needs. While Anne's guardian, Marilla, is painted somewhat sympathetically, Pollyanna's "stern, severe-faced" Aunt Polly (Porter, *Pollyanna* 3) and Rebecca's grim Aunt Miranda are not; moreover, the books imply that they have acquired their harsh natures because they have not allowed themselves to love men. In Pollyanna's case, the reader learns Aunt Polly's pride had blighted a promising romance and, as a servant puts it, "[S]he's been feedin' on wormwood an' thistles ever since" (Porter 13); once reunited with her former fiancé, she is transformed into "a wonderfully tremulous, wonderfully different Aunt Polly" (Porter 307). Rebecca's two aunts, Miranda and Jane, also illustrate the presumed effect of a man—or lack thereof—on a woman's life: as Wiggin explains, Aunt Miranda's heart "had never [been] used for any other purpose than the pumping and circulating of blood" (31) and even in her last days she remains filled with "petty cares and sordid anxieties" (255), leaving Rebecca "wonder[ing] if old age must be so grim, so hard, so unchastened and unsweetened" (258). Rebecca's more kindly Aunt Jane, however, had once loved a young man and gone to nurse him when he was mortally wounded in the war, "to show him for once the heart of a prim New England girl when it is ablaze with love and grief," and "[h]aving learned the trick of beating and loving . . . the poor faithful heart persisted" in doing so (Wiggin 33), thereby enabling Jane to live a richer life ever after.

Not only does it take a man to fulfill a woman and make her a better person, but the books also suggest that, at least initially, it takes a man to recognize the protagonist's special qualities. In *Rebecca*, it requires only the ride from the station to Rebecca's aunts' home for Mr. Cobb, the stagecoach driver, to realize that Rebecca is an extraordinary child, bright and imaginative; from then on, she can turn to him for comfort and advice when life with her aunts becomes too difficult or emotionally barren. Similarly, Matthew discovers Anne's fine qualities on the drive to Green Gables and then offers Anne gentle suggestions and support in overcoming initial difficulties with Marilla; throughout *Green Gables* he remains more receptive to Anne's creative talents and abilities than does Marilla. Although Pollyanna has no older man alive to guide her, she continually reminds everyone that her entire philosophy—the "glad game"—came from her Papa and still sustains and directs her in his absence. Even in *Daddy Long-legs*, it is a man, Jarvis Pendleton, who recognizes Judy Abbott's potential and arranges for her college education. The protagonist and reader thus learn that a superior female—for the protagonists are all superior females—in need of succor and advice must turn not to a woman but to a man.

Additionally, the books' conclusions or sequels reinforce the idea that woman is incomplete without man since all contain what has been called the "waif to wife theme" (Cadogan and Craig 106). As Cadogan and Craig observe in *You're a Brick, Angela! A New Look at Girl's Fiction from 1839 to 1975*, all the protagonists except Pollyanna are "educated to an advanced level, yet . . . [e]ach sees herself ultimately as a nest-maker and breeder" (109). *Daddy Long-legs* concludes with Judy's engagement to Jarvis, and in *Dear Enemy,* the sequel, Judy's voice is virtually silent: focused on her husband and child, she has left the responsibility for reforming orphanages—and narrating books—to a friend. Anne spends several books establishing a career as a talented teacher and promising writer before abandoning both to manage Gilbert's "house of dreams";[6] Pollyanna weds Jimmy Pendleton; and Rebecca, while still unmarried, clearly anticipates a future with Adam Ladd.

Perhaps because she was writing more than a decade after the last of her predecessors, perhaps because she was a single, working woman in her thirties, Lawrence dispenses with these images, creating females who manage admirably on their own or with other women's support. This is first seen in the case of Miss Gilly. From the very beginning when Miss Gilly resolves to "take a little girl and try to make her happy" (unlike Marilla or Aunt Polly who acquire their female charges by fate, not choice), she already possesses the capability of loving a child and the ability to direct her own course (*Linda Lane* 39). There is no mention of a man in Miss Gilly's past—and no indication that his presence or absence has affected her character or development in any way. Miss Gilly's one flaw is her timidity or meekness, but even here, although Lawrence describes Miss Gilly as timid, this does not prevent Miss Gilly from taking action when needed; rather, it serves as a way of creating a balance between her personality and Linda's.

Lawrence's decision to create Miss Gilly as a female who wants Linda in her life and is able to show her affection obviates the need for a male voice to point out Linda Lane's fine qualities or to offer Linda advice or guidance. Linda and Miss Gilly get along immediately, recognizing they balance each other's weaknesses with their own strengths, and it is Miss Gilly who, in turn, provides the support and suggestions that help Linda to adapt more smoothly to her new environment. Moreover, Miss Gilly is not the only female to serve this function. Adrienne Rich's observation that "there is a unique quality of validation, affirmation, challenge, support that one woman can offer another" (240) is echoed throughout the series. Rather than using males to reassure the protagonist of her worth, Lawrence repeatedly creates situations that allow females to encourage one another and to help develop each other's strengths. When Linda begins school, she bristles at a question from the male principal—one of the only two men even included in the opening chapters—but the female secretary who shows Linda to her new classroom "assured Linda that she would like the girls and the teacher and, what was more encouraging, predicted that she would [succeed]" (*Linda Lane* 54). Linda's teacher—another woman—then assigns two female classmates to coach her in English and math, telling Linda that she "should be able to make rapid progress" (60). The girls not only tutor Linda willingly and effectively, but also invite her to join their girls' club, a club whose initiation ritual asks each girl to identify the area in which she excels, again encouraging positive assessment of one's abilities. At the club meeting, when Linda announces that her talent is for "bossing" because she "doesn't mind responsibility and . . . [likes] to tell people what to do" (86), instead of being jealous or threatened, the club president immediately identifies a means of employing Linda's skills, "pleasantly" remarking that if Linda "like[s] to run things it must be because [she has] a gift that way" and promptly makes her program chairman (87). This attitude continues throughout the series, culminating in the final volume that includes, among other instances of girls assisting one another, a big sister program in the local high school whereby older girls "can give [younger ones] a lift over some of the hard places" (*Big Sister* 21), and Linda and her friend Katherine aiding Mary Rice first by finding her family an affordable home and then by guiding her toward a promising career.

Finally, the books never imply that ultimately girls need to marry to be complete. Admittedly, the series ends while Linda is still a freshman in high school, far too young to be considering marriage, and *Girls' Series Companion* feels that "[i]f the series had gone on longer . . . it would certainly have included romance in the person of Jimmie

Andrews" (Society of Phantom Friends 156), a boy who remains a close friend of Linda's throughout the series. While Lawrence's intentions—if any—for later volumes in the series are not known, her treatment of marriage within the existing texts is clear: not one female marries, becomes engaged, or even expresses a strong interest in romance in the course of the series, and all the major female characters are unmarried or widowed. Even in the final book, although Linda's friends are juniors and seniors, there is no mention of marriage; instead those girls who speak of their future plans refer to college or employment. If anything, rather than endorsing marriage, the series suggests that women should be prepared to live independently—and even undercuts the necessity for having a man in the home. Linda manages to assemble an entire family—*sans* adult males—for Miss Gilly without the assistance of men (unless one considers David's grandfather, who helps her by dying and leaving David orphaned and available for adoption).[7] With few exceptions, married women—all minor characters in the series—are painted unflatteringly: those who visit Miss Gilly's dressmaking establishment are often unable to make up their minds about styles or treat her rudely; those with children are often unable to control them; one married woman who initially plans to adopt a child even changes her mind because she decides the boy is too much trouble. In contrast to works like *Pollyanna* and *Rebecca,* which suggest that loving a man improves a woman, the Linda Lane series frequently depicts married women less sympathetically than those without men.

Character Traits

The Linda Lane series also conveys messages about desirable character traits by presenting traits favorably associated with Linda or praised by the narrator or sympathetic characters in the series. Lawrence may have intended these as advice to readers, a rough blueprint on which to model their own character. Here, too, she draws on and modifies concepts in earlier orphan fiction, at times moving toward a more feminist outlook, at times adhering to traditional feminine perspectives.

One of the key differences between Linda and her predecessors is in the traits that distinguish the protagonists from their peers. *Anne of Green Gables, Rebecca of Sunnybrook Farm,* and *Daddy Long-legs* present characters whose outstanding traits include their sensitivity and imaginative ability, which are often contrasted with that of their more prosaic friends. The girls frequently express their sentiments through their literary efforts—and the type of writing they choose (or that the authors choose for them) places them firmly within a feminine, flowery world. Thirteen-year-old Anne's literary endeavors include an overly sentimentalized melodrama, "The Jealous Rival; or, In Death Not Divided" (Montgomery, *Green Gables* 265); a few years later, she has progressed to penning "a most interesting dialogue between the asters and the sweet peas and wild canaries in the lilac bush and the guardian spirit of the garden" (Montgomery, *Avonlea* 205). The child Rebecca indulges in cloyingly sweet poetry; at age fifteen, she adopts the title "The Rose of Joy" for her entry in an essay contest, telling a confidante that she "hasn't any beginning [yet], nor any middle, but there will be a thrilling ending, something like this . . . 'Then come what will of weal or woe/(Since all gold hath alloy),/Thou'lt bloom unwithered in this heart,/My Rose of Joy!'" (Wiggin 227-28). As Cadogan and Craig observe, "The strain in her which has been allowed to predominate is the enfeeblingly sentimental one" (93).

In contrast, Linda Lane's most remarkable traits are her strong sense of self-worth and her leadership abilities—more androcentric or androgynous qualities (especially given the nature of many of Anne's and Rebecca's early literary efforts). In this respect, the series reflects—or anticipates—heroines found in many popular girls' series of the 1920s and 1930s, which, as Romalov notes, "[incorporate] intelligence, self-respect, independence, [and] ambition . . . as desirable female traits" (154). Linda Lane also contains some of the same type of "tensions" concerning "the proper exercise of power" (Romalov 182) that Romalov found in girls' high school and college series, tensions which she feels stem from "the authors' ambivalence toward the women's rights movement, or more precisely, toward women's flagrant and conspicuous use of power" (183)[8] and from "the contradictory tensions pulling [the series] toward a conservative definition of femininity or into authentic feminism" (153).

Throughout the series, Linda worries about balancing her desire to lead with a fear of being "too domineering" or failing to "respect the rights and ideas of others" (*Plan* 52). Tellingly, in the first two books Linda's ability to stand up for herself and to direct others is also specifically endorsed as a means of success by two different characters, the millionaire Mr. Pine and the mild Miss Gilly, but in two different ways. When Mr. Pine speaks admiringly of Linda to his wife, he remarks, "To get anywhere, aggressiveness is necessary . . . [I]f there is one quality an orphan with her own way to make, [*sic*] should have it's that—aggressiveness and initiative" (*Helps Out* 68). Here, he not only uses the term "aggressiveness," a much stronger word than "assertiveness," but also cites only those two qualities, aggressiveness and initiative, as necessary for success. In contrast, when Linda initially broaches the subject of her bossiness with Miss Gilly, Miss Gilly praises Linda for her "assertiveness" (which she also labels "spirit" or "the gift of management") (*Linda Lane* 84-85), admits it is a quality she lacks, then reflects, "If I had half your spirit I would have been head of a successful dressmaking establishment in the city years ago" (*Linda Lane* 85). However, Miss Gilly does not give an unqualified endorsement: she also tells Linda that assertiveness must be tempered with tact, stating that tact is "a gift every girl needs and every woman" (*Linda Lane* 85). She even continues that "a tactful woman who isn't very clever can do a great deal more than the brilliant woman who hasn't an ounce of tact in her make-up" (*Linda Lane* 85). For a man, to be assertive (or aggressive) is sufficient; for a woman, it is not.

The series reinforces Miss Gilly's interpretation both through Linda's constant worry about being overbearing and through comments about other women who lack tactfulness. One such instance follows several chapters after Linda's conversation with Miss Gilly, when Linda encounters their next-door neighbor, Mrs. Hampton, a character Lawrence frequently employs as a foil. Mrs. Hampton is blunt and outspoken and frequently blind to situations where others' rights conflict with her own desires; the omniscient narrator comments that "Linda's spirit . . . appealed to Mrs. Hampton who was plentifully endowed with the same quality, but who unfortunately had not had a Miss Gilly to show her into what mistakes independence may lead one" (*Linda Lane* 134). Similarly, in other situations when a girl speaks freely or bluntly, either Linda or the narrator will occasionally observe that "that wasn't the most tactful remark" (*Plan* 97). And, especially in the first volumes Linda is placed several times in situations where she finds herself remaining silent or yielding to another's suggestion rather than promoting her own ideas. The combination of leadership and tact can thus be read either as Linda learning to assume a more traditionally feminine role by silencing or suppressing her own needs and voice to accommodate others *or* as Linda's successful integration of traditionally masculine and feminine qualities into an androgynous self, blending an awareness of others with an ability to assert her own rights and to lead others.[9]

The second key characteristic the Linda Lane series stresses—increasingly so in later volumes—is the importance of a positive attitude. Like the "sunny-dispositioned" protagonists of classic orphan fiction (Cadogan and Craig 89) as well as characters in contemporaneous series fiction, Linda possesses a cheerful, enthusiastic nature; even the matron at the orphanage notes that "Linda never seemed to feel 'blue'" (*Linda Lane* 64). Lawrence also highlights Linda's good nature and its effect upon others through the use of foils. In the second volume, for example, the wealthy Miss Cummins regularly complains even amid what Linda considers a life of luxury, and one of Miss Cummins's nieces compares her unfavorably with Linda, remarking, "Auntie always scolds when she is going anywhere because nothing ever suits her; but Linda laughs and likes it and says she is glad she came" (*Helps Out* 80). Later volumes contrast Linda's optimistic outlook with Mary Rice's pessimism. At one point, Linda—or Lawrence—even suggests that positive thinking can affect one's circumstances, for Linda tells a mutual friend "[Mary] does have a tough time . . . but she always seems to expect the worst; I think nice things happen to you more often if you expect them to happen" (*Big Sister* 72). This echoes a philosophy voiced by Mr. Pine in the first book, when, after telling Linda the secret that he, too, was an orphan, he advises her, "Here's another little secret—don't waste any time in self-pity; it's a kind world, after all, if you smile at it persistently" (*Linda Lane* 242). Linda does smile at the world persistently, but her success actually comes from a combination of attitude and action (coupled with some good fortune): she not only expects good things, but has the assertiveness and initiative to implement her plans and a strong enough sense of self-worth to stand up for her rights when necessary. It is this combination that helps her to advance, in part by making her appealing to others, who reward her efforts accordingly.

For Linda then, as for Mr. Pine, this "smile at the world" philosophy is one that works—especially since Lawrence does not extend the series far enough into Linda's future for her to discover that Mr. Pine, merely by being born male, had advantages not available to most females. And it is in this respect that Mr. Pine's philosophy becomes problematic, an issue Lawrence both introduces and avoids. For while one side of Mr. Pine's philosophy is that complaining and indulging in self-pity are ineffective and that one can be cheerful by resolving to be content with one's fortunes, the other side suggests that the unfortunate and marginalized should also make the best of their misfortunes. This hearkens back to the classic orphan fiction, which, as Cadogan and Craig observe, "preaches the desirability of contentment with the *status quo*" (94). In *Linda Lane's Plan*, Lawrence creates a character who embodies Mr. Pine's "smile at the world" philosophy: Emily Poore, an elderly widow who "has had a hard life, with little else in it but sickness and loss and trouble" and whose finances are so limited that "she never dares spend a cent on luxuries of the simplest kind" (*Plan* 131). Despite Mrs. Poore's adversities, the narrator explains, "Mrs. Poore's most marked characteristic was a sense of humor. She laughed over mishaps and what another woman would have regarded as a trial or trouble, she treated as a joke. She was an excellent foil to Mrs. Hampton who constantly saw the darker side of life" (*Plan* 145). While Lawrence clearly intends the aptly named Mrs. Poore—who is always presented in the most favorable light—to show the value of making the best of a difficult situation, the character also illustrates one side of the classic double bind women faced. As Marilyn Frye explains in *The Politics of Reality: Essays in Feminist Theory*,

> It is often a requirement upon oppressed people that we smile and be cheerful. If we comply, we signal our docility and our acquiescence in our situation. . . . On the other hand, anything but the sunniest countenance exposes us to being perceived as mean [or] bitter. . . . This means, at the least, that we may be found "difficult" or unpleasant. (2)

And this is precisely what happens when Lawrence introduces another character in a similar situation. Sixteen-year-old Mary Rice's life is as bleak as, if not bleaker than, Mrs. Poore's. She lives with her ailing, widowed mother and five siblings; the family barely ekes out an existence from the limited wages the boys earn at part-time work, while Mary struggles to complete high school and win a scholarship so she can become a teacher. She does this not because she wants to teach—she actually "loathe[s] and despise[s]" the idea (*Big Sister* 45)—but pursues this goal because "you can get through Normal in two years" (*Experiments* 129) and "you get better pay for [teaching] than for anything else you can be trained for in that length of time" (*Big Sister* 37). To Mary, life is full of joyless duty, and she is not smiling or cheerful about her situation. However, as Linda's comment about Mary illustrates, although Linda acknowledges the obstacles Mary faces, she still places some of the blame on the victim.[10]

Ultimately, Lawrence's resolution of both Mrs. Poore's and Mary Rice's situations embraces both the philosophy of optimism and that of speaking out about perceived injustices. In Mrs. Poore's case, when Miss Gilly receives a sizable inheritance from a cousin, she and Linda promptly invite Mrs. Poore to live with them permanently as a resident grandmother for the family of orphans Linda plans to assemble. It is precisely *because* Mrs. Poore's amiable and cheerful attitude makes her a pleasant companion that Linda and Miss Gilly feel she would be a welcome addition to the family: thus, her smiling, uncomplaining demeanor earns the desired reward of financial security, albeit within a traditional female nurturing role.

Lawrence employs a different strategy for Mary Rice. Linda—the character with whom the reader feels the most empathy—recognizes that Mary complains because she is trapped by her circumstances (although Lawrence attributes this to financial problems, not gender) and repeatedly mentions this when discussing Mary's pessimism, yet she still feels that things would improve for Mary if she would just cheer up. However, Lawrence also allows other sympathetic characters to defend Mary's position. In a conversation with Linda, Jimmie Andrews (whose own mother is, ironically, quite similar to Mrs. Poore) raises the issue of privilege, claiming that "if Mary Rice had had as pleasant and easy a life [as Katherine, one of their affluent friends], she would also have been almost as friendly and sweet as Katherine" (*Big Sister* 77). Moreover, Lawrence's solution to Mary's problems indirectly attributes her success to her continual complaints. Because Mary refuses to be silent, to "signal [her] docility and [her] acquiescence" (Frye 2), Linda is unable to ignore the problem. She becomes determined to find something Mary enjoys and finally prods Mary into admitting she would like to pursue a career in interior design, then helps her learn about the field. She even encourages Mary to enter a contest for amateur designers, which Mary wins. A mutual friend, also aware of Mary's unhappiness over the prospect of teaching, then volunteers to get Mary a position with her aunt, a well-known interior decorator, who "has trained a number of girls who have opened shops of their own" (*Big Sister* 238). Thus, both strategies yield the desired result. And while these fortuitous circumstances conveniently permit Lawrence to skirt the issue of the societal situations and inequalities causing Mrs. Poore's and Mary's problems, the resolution allows her to reinforce and reaffirm the important message that women must help other women if they are to succeed.

Conclusion

With the Linda Lane series, Lawrence re-envisioned some of the elements in classic orphan fiction. As Annette Kolodny writes, "The fictions that women compose about the worlds they inhabit may owe a debt to prior, influential works by other women or, simply enough, to the daily experience of the writer herself or, more usually, to some combination of the two" (155). Essentially, the heart of orphan fiction is the story of a disempowered female, a lone figure initially without family or community, who, through others' assistance and her own character, survives in the world. The Linda Lane series adopts that idea but shifts it from a turn-of-the-century feminine sentimentality to a more contemporary perspective. Lawrence lived at a time when more women were entering the work force while contending with low wages and limited options; she also dealt with correspondence of the readers of her *Newark Sunday Call* woman's page: she thus saw both the potential and the problems facing women, especially single women. Although at times the Linda Lane series still reflects earlier attitudes and balks at directly addressing gender inequalities, it also continually presents an array of girls and women who are without men and who, while facing varied obstacles, still manage to unite and thus survive. Like the question-and-answer column in Lawrence's woman's page, which gave women a voice and allowed them to share their ideas and strategies with each other for mutual benefit, Lawrence's Linda Lane series reaffirms women's ability to manage independently, acknowledges that they will face difficulties, and encourages them to support one another in their endeavors.

Notes

1. Early biographical sources list her birthdate as "1897?"; the confusion occurred after her *New York Times* obituary in 1978 gave her age as 88. After that, some sources began using 1890 as her year of birth.

2. The topics listed were among those either posed as prompts or used as headlines for Lawrence's question-and-answer column in the *Newark Sunday Call* for the first eight weeks of 1924.

3. In a typical publisher's quirk, although the series was advertised as "Josephine Lawrence Stories for Girls," there was actually a ninth book in the series, *Joyous Peggy*, by Lillian Grace Copp.

4. Information about some of the series comes from James Keeline, manager of The Prince and The Pauper Bookstore. Personal communication, September 1995.

5. Technically, Rebecca is only a half-orphan, but since she spends most of the book in the care of her aunts, the impression is the same. The fifth title, Gene Stratton Porter's *A Girl of the Limberlost* (1909), also deals with a half-orphan and actually contains many of the same attitudes about male-female relationships found in the four titles discussed.

6. Mary Atwell's study of the Anne series, "Anne Shirley: The Heroine Shines and Fades," also comments on this phenomenon, noting that "Anne's creative powers seemed to change, and even to shrink from reality to metaphor as she aged and the series progressed. . . . With her marriage it seems Anne moved into [her husband] Gilbert's world . . . one in which she became less and less empowered" until "vibrant Anne faded out of the picture . . . replaced by her youngest daughter."

7. In *Linda Lane Experiments*, while a man, Dr. Copely, introduces Linda to baby Joy, the final addition to Miss Gilly's family, he also makes it clear that the idea came from Miss Gowan, the nurse. He tells Linda, "[T]he moment we began to discuss plans for having this baby adopted, up pipes Miss Gowan with 'Can't you persuade that nice Linda Lane to take her, doctor?'" (205).

8. Although Romalov is speaking of power in terms of "being actively involved in student government, holding class offices" and such, the central issue remains the same (182).

9. However, it should also be noted that such conflicting messages are not limited to girls' series or even girls' books, but have also been considered an elemental aspect of most works for children. In analyzing mainstream children's literature from the 1900s to the 1970s, Perry Nodelman offers another interpretation, observing that

such paradoxes are at the heart of children's fiction, which is often both revolutionary and conservative, both anarchistic and highly conventional. . . . In this determined insistence on contradiction, children's literature does not so much blend male and female into genderless androgyny as it salvages both masculinity and femininity as traditionally understood, and keeps both intact and in battle with each other. (34)

10. A similar situation illustrating both perspectives occurs in the fifth book. Linda and Jimmie Andrews's mother are going to the seashore and Mrs. Andrews tells Linda "how excited" she is about the vacation.

Linda looked at her. Mrs. Andrews had had plenty of trouble—her husband had died soon after Jimmie's birth and she had had to bring him up an earn the living for both. She had had to contend with poor health, poverty and endless anxiety. Yet she had not lost her capacity for enjoyment and she had taught her son not to grumble.

"There is no use talking," thought Linda . . . "being cheerful does make you more attractive. Mary Rice probably has just as good qualities as Mrs. Andrews, but no one would ever guess it." (*Problems* 235)

Works Cited

Atwell, Mary. "Anne Shirley: The Heroine Shines and Fades." Paper presented at the 19th Annual Popular Culture Association Conference/11th Annual American Culture Association Conference, St. Louis, Missouri, April 5, 1989.

Cadogan, Mary, and Patricia Craig. *You're a Brick, Angela! A New Look at Girls' Fiction from 1839 to 1975*. London: Gollancz, 1976.

Frye, Marilyn. *The Politics of Reality: Essays in Feminist Theory*. Trumansburg, NY: Crossing, 1983.

Guilfoil, Kelsey. "Josephine Lawrence: The Voice of the People." *English Journal* 38.7 (1949): 365-70.

"Josephine Lawrence, 88, Author; Novelist of Middle-Class America." *New York Times* 24 Feb. 1978: msg. pg.

Kolodny, Annette. "Dancing Through the Minefield: Some Observations on the Theory, Practice, and Politics of a Feminist Literary Criticism." *The New Feminist Criticism: Essays on Women, Literature, and Theory.* Ed. Elaine Showalter. New York: Pantheon, 1985. 144-67.

Lawrence, Josephine. *Linda Lane.* 1925. Rpt. in *Linda Lane's Adventures.* New York, Grosset, 1939.

———. *Linda Lane Experiments.* 1927. Rpt. in *Linda Lane's Adventures.* New York: Grosset, 1939.

———. *Linda Lane Helps Out.* 1925. Rpt. in *Linda Lane's Adventures.* New York: Grosset, 1939.

———. *Linda Lane's Big Sister.* New York: Grosset, 1929.

———. *Linda Lane's Plan.* 1926. Rpt. in *Linda Lane's Adventures.* New York: Grosset, 1939.

———. *Linda Lane's Problems.* New York: Grosset, 1928.

"Miss Lawrence's Latest." *Newsweek* 4 Sept. 1950: 78-79.

Montgomery, L. M. *Anne of Avonlea.* Boston: Page, 1909.

———. *Anne of Green Gables.* Boston: Page, 1908.

Nodelman, Perry. "Children's Literature as Women's Writing." *Children's Literature Association Quarterly* 13.1 (1988): 31-34.

Porter, Eleanor H. *Pollyanna.* 1912. Reprint, New York: Grosset, n.d.

———. *Pollyanna Grows Up.* 1914. Reprint, New York: Grosset, n.d.

Rich, Adrienne. *On Lies, Secrets and Silence: Selected Prose, 1966-1978.* New York: Norton, 1979.

Romalov, Nancy. "Modern, Mobile, and Marginal: American Girls' Series Fiction, 1905-1925." Diss. U of Iowa, 1994.

Society of Phantom Friends. *Girls' Series Companion.* Highlands, CA: Society of Phantom Friends, 1994.

Webster, Jean. *Daddy Long-legs.* 1912. New York: Grosset, n.d.

———. *Dear Enemy.* 1915. New York: Grosset, 1970.

Wiggin, Kate Douglas. *Rebecca of Sunnybrook Farm.* 1903. Middlesex: Puffin, 1985.

4

Mobile and Modern Heroines:
Early Twentieth-Century Girls' Automobile Series

Nancy Tillman Romalov

In her keynote address given at the Nancy Drew Conference at the University of Iowa in April 1993, Carolyn Heilbrun identified Nancy Drew as a model for early second-wave feminists, citing as a requisite for that identification, among other things, Nancy's blue roadster. Heilbrun noted: "She can not only back it out of tight places, she can get into it and go anytime she wants. She has freedom and the means to exercise it. That blue roadster was certainly for me, in my childhood, the mark of independence and autonomy: the means to get up and go" (18).

Yet preceding the second wave that Heilbrun refers to, there came the first, that generation of Progressive Era feminists to whom Nancy Drew is so indebted. Not surprisingly, the fictional feminists who serve as Nancy's foremothers also marked their independence and autonomy through means of motorized vehicles.

As early as 1910 mass-market publishers had begun to capitalize on the interest in the exotic new toys of the technological age by offering girls stories involving adventures with airplanes, motorboats, and, above all, automobiles. In 1910 *The Automobile Girls* (Altemus Co.) and *The Motor Girls* (Stratemeyer Syndicate/Cupples and Leon) were both created around the exploits of a group of teenage girls who tour the countryside in their own automobiles. A year later Hurst Publishing Company offered two sets of traveling teens, *The Motor Maids* and *The Girl Aviators*. These groups were soon joined by *The Outdoor Girls* (Stratemeyer/Grosset and Dunlap), one of the most popular girls' series of all time. In addition, other existing series added new volumes that capitalized on the current trend in girls' automobile adventure tales by eventually setting their heroines at the wheel: *The Meadow-Brook Girls* (Saalfield), *The Ranch Girls* (Winston), *Ruth Fielding* (Stratemeyer/ Cupples and Leon), *Aunt Jane's Nieces* (Reilly & Britton), and *Polly Brewster* (Grosset and Dunlap). By the mid 1910s, girls wanting to take to the

75

road in search of vicarious adventure could choose from among dozens of series books.

By giving the heroines the technological expertise to master automobiles and airplanes, and imbuing them with a relish for action and strenuous physical activity, the authors marked their protagonists as new women ready to inhabit a modern era. As series protagonists venture into the wide unknown—as travelers, tourists, adventurers, and thrill seekers—they seem far removed from obligations of home and family. Often traveling alone, frequently without male companionship or protection, heroines are set up to cross not only physical boundaries but social and cultural ones as well. Potentially free from the restrictions that space, time, and gender impose on them in a domestic or institutional setting, girls on the move are given the opportunity to demonstrate those modern virtues the public had come to expect of "New Women": courage, stamina, physical strength, independence, and leadership qualities, as plot after plot placed them in dangerous, alien, and challenging situations. Yet this implicit resistance to Victorian notions of women's inherent fragility and to sexist valuations of women's abilities and rights was not an unequivocal one. Anyone who has read these books quickly discovers that the girls' adventure series is a genre often at odds with itself, replete with contradictory impulses and convoluted narrative strategies, meant, it seems, to reconcile greater freedom and fitness for girls with their continued subordination to a patriarchal, genteel order.

To some degree the obvious contradictions are the result of a certain amount of genre confusion. On first read the books appear to follow the narrative formula of boys' adventure stories, a formula that clashes with another, the contemporary romance formula. The girls' adventure series might also be profitably viewed as a form of travel, or quest literature; and nearly without exception, the series books deserve to be classified as melodrama.

Authors of the girls' series books, finally, had to become quite adept at genre mixing. The resulting pastiche of forms, the confusions of plots and formulas that characterize the girls' series can be explained, in part, as the result of production constraints and conditions: the frequent changes of authors, the necessity of keeping on top of trends and ahead of competitors, an effort to please different audiences, for instance. Yet just as importantly, such mixing is indicative of the larger confusions, motives, and tensions of a society in the process of negotiating the changing dynamics and meaning of modern womanhood. When authors mixed adventure and romance genres, they were attempting to harmonize contradictory impulses, and the effect was simultaneously to challenge and to reaffirm femininity. It is here, in the clash of narrative formulas, I would argue, where the struggle for meaning in the series books is most apparent. Raymond Williams might point to this literature as representative of the "Janus-faced" nature of popular culture in its articulation of the uneasy co-existence of residual and emerging cultural meanings. Popular culture is both dominant *and* oppositional, according to Williams and other cultural studies theorists; it not only contains contradictions, but it functions in a highly contradictory manner (Williams, Eagleton, Davis). Thus, one of the critic's tasks is to locate ideological struggle—here over gendered meanings—in those instances where the narrative appears to contradict itself; where the apparent message is at odds with the process of narration; where, for instance, traditional values of feminine virtue are negotiating with newer, feminist perspectives of reality.

The attempt to blend the old-fashioned girl with the new woman on the go is evident in Cupples and Leon's 1910 advertisement for their new *Motor Girls* series:

The adventures of Cora Kimball and her friends are many and varied. They go on automobile tours, spend vacations by the seashore and even take a yachting trip to the West Indies. While their adventures are exciting enough for the veriest tomboy, the distinctive feminine appeal is not lacking. Cora and her friends are, in the final analysis, just wholesome, everyday girls. In spite of their unusual adventures their daily lives are filled with the sort of activities that every girls knows and enjoys. They design clothes, they shop for the newest in hats and they give marvelously clever parties. What girl doesn't enjoy these things? What girl doesn't enjoy reading about them? (Penrose, jacket blurb)

Such combinations did not always take, and often resulted in incongruities and tensions in the narratives that had to be continually balanced and resolved.

In examining the girls' automobile series books, I am interested in how gender ideologies were mediated once heroines were given the means and mobility to trespass into male territory. How are the narratives structured to accommodate the inevitable tensions that accompany that trespass? What is the meaning of their travel? How do they behave once in public spaces? What might these books have meant for the way American girls living in the early twentieth century learned to think about themselves and how might these stories have helped influence beliefs about future possibilities?

In her historical account of women's involvement in the early years of the automobile age in America, Virginia Scharff shows how the first automobiles collided with Victorian notions of woman's nature and abilities and how women appropriated that icon of masculinity and made car culture into women's culture. She writes:

Women in automobiles entered public space at a time of unprecedented debate over women's rights and capacity to step into public life . . . where the distinction between public and private places served as a boundary defining proper masculine and feminine roles . . . women's inroad into the automobile world reverberated with cultural significance. (23)

When middle-class women took to open spaces with the aid of the automobile, they were conspicuously invading a male domain. Not surprisingly, this invasion met considerable resistance and backlash. Just as opponents of women's entry into competitive sport had tried to argue that "nice girls don't sweat," so too opponents of women drivers worried that women could only dirty themselves by venturing beyond the front door. And motoring *was* a dirty sport; speeding down the dusty byways dressed in a heavy overcoat ("duster") and wearing unflattering goggles, this new passion was hardly conducive to preserving female decorum. Early critics of women drivers cited three presumed sources of women's inferiority at the wheel: emotional instability, physical weakness, and intellectual deficiencies (Scharff 30); the same arguments, it is interesting to note, that were used by those opposed to women's entry into higher education and suffrage for women.

Yet, by 1912 women were eagerly participating in races, cross-country tours, and competitions. Whether they intended to or not, women motorists made a conspicuous statement about female assertiveness, and the automobile became both a symbol and an actual source of independence for women.

The automobile's popularity with women was aided by the visible presence of prominent women motorists. Edith Wharton was one who proclaimed the joys of motoring, as was President Theodore Roosevelt's indomitable daughter Alice, who stirred up considerable controversy when she drove from Newport to Washington alone, an act which she admitted was a mild protest against her father's rather staid notion of femininity (Scharff 72).

Progressive Era women used the car for different ends. Some women were seeking new thrills and adventure and yet took pains to avoid appearing feminist, a common connection in the press of the day.[1] Other women saw more radical potential in women's driving and made direct connections between the autonomy that the car afforded and the women's rights campaign. The women's suffrage movement made effective use of the automobile, conducting tours for suffrage, holding open air meetings and auto parades.[2] World War I presented new opportunities for women to put their driving skills to work, whether they joined the Motor Corps as volunteers or capitalized on professional opportunities as mechanics at home.

For whatever reason women were taking the wheel, whether carrying out domestic duties, pursuing personal pleasure or political and social agendas, women drivers gave evidence of a new perception of modern women as mobile, active, and public. It was in this controversial climate that juvenile publishers joined the cultural forces that mediated popular understanding of women's spatial, social, and political spheres. In 1910 and after, when the Motor Girls, the Motor Maid, and their fictional companions set out to find adventure in their motor cars, the authors who sent them understood the potential political and social meaning these adventures held. To varying degrees authors structured their narratives to realize or to avoid the radical possibilities of such apparently limitless freedom.

When the girls of the series take to the wheel in search of adventure, their creators imbue them with a knowledge that they are pushing at gender barriers and initially, at least, they frame the heroines' undertakings in progressive, if not feminist, terms. When Ruth Stuart, leader of the Automobile Girls, is given a car by her father she proposes an auto tour with her friends:

All my life I have longed to travel by myself; at least with the people I want, not in a train, or a big, crowded boat. Dad knows the feeling; it's what makes him run away from Chicago and get out on the prairie and ride and ride! I'm a girl so I can't do that or lots of things. But I can run an automobile. (Crane, *Newport* 32)

Ruth has a taste for mechanics, "even though I am a girl" (49), has studied the automobile manual, and helps her father with car repairs and maintenance. She has her father's full support: "[Ruth] loves fun and adventure and 'getting there' like a man. I am not going to stand in her way" (49-50).

Where they "get" is not always relevant, as a character in another series notes: "It's hard to say where any person in an auto is going . . . or when they'll get there" (Penrose, *Road* 130). The Outdoor Girls embark on a two-hundred-mile auto tour without a fixed itinerary: "It's nicer not to know exactly what you are going to do . . . we're going to be as carefree as we can" (Hope, *Motorcar* 91). Abandoning prescription and setting their own agenda invites risk, but that is precisely the point, as Bab, an Automobile Girl, argues. The whole value of adventure, she says, is "choosing to proceed in spite of risks" (Crane, *Hudson* 62).

The motoring heroines are cast as modern women; impulsive, spunky, and athletic: "Well, a girl has to be impulsive to get ahead," says the brother of one of the Motor Girls, "she is so ridiculously hampered by conventionalities" (Penrose, *Tour* 63). Operating an automobile gives the girls the chance to prove parity with, if not superiority over, men. When they enter races with men they invariably win: "It'll do them good to take some of the conceit out of them" (Penrose, *Mountains* 29), Cora of the Motor Girls crows after beating the boys at a cross-country race. Cora's model for such chutzpah is a female aviator who has landed in a field where Cora is stranded. The woman, on a cross-country flight from Chicago to New York, is intent on beating the best record set by "either man or woman."

> "I don't see how you dare to take such risks. It must take a tremendous amount of courage," says the awe-struck Cora.
> "Oh, I don't know, . . . But there is a lot of satisfaction in beating the men at their own game," she added mischievously.
> "We women all owe you a lot for doing it," Cora replies. (139-40)

When Cora apologizes for having delayed her flight, the aviatrix assures her, "Don't worry about lost time. . . . We girls can give the men a handicap and yet beat them out" (144). The effect on Cora of this potential role model is short-lived, however; Cora's first act after her rescue is to freshen up: "Her purely feminine instincts coming to the fore, now that she was once more in touch with civilization" (144). Liberated in limited ways, Cora nonetheless embodies the era's notion of the ideal woman: independent, yet feminine.

When faced with mechanical trouble, the heroines usually know how to handle it: "We have been taught to run them carefully," says Motor Girl Cora (Penrose, *Lookout Beach* 46). And if they don't, they set out to learn: "If young men could fix it, it surely could not have been difficult for her to have understood and set it right," Cora reasons (134). They insist on cranking their own motors: "I've got a strong right arm. . . . I don't row and play tennis for nothing," boasts Motor Girls' leader, Ruth (Penrose, *Mountains* 77). They recognize when a cylinder is stuck, how to prime it, how to adjust the carburetor, or fix a flat tire, if they must. Their competence is meant to impress:

> "Suppose you had a blow-out?" asks an admirer of the Outdoor Girls.
> "We'd fix it. Engine trouble? We fix it—just like that," Betty tells her. (Hope, *Cape Cod* 19)

These independent young women of the series introduce the hinterland to the spectacle of new womanhood: "I sh'd think them gals w'd be skeered to death to ride in one ov them," a local villager remarks to Cora's brother (Penrose, *Mountains* 69). His reply: " 'They drive them as well as ride in them. . . . My sister can handle one of them as well as any man can. Y' don't say so!' . . . It was evident that his respect for the feminine members of the party had gone up several degrees" (69).

It is not surprising that these assertive, independent young women who insist on traveling only in the company of females should be taken for suffragettes, a catch-all term for emancipated women of the early part of the century. On meeting the five brave Automobile Girls, an older man compliments them: "I don't think I ever met a really brave woman before, and to be introduced to five at once! Why, I feel as if I were at a meeting of suffragettes" (Crane, *Newport* 98). When Automobile Girl Ruth boasts of her strength and skill at motoring, her friend Grace counters, " 'Whew, Ruth! You talk like a suffragette!' 'Well, maybe I am one,' " Ruth says, " 'I'm from the West where they raise strong-minded women. . . . Anyhow . . . I should be allowed to vote on laws for motorcars, as long as I can run a machine without a man' " (Crane, *Hudson* 98).

"Suffragette" is a term the girls of the series are not entirely comfortable with, however. For all their boasting of being modern American women who can compete with men, "ride horseback, run a motor car, repel a highway man with a pistol and not loose their heads . . . " (Crane, *Hudson* 134), the series heroines are quick to disassociate their activities from any political intent. When the Outdoor Girls are asked by villagers if they are suffragettes they respond: "Oh, mercy! What will we be taken for next? . . . Do we look so militant?" (Hope, *Deepdale* 117). When in another town a woman asks, "Are you a votes for women crowd?" Betty assures her, "No, we're a walking club." "No politics?" the woman presses. "None whatsoever" (Hope 169). Frequently humor in the series books is achieved at the expense of feminists. When an Englishman asks why the Automobile Girls carry firearms, one of the characters replies: "Don't you know it's dangerous in this country for a woman to walk on the streets unarmed unless she is dressed like a suffragette? And then she doesn't need a pistol to make people run from her" (Crane, *Hudson* 97). Although Ruth originally responded sympathetically to being associated with the suffrage movement, in the end she is mostly indifferent: "My dear Ruth," her aunt says "I beg of you, don't vote in my lifetime. Girls, in my day, would never dream of such a thing." To which Ruth replies, "Oh well, Auntie . . . I wouldn't worry about it now. Who knows when I may have a chance to vote?" (Crane, *Newport* 78).

Having set their heroines up with the ability, courage, independence, and athleticism required to enact the heroic adventures that the genre calls for, the authors then set about negating, disrupting, or dismissing the radical possibilities that might have been realized. The girls on the move may be shockingly independent, but they are nevertheless governed by strong moral, class, social, and gender codes. They assertively trespass into male territory, then dissemble once they get there.

Hidden behind long coats, goggles, and gloves, motoring females could easily camouflage their sex. A Motor Girl, the author notes, looked almost "boyish" at the wheel. The reclaiming of femininity begins, then, with appropriate attire, "the ever-necessary feminine adornment" (Crane, *Hudson* 59). While touring, the Automobile Girls make sure they have fresh clothes sent to destinations along the way: "It so happened that the Motor Girls afforded a peculiar variety, no two wearing similar outfits" (Penrose, *On Tour* 69). Clothing the protagonists to make a fashion/gender statement restricts the girls' freedom, however: "The speed of the car was playing havoc with [Cora's] costume and she was not too independent to want to look well when she got into her home-town" (191).

The best intentions of the protagonists to have adventures on their own are seldom realized, for despite protests to the contrary, it seems their wish for independence is somewhat disingenuous. The heroines value their independence but tend to betray it, either by acting against their will or by rationalizing the advent of male power into their autonomous but incomplete lives. Although virtually all of the motoring series begin with the heroines' declaration of the desire to be left alone, that resolve weakens, so that on their first night of a two-week tour, one of the Motor Girls laments: "I fancy it might be rather lonely evenings without the boys." When the boys show up, they rationalize: "There's nothing on earth pleases a girl so much as to have a boy run after her when she distinctly says you shall not go . . . " (Penrose, *Lookout Beach* 153).

With their boyfriends present, the girls' adventures, and the meaning of them, gradually changes. The thrust of the stories is still toward the adventure, in which individually and as a group, the girls (now with boyfriends) are put through paces of overcoming obstacles and dangers, usually the result of the machinations of a villain, on their way to accomplishing a moral mission. Eventually though, by the end of a series and with few exceptions, the adventure is subsidiary to the growing relationship between the sexes, which in all the motoring series end in marriage or a promise of it.[3] This acquiescence to the reassertion of male controls pervades the stories, which finally celebrate home over wandering, marriage over the life of spinsterhood, male-identification over the female collective identity that had been a source of strength and protection for the protagonists. In this way, a pattern is reinforced that positions the girls' heroic adventures as a passing phase, a necessary prerequisite perhaps to a companionate marriage. The marriage finale in itself does not necessarily negate or render meaningless the preceding assertions of independence and ambition. It does, however, create irreconcilable structural and genre differences with which series creators had to deal.

The narrative turn toward marriage at the end of a series represents one strategy the authors and editors used to resolve tensions that resulted from ambiguous and changing attitudes of the period. These stories can be seen mediating two contradictory impulses evident in popular culture: the desire to assimilate into the modern world and the desire to flee from it. We should keep in mind that decisions made in the creation of mass-market books also are structured by the imperatives of profitability and minimalization of financial risks. The surest way to this end, series' publishers perhaps felt, was to portray a happy blend of old-fashioned, family-oriented female and the new young woman on the go. The result is that the more radical values of the new era become sanitized and incorporated into the mainstream, but, quite evidently, at the expense of narrative cohesion.[4]

Central to the girls' motoring series books definition of modern womanhood is a slippery concept of the notion of "independence"; a value that has less to do with political and economic emancipation that it does with leisure and wealth. In spite of an Automobile Girl's assertion that "I'd rather be independent than rich" (Crane, *Berkshires* 126), those two conditions are intimately bound within the narrative world of the series, for the girls' independence itself depends on other people's money, i.e., on family wealth, unexpected inheritances, and sudden windfalls that come without the effort of labor. In fact, the series definition of "new womanhood" depends upon the construction of race and class bias, which are reinforced through various conventions and devices of the narratives. While the stories appear to carry the overt message of gender solidarity and equality, these fictions rest heavily on white supremacist assumptions. As the young girls match wits with and triumph over the highway men, gypsies, tramps, anarchists, and foreigners they meet on their travels, they continue to establish and reassert their position as genteel American women, well-bred capitalists, and emissaries of leisure.[5]

The presence of adolescent girls in their own automobiles is the most obvious marker of their class, and the heroines use the power cars afford to claim their privileged class status. Although they are variably described as "vagabonds" or "gypsies of the road," their adventures are supported by aristocratic comforts. To sustain their adventurous lifestyle requires money, which they come by handily: Cora's (Motor Girl) mother is a wealthy widow and Cora's boyfriend is planning a career as a stock broker; Motor Girls Bess and Belle have "an immensely rich Papa" (Penrose, *Tour* 10) who made his money from the railroad; Ruth of the Automobile Girls is supported by her father who sells real estate in Chicago, having first made money from a gold mine out West; the Ranch Girls have received a generous inheritance from their deceased father. Members of the collective who do not come from wealthy backgrounds come into money in the course of the series, either through marriage or fortunate coincidences.

That the automobile was a picture of the arrogance of wealth was a perception debated at the highest levels of public life during the early part of the century. Present Woodrow Wilson felt that the new automobile culture had dangerous class implications, and he feared that "the masses" would only become more resentful when confronted with the daily spectacle of the independent and careless touring leisure classes. "Nothing has spread socialistic feeling in this country more than the use of the automobile," he wrote (qtd. in Jakle 102).

The series heroines and their friends model the arrogance Wilson described, although they rarely meet with the resentment he feared. One convention of the genre, included for its comic effect, involves an encounter between the young motorists and local villagers, whose livestock have a habit of getting in the girls' way. The Motor Girls run into a herd of sheep, pay for the damage and are on their way. The Automobile Girls hit a cow, but don't stop. The Girl Aviators likewise collide with a herd of sheep on the road; the Meadowbrook Girls run over a calf. The heroines usually bribe their way out of predicaments, if they bother to stop at all. The Motor Maids are particularly egregious in their disregard for the rights of the under-privileged. When their car gets stuck in mud, they dismantle a hermit's house to use the boards as a make-shift roadway. They find a box in the foundation of the house which they also take because, they rationalize, "having walked off with . . . boards, why pause at boxes?" (Stokes, *Palm and Pine* 191).

The markers of class are inherent in the narrative structure of the girls' adventure stories. Time and again, series plots set up the heroines as protectors of property and champions of genteel (old) wealth, as authors engage protagonists in search of lost wills, in restoring estates, gold mines, investment stocks, and heirlooms to the authentic owners, in settling title disputes over property, and defending against the impostors who would deceive their way into high society.[6]

John Jakle has written that promoters of early car travel saw the automobile as an educational device, one that would inspire cultural nationalism by defining America for the travelers. More than defining America, however, the series heroines' travels are a *self*-defining activity; travel is the means by which they learn to differentiate themselves from others and to secure their sense of identity as not only Americans, but as women of a privileged class and dominant race.

As tourists, series heroines are amateur semioticians, to borrow from Jonathan Culler; they are interested in everything as a sign of itself; they travel to France in search of signs of Frenchness; to Italy in search of typical Italian behavior; to Asia to take in exemplary Oriental scenes (Culler 127). Their travels teach them to recognize the signs that signify certain behaviors and values: swarthy, beady-eyed people signify evil; loud clothing and boisterous behavior signifies lower classes. They immediately "understand" "cowboyness" or "Asianness" because their search for stereotypes is continually validated. Their superficial understanding of their travel experiences is captured in this quotation from *The Motor Maids in Fair Japan*: "Everything is picturesque in this country, from beggars to railroad bridges . . . everything is like a decoration. I can't imagine anything really seriously [*sic*] happening, it's all so gay and pretty and the people are all like dolls" (Stokes 22).

One might argue that the inherent form of mass-marketed formulaic fiction, with its focus on action, does not allow protagonists to seek meaning in the lives of others. Yet, it is in part the very structure of this fiction that allows for certain meanings to be conveyed. Although travel essentially implies liminality, according to John Urry, in that it involves social and spatial separation from the normal (10), in the series books the potential liminal experience is inverted so that the centrality of the heroines' position as middle-class white women is constantly reestablished.

Finally, the series heroines' outward movement must be understood in terms of social movement, from the familiar to the unknown, from the security of their own culture to contact with the "Other." It is through such contact that the social and cultural meaning of their adventures is determined. The whiteness and class bias of these stories of modern girlhood reflect practices of editors and authors as well as the failure of the pre-suffrage women's movement to make race or class a priority for women's rights. These books operate within an accommodationist framework, highlighting race and class privilege behind the challenge to sexism, which makes them valuable to cultural historians as we seek to understand the processes of cultural hegemony in a given era.

Notes

1. Writing to *Motor* magazine in 1914 on the topic of whether women make good drivers, one reader commented: "Discussing women's fitness for driving . . . is on a par with discussing her ability to use the ballot" (qtd. in Scharff 32).

2. The Congressional Union sponsored a cross-country trip from Oregon to Washington, D.C., in 1915 to capitalize on the media attention that normally attended women's motor treks. A story in *Motor* magazine in 1919 related how "the motor vehicle has aided in the long fight for suffrage" (Scharff 87).

3. *Ruth Fielding* and *The Ranch Girls* series are exceptions to the rule of total reassertion of male control. Although each series also ends with the marriage of the protagonist, these two series offer a more complex view of the negotiations needed to reconcile their independence with marriage, and both tend to resolve the dilemma with a portrayal of companionate marriages in which the protagonist is able to live out the convictions that she and other series heroines proclaim at some point but few are able to enact. Ruth doesn't marry until the twenty-fourth book in the series, and when she does marry her best friend's brother, he supports her career as film producer and decision to keep her own name. Yet, as Carol Billman points out, after Ruth Fielding's marriage the series suffers from a kind of narrative schizophrenia by trying to have it both ways. Ruth repeatedly proclaims her complete submission to husband Tom and to family life, only moments later to defend, just as passionately, her work. What happens to Ruth's character as a result ultimately makes for irreconcilable structural differences in the series, as Billman rightly asserts (74-77). Jack, heroine of the *Ranch Girls* series, marries twice before the series' conclusion and likewise is able to keep her career as ranch manager and business woman.

4. Carol Billman writes that the Stratemeyer Syndicate learned from the dilemma of Ruth Fielding to restrict their characters spatially, to distance them from the options and complexities of the real world. Having sent Ruth into the world where she became successful and famous, she could never really come home again (77). As the Ruth Fielding series was winding down, the syndicate put its author, Mildred Wirt, to work on a new series, *Nancy Drew*, that would skirt this problem. Nancy would remain a teenager throughout the series and rarely leave her secluded hamlet of River Heights.

5. These motoring girls give fictional evidence of T. J. Jackson Lears's theory of a Progressive Era shift from the Protestant ethos of salvation through self-denial to a therapeutic ethos stressing self-realization. The pleasure-seeking, well-to-do adventurers seem to confirm the existence of a new set of values which, according to Lears, sanctioned leisure, compulsive spending, and the morality of individual fulfillment.

6. The theme of "old" versus "new" wealth is evident in a Motor Girls book, *On Crystal Bay*. In this work, Cora and her friends stop landsharks from re-routing the bay water for use in a mill that will destroy the bay's attraction for tourists. The land on which the mill will be built has been illegally procured from Freda's family. The landsharks have little regard for the land: "So what if it [the factory] ruins the park?" (169). The outcome of the story, in which the land is returned to Freda's mother, is not anti-capitalist, although this might be one reading. It shows, rather, the triumph of gentile wealth (Freda's New England family who has owned the land generations) versus intruding (outsider) wealth.

Works Cited

Billman, Carol. *The Secret of Stratemeyer Syndicate: Nancy Drew, The Hardy Boys and the Million Dollar Fiction Factory*. New York: Ungar, 1986.

Crane, Laura Dent. *The Automobile Girls Along the Hudson; or Fighting Fire in Sleepy Hollow*. New York: Altemus, 1910.

——. *The Automobile Girls at Newport; or Watching the Summer Parade*. New York: Altemus, 1910.

——. *The Automobile Girls in the Berkshires; or The Ghost of Lost Man's Trail*. New York: Altemus, 1910.

Culler, Johnathan. "Semiotics of Tourism." *American Journal of Semiotics* 1 (1981): 120-32.

Davis, Lennard J. *Resisting Novels: Ideology and Fiction*. New York: Methuen, 1987.

Eagleton, Terry. "Ideology, Fiction, Narrative." *Social Text* 2 (1979): 62-80.

Heilbrun, Carolyn G. "Nancy Drew: A Moment in Feminist History." *Rediscovering Nancy Drew*. Ed. Carolyn Stewart Dyer and Nancy Tillman Romalov. Iowa City: U of Iowa P, 1995: 11-21.

Hope, Laura Lee. *The Outdoor Girls in a Motorcar; or The Haunted Mansion of Shadow Valley*. New York: Grosset, 1913.

——. *The Outdoor Girls of Deepdale; or Camping and Tramping for Fun and Health*. New York: Grosset, 1913.

——. *The Outdoor Girls on Cape Cod; or Sally Ann of Lighthouse Rock*. New York: Grosset, 1924.

Jakle, John. *The Tourist: Travel in Twentieth-Century North America*. Lincoln: U of Nebraska P, 1985.

Lears, T. J. Jackson. "From Salvation to Self-Realization: Advertising and the Therapeutic Roots of the Consumer Culture, 1880-1930." *Culture of Consumption: Critical Essays in American History, 1880-1980*. Ed. Richard Wightman Fox and T. J. Jackson Lears. New York: Pantheon, 1983: 3-38.

Penrose, Margaret. *The Motor Girls at Lookout Beach; or In Quest of the Runaways*. New York: Cupples, 1911.

——. *The Motor Girls in the Mountains; or The Gypsy Girls' Secret*. New York: Cupples, 1917.

——. *The Motor Girls on Crystal Bay; or The Secret of the Red Car*. New York: Cupples, 1914.

——. *The Motor Girls on a Tour; or Keeping a Strange Promise*. New York: Cupples, 1911.

——. *The Motor Girls; or a Mystery of the Road*. New York: Cupples, 1910.

Scharff, Virginia. *Taking the Wheel: Women and the Coming of the Motor Age*. New York: Free P, 1991.

Stokes, Katherine. *The Motor Maids by Palm and Pine*. New York: Hurst, 1914.

——. *The Motor Maids in Fair Japan*. New York: Hurst, 1915.

Urry, John. *The Tourist Gaze: Leisure and Travel in Contemporary Societies*. Newbury Park: Sage, 1990.

Williams, Raymond. *Marxism and Literature*. Oxford: Oxford UP, 1977.

5

Girl Scouts, Camp Fire Girls, and Woodcraft Girls: The Ideology of Girls' Scouting Novels, 1910-1935

Sherrie A. Inness

In his article "The Boy Scout Handbook," Paul Fussell argues that scholars are not paying adequate attention to many literary works that do not qualify as masterpieces. "It's amazing how many interesting books humanistic criticism manages not to notice," he comments. "Staring fixedly at its handful of teachable masterpieces, it seems content not to recognize that a vigorous literary-moral life constantly takes place just below (sometimes above) its vision. . . . The culture of the Boy Scouts deserves this sort of look-in" (3). On this point, I concur with Fussell. Humanist criticism (or Marxist or Lacanian or feminist criticism) has managed to overlook or disregard a vast number of texts that do not achieve "masterpiece" status. Feminist critics (as well as others) have challenged the established canon of Anglo-American literature, but, for the most part, old great books have been replaced with new great ones. Thus, in an American literature survey course, Melville, Faulkner, Hemingway, Emerson, and Hawthorne are commonly taught along with Sarah Orne Jewett, Mary Wilkins Freeman, Jean Toomey, Agnes Smedley, Charles Chesnutt, and a host of other writers being touted as desirable additions to the canon. Literary critics, however, have had a more difficult time getting past the "masterpiece mentality": a mindset in which the critic must proclaim a text's "greatness" in order to justify its right to be read, criticized, and inserted into Norton anthologies. This strategy has been and continues to be a highly successful way to alter the traditional canon, but it fails to challenge the notion of the canon itself and of the literary masterpiece. Thus, a vast variety of texts still fails to find a home or a voice in literature departments, creating a lopsided, elitist view of literary history. Many works of children's literature are not considered "great" by critics who condemn them as insignificant; this results in the marginalization of countless works of popular children's literature, including series books.

I am not, however, in complete accord with Fussell's argument, particularly when he appears to suggest that scholars neither have to pay close attention to the historicity nor the ideology of a particular text. He analyzes the rhetoric of *The Official Boy Scout Handbook* (1979) and has nothing but praise for what he considers to be its high moral standards. He lauds the "pliability and adaptability of the scout movement" (4) that have helped it to exist for so long. Although he admits that the term "free world" (5) appears too frequently in the Handbook, Fussell quickly bypasses this phrase to discuss the "slightly archaic liberal" politics of the Handbook (6), praising the book's ethics as the best gauge "for measuring the gross official misbehavior of the seventies" (7). "The generously low price of $3.50 [for the Handbook]," he remarks, "is enticing, and so is the place on the back cover where you're invited to inscribe your name" (8). But are we *all* "invited" to inscribe our names? Certainly, women and girls are not invited (perhaps they are supposed to inscribe their names on the Girl Scout's Handbook), while boys who refuse to pledge allegiance to the flag need not sign, because they will not be allowed to stay in scouting. Before we sign on the dotted line, perhaps we should learn more about scout ideology and its origins. Fussell establishes an overly simplistic dichotomy between the upright morals espoused in the Handbook and the general decay of American government and civilization. We have to go beyond this bipolarism and examine the ideology behind the scouting movement and how scouting was perceived by the general public at various times, as textual criticism of popular texts gains in depth and breadth if grounded in historical research.

To this end, this chapter examines the beginnings of the Girl Scout/Camp Fire Girl movements in the United States, particularly their representation in popular United States girls' series novels written from 1910 to 1935.[1] The numerous Girl Scout, Camp Fire Girl, Junior Guide, and Woodcraft Girl novels as well as Boy Scout and Camp Fire Boy novels that were published during this period are an important source of information about changing gender roles and United States imperialism. Also, we shall discover how the commodities of a capitalist system (in this case, serial novels) can function to promote and sell the system of which they are a product.

From analyzing these novels and the early development of scouting for girls, we shall be better able to understand that the scouting movement functions as a disciplinary agent of the state, which wishes to control and regulate the movements of youths; as Foucault informs us, "discipline fixes; it arrests or regulates movements; it clears up confusion; it dissipates compact groupings of individuals wandering about the country in unpredictable ways" (219). Compact groupings of people, however, that act in predictable and socially sanctioned ways are one of the essential sources of power for the state. Whether scouts, members of the military, or college students, organized groups help to ensure obedience to state regulations and control. Although scouting in fiction and in reality might offer girls a fleeting feeling of agency, ultimately scouting is only one of many state-sanctioned institutions that produces more malleable subjects for the nation. Thus, a reader should hesitate before inscribing his or her name on the official Boy/Girl Scout Handbook and question whether its ideology is, as Fussell implies, "enticing."

History of the Scouting Movement[2] and Popular Scout Fiction
The scouting movement originated in England when Lord Baden-Powell established scouting for boys in 1908. After his military campaigns in South Africa, he sought to create a pseudo-military organization for boys that would provide the discipline of a military unit during a non-war period. Boy Scouting was a clever combination of paramilitary style (uniforms, badges, and military organization) and imperialist ideology (emphasizing the "natural" dominance of the Anglo-Saxon races over all other peoples) combined with a large dose of camping and woodsmanship that proved to be remarkably attractive to large numbers of boys and girls, too. Thousands of girls wrote to Baden-Powell, pleading to be included in scouting activities. Although Baden-Powell, a strong believer in male supremacy, had no intention of allowing girls into the Boy Scouts, a separate group—the Girl Guides—was founded in England in 1910 and exported to the United States as the Girl Scout movement in 1912. From slightly different roots, the Camp Fire Girls began in 1910 in the United States. Both the Girl Scouts and the Camp Fire Girls spread rapidly across the globe. Girl Aides developed in Australia while Peace Scouting was organized in New Zealand. By 1912, there were an estimated 60,000 Camp Fire Girls, and Camp Fire circles were established in Japan, Canada, Siam, Panama, Scotland, the West Indies, and several other countries (Buckler 83-84).

The interest in scouting was reflected in the massive production of commodities with a scouting theme, and scouting quickly became a capitalist enterprise. For example, *The Vacation Book of the Camp Fire Girls* (1914) assures its early twentieth-century readers that the Camp Fire Outfitting Company stocked everything from short skirts and bathing suits to outing hats, middies, and bloomers for the well-dressed Camp Fire Girl (32). The scouting craze reached such grand proportions that a number of Girl Scout and Boy Scout moving pictures were filmed, while dozens of scouting serial novels were published by firms such as

Lothrop, Lee & Shepard, A. L. Burt, D. Appleton, Cupples & Leon, and Penn Publishing. Only a few of these novels received official sanction from the organization that they represented: I. T. Thurston's novel, *The Torch Bearer*, was one of the few officially endorsed Camp Fire stories (Buckler 88), while Lillian Roy's novel *Norma: A Flower Scout* was published with the approval of the National Girl Scouts. The lack of official endorsement, however, did not hinder scouting fiction from becoming tremendously popular. It is extremely difficult (if not impossible) to discover exact reader statistics for these series novels, but we can judge their popularity from other sources. For instance, the companies publishing the five to fifteen novels in a typical series would not have been so eager to produce these books if they had failed to sell. Moreover, authors would not have maintained and copied the standardized format for a scouting novel unless it was a format that was marketable.

A girls' scouting novel (when I refer to "scouting" I also include Camp Fire Girls' novels) was a rationalized, standardized product, as are most series books, that was churned out by the score by various obscure writers working for slim salaries. A typical book was approximately 225 pages long, hardbound, stamped on the cover with a colored picture of a group of girls engaged in some scouting activity, and it cost a nominal fifty to seventy-five cents. The words "Camp Fire" or "Girl Scout" were inevitably prominent in the title. Furthermore, the reader was obviously expected to read, and even encouraged to read, all the novels in a particular series. Commonly, the books would self-consciously refer to the other novels in a series and urge the reader to purchase them. For example, in Lilian Garis's *The Girls Scouts at Rocky Ledge*, a group of Girl Scouts (Betta, Doro, Pell, Alma, and Tremble) are discussing the merits of the last books in the series that center on their scouting exploits:

They were referring to the first volume, 'The Girl Scout Pioneers,' but others of the group spoke up for their particular choice of the series, naming, 'The Girl Scouts at Bellaire' and 'The Girl Scouts at Sea Crest.'

'You may have those,' offered Doro, 'but I perfectly love this.' She held up the last book published. It was entitled 'The Girl Scouts at Camp Comalong.'

This brought about a general discussion of the entire series, and although the method being used is not usually employed to remind readers of the other books in a series, perhaps, since the girls were speaking for themselves, it will be accepted. (74)

The fictional scouts sold themselves. Also, the novels sold their readers on the importance of scouting activities. In Amy Blanchard's *In Camp with the Muskoday Camp Fire Girls* (1917), the author writes in the foreword, "To those girls who know nothing about the joys of camp life such experiences as those of the Muskoday Camp Fire Girls must come as a revelation. . . . The doings of the Muskoday Camp Fire Girls I hope may inspire others" (n.p.). Similarly, the narrator in Lilian Garis's *The Girl Scout Pioneers* questions the reader, "Have you ever been called upon to lead others? Do you know the joys of using your own personal power in a well-organized and carefully directed plan?" (143). The reader is not expected to read passively but to view her reading experience as a direct reflection of the potential enjoyment that she, too, could receive from joining a Camp Fire or Girl Scout troop.

It is unlikely, however, that any real scouting troop could meet with a fraction of the adventure enjoyed by one of the many fictional scouting troops. Always undaunted, always high-spirited, scouts in novels go through dangers that would be insurmountable to non-scouts, their only worry being that their new uniforms might become wrinkled. In Hildegard G. Frey's novel *The Camp Fire Girls Go Motoring*, the plucky girls are involved in several car accidents, have an automobile stolen, drive a thousand miles with no chaperon, and escape from a burning building, yet are still chipper enough to sing camp songs on a dismally wet, cold night. (And all my scouting troop had a chance to do was tour the local ice cream shop and take nature walks at the park.) Not all scouting novels paint such an unrealistic picture of scouting; in Elizabeth Duffield's *Lucile, the Torch Bearer*, the title character enjoys "fishing on the banks of the stream . . . swimming—tramping—canoeing" (115), while Olive in Isabel Hornibrook's *Camp Fire Girls in War and Peace* benefits from "hiking, climbing, sleeping out on mountain-tops, or by the seashore" (24). Girls are lured into scouting because serial fiction depicts scouting as offering them escape from stereotypical gender roles, along with a great amount of physical freedom. As the next section explains, however, the degree of liberty allowed to girls does not hinder the scouting movement from working to construct suitably socialized bourgeois women.

Domestic Training: Building a Better Mother

James F. Page, in his book about juvenile organizations entitled *Socializing for the New Order* (1919), points out that "if girls are to possess the highest type of feminine traits which will enable them to serve adequately the needs of society, they must pass through the race history of women, as the boy to attain to maximum proficiency must recapitulate the history of man" (79). According to Page, the Camp Fire Girls and the Girl Scouts facilitate a pseudo-return to a more primitive racial past. The Camp Fire Girls and the Girl Scouts "will tend to restore [woman's] original and true status; and prepare her subsequently to function in the domestication of the larger social community" (81). "The general aim of the Camp Fire Girls," Page writes, "is to help girls prepare for the new social order, and to enable them to overcome the grinding tendency of modern machine work; to develop in girls the power of cooperation, the capacity to keep step" (81). His words reveal a dark underside to scouting ideology. Girls participate in camping activities, build nature crafts, and engage in the rituals of the Camp Fire Girls (coining Native American names such as "Nyoda" and "Hinpoha," building campfires, and adopting pseudo-Native American rituals) so that they will be closer to their "original and true status," not so that they experience a feeling of personal agency or empowerment. Scouts are taught not to question modernization and technological innovation; instead, they must "keep step" with the "new social order."

Dr. Luther Gulick, co-founder of the Camp Fire Girls, had no intention of subverting social norms of gender behavior in his organization. "I believe the keynote [of the Camp Fire Girls]," he stated, "is . . . that we wish to develop girls to be womanly . . . [T]o copy the Boy Scout movement would be utterly and fundamentally evil, and would probably produce ultimately a moral and psychological involution which is the last thing in the world that . . any of us want. We hate manly women and womanly men" (qtd. in Buckler 22). He continued, "the bearing and rearing of children has always been the first duty of most women, and must always continue to be. This involves service, constant service, self-forgetfulness and always service" (22). In light of Gulick's comments, we must consider the many physical activities (hiking, camping, swimming, and other outdoor sports) offered to scouts as aimed at developing and encouraging traditional gender roles. Thus, it comes as little surprise to the reader that both the fictional and the actual Boy Scout is allowed far more physical freedom than the Girl Scout or Camp Fire Girl.[3]

In the first quarter of the twentieth century, scouting did not always undermine the role of the woman as wife and mother. One way this was accomplished was by encouraging domestic training as a part of scouting. *Campward Ho! A Manual for Girl Scout Camps* (1920) insists on domestic training for all girls; "There are many young women with homes of their own whose houses are badly run because they have no idea how the daily housework should be done. They cannot do it themselves and they cannot direct another. The camp is the one place where the scout can learn what to do and how to do it" (45). Many of the early Girl Scout training manuals emphasized that the Girl Scout should be both a good mother and a fanatic housewife. "Every Girl Scout knows the deep and vital need for clean and healthy bodies in the mothers of the next generation" (11) states the *Official Handbook of the Girl Scouts* from 1920. The *Handbook* informs its readers, the Girl Scout "is honor bound to have no dark, damp, hidden, dirt-filled corners in any part of house, not even in shed or cellar" (121). From this rhetoric, it is clear that cleaning the house is represented not as merely a job, but a moral crusade.

Such scouting ideology is also depicted in scouting fiction, which is very much aware of its responsibility to instruct young girls about socially acceptable gender behavior. Thus, in Garis's *The Girl Scout Pioneers*, the narrator remarks:

[I]t may not be amiss to call attention here to the value of such training given almost in play, and without question in such attractive forms as to make character building through its influence an ideal pastime, a valuable investment, and a complete program for growing girls, who may emerge as . . . nicely trained little helpers for the home. (16)

In Jane Stewart's novel, *The Camp Fire Girls in the Mountains*, the Camp Fire leader is even more explicit about the future responsibilities of the Camp Fire Girl: "the job every girl ought to get sooner or later," she admonishes, is "running a home" (75). Scout training is a "valuable investment," but for whom? Certainly, scouting is a worthwhile investment for a society intent on reminding the increasingly independent women of the 1920s that they must not disregard their ultimate responsibilities as future American mothers and housewives. In addition, as the next section discusses, scouting fiction promotes the socioeconomic hegemony of the Anglo-Saxon girl by portraying working-class girls, African Americans, and foreigners as inferior citizens who deserve only condescension.

Americanization in Scout Fiction

If Fussell thinks the ideology of the Boy Scouts (or Girl Scouts) is pliable and adaptable, he should read *Anne Thornton, Wetamoo*, in which the Woodcraft girls work at a local community center "teaching the foreigners and helping them to become good citizens" (Anthony, n.p.). Or Fussell should examine Latharo Hoover's novel, *The Camp-Fire Boys in the Philippines*, in which "three clean-minded American youths" are pursuing a "vile leprous [*sic*] Chinaman" (229) who is planning to marry not one but *two* "beautiful white girls" (229).[4] Of course, the "vile" Chinaman is killed, while the beautiful white girls are saved by the stalwart Camp Fire Boys.

The connections between American imperialism and scouting are impossible to escape, both in fiction and in reality.[5] For example, Jean Large's book *Nancy Goes Girl Scouting* openly proselytizes for United States' values and culture. Not only does Mrs. Herbert Hoover (honorary President of the Girl Scouts) write the introduction for the book, describing herself as an "extremely enthusiastic Girl Scout" (v), but fictional Girl Scout Nancy discovers "the numerous ways the people of the United States have benefited the world" (129). Nancy is only one of countless fictional Girl Scouts or Camp Fire Girls who praise the superiority of American values, while implicitly or explicitly downgrading the values of other countries. In Margaret Vandercook's *The Camp Fire Girls by the Blue Lagoon*, one Camp Fire Girl desires to go into social settlement work "to teach our immigrants more of the spirit and opportunities of the United States" (31), while in *The Girl Scout Pioneers*, the Girl Scouts of the True Tred troop are elated that they can start a troop for some poor mill girls: "The girls of True Tred were radiant with the prospect of their work—that of assisting the mill girls and actually taking part in real Americanization" (63). Both fictional and real Girl Scouts could earn a merit badge in "Americanization." Whether in fiction or in actuality, early twentieth-century scouting offered a convenient way to export Anglo-Saxon values to the rest of the world. It comes as no surprise in *The Campfire Girls as Federal Investigators* by Julianne DeVries[6] that the first task Mrs. Evans's Camp Fire Girls do when shipwrecked on a South Pacific Island is establish a Camp Fire circle for the native girls and instruct this new circle in how to start other Camp Fire groups on the neighboring islands.

In conclusion, texts that are by no means literary masterpieces, such as Girl Scout serial books and other girls' series, can still offer valuable insights into the construction of gender roles and, more generally, United States culture. Such texts, however, remain shallow and one-dimensional if they are studied only as representations of our modern historical period. For example, *The Official Boy Scout Handbook* may be interpreted as a gauge "for measuring the gross official misbehavior of the seventies," but an earlier edition also must be analyzed as a gauge of the rampant American nationalism of the early twentieth century. Similarly, the scouting movement undoubtedly has offered individual girls and women a sense of agency and autonomy; but, as we have seen, the Girl Scout and Camp Fire girl movements between World War I and World War II were also actively engaged in convincing women that domesticity was the *sine qua non* for feminine happiness. Furthermore, the scouting movement, whether in reality or fiction, helped perpetuate the idea that the "true" American girl was middle class and white.

Insights such as these would not be possible if critics ignored popular texts like girls' series books and studied only a "handful of teachable masterpieces." Although Fussell made his claim in the mid-1970s, it still has validity in the 1990s. Today, many scholars still wear blinders when it comes to recognizing the importance of texts that will never be touted as "good books." Of course, there are critics (Allen Bloom springs to mind) who condemn efforts to bring high and low culture together, and claim that popular culture studies should be excluded from the academy, or, at most, given a marginal position. These scholars generally argue that a call for popular culture in the classroom is a call for cultural anarchy; they wish to build an impenetrable barrier between the literary classics suitable for teaching, and the innumerable other popular texts, which would remain in an outer purgatory reserved for "bad" books. Even scholars who wish to have Agnes Smedley's or Sarah Orne Jewett's works taught in the classroom balk at the thought that Carolyn Keene's novels might also be included. Such an approach to pedagogy, I believe, is narrow, elitist, and helps to perpetuate a skewed vision of the past. Such scholars fail to recognize that "bad" literature in all its myriad forms has just as much (if not more) impact on United States culture than does "good" literature. Moreover, excluding popular literary works from the classroom establishes a dangerous precedent for students, who are led to believe that critical thinking about texts should be limited to certain canonical or semi-canonical works, failing to recognize that a critical approach to popular culture is vitally important in a world inundated with countless popular art forms.

Combining popular literary works, such as girls' series, with more traditional texts in the classroom has the potential to enrich the academic experience. As cultural critics, we can better interpret the ideological density of any historical era by integrating popular works into our pedagogy (and, I would add, our own scholarship). The possible combinations of works to teach together are exciting: visions of the West in both Willa Cather's novels and Owen Wister's western *The Virginian*; images of the city in Theodore Dreiser's novel *Sister Carrie* and in Raymond Chandler's detective novels; gender roles in Edith Wharton's society romances and in Girl Scout novels. By juxtaposing texts in this manner, we not only encourage new insights into United States culture, but also create a more nuanced vision of how society constitutes itself, at least partially, through literary representation.

Notes

1. In England, there were also Girl Guide novels and Camp Fire Girl stories published. For an account of these books, see Mary Cadogan and Patricia Craig, *You're a Brick, Angela! A New Look at Girls' Fiction from 1839 to 1975*, 140-77.

2. Histories of scouting are typically saccharin and uncritical. For examples of this genre, see Helen Buckler, Mary Fielder, and Martha F. Allen, *Wo-He-Lo: The Story of Camp Fire Girls 1910-1960*; and Anne Hyde Choate and Helen Ferris, *Juliet Low and the Girl Scouts: The Story of an American Woman, 1860-1927*.

3. Boy Scout series allow their boys much more physical freedom than do Girl Scout series. For instance, in Herbert Carter's *The Boy Scouts Along the Susquehanna*, many of the troop members carry guns and go on more strenuous hikes than fictional Girl Scouts are ever allowed. Other Boy Scout books of interest include Thornton Burgess, *The Boy Scouts of Woodcraft Camp* in which the scouts go through what one character calls a "man factory" (343): a wilderness camp; Herbert Carter, *The Boy Scouts Afoot in France*, which features the Boy Scouts in World War I; Latharo Hoover, *The Camp-Fire Boys in the Philippines*, which stars "three clean-minded American youths" complete with rifles and twin machine-guns on their private airplane; Howard Payson, *The Boy Scouts at the Panama Canal*; G. Harvey Ralphson, *Boy Scouts in a Motor Boat or Adventures on the Columbia River*, which features Boy Scouts who camp and also work for the United States Secret Service. A more comprehensive listing of Boy Scout series is found in *American Boys' Series Books 1900-1980*.

4. Scouting fiction is openly racist: "Chinamen" are described as lepers; the Japanese are scornfully referred to as "Japs," and African Americans and Mexicans are portrayed as foolish and lazy. Some writers of series fiction perpetuated truly dreadful stereotypes of racial and ethnic groups. For instance, in Hildegard Frey's *The Camp Fire Girls Go Motoring*, Katherine, a widely admired Camp Fire Girl, nonchalantly describes Negroes as looking "like apes, but they're quite harmless. They're shiftless to the last degree, but not violent. They're too lazy to do any mischief" (50). For information about the racism in series books, see J. Frederick MacDonald, "'The Foreigner' in Juvenile Series Fiction, 1900-1945."

5. Of course, both fictional and real scouts were engrossed with war work during World War I, and strongly supported the pro-America jingoism of the war period. See Margaret Widdemer, *Winona's War Farm*. There are also numerous other series books for boys and girls that incorporate World War I or II.

6. Julianne DeVries is actually the pen name of Julian DeVries. The ramifications of this are beyond the scope of this essay.

Works Cited

American Boys' Series Books 1900-1980. Tampa: U of South Florida Library Associates, 1987.

Anthony, Lotta Rowe. *Anne Thornton, Wetamoo*. Philadelphia: Penn, 1922.

Blanchard, Amy E. *The Camp Fire Girls of Brightwood: A Story of How They Kindled Their Fire and Kept It Burning*. Boston: Wilde, 1915.

——. *In Camp with the Muskoday Camp Fire Girls: A Story of the Camp Fire by the Lake*. Boston: Wilde, 1917.

——. *Lucky Penny of Thistle Troop: A Girl Scout Story*. Boston: Wilde, 1920.

Buckler, Helen, Mary F. Fiedler, and Martha F. Allen. *Wo-He-Lo: The Story of Camp Fire Girls 1910-1960*. New York: Holt, 1961.

Burgess, Thornton W. *The Boy Scouts of Woodcraft Camp*. Philadelphia: Penn, 1920.

Cadogan, Mary, and Patricia Craig. *You're a Brick, Angela! A New Look at Girls' Fiction from 1839 to 1975*. London: Gollancz, 1976.

Carter, Herbert. *The Boy Scouts Along the Susquehanna or The Silver Fox Patrol Caught in a Flood*. New York: Burt, 1915.

——. *The Boy Scouts Afoot in France; or, With the Red Cross Corps at the Marne*. New York: Burt, 1917.

Choate, Anne Hyde, and Helen Ferris. *Juliet Low and the Girl Scouts: The Story of an American Woman, 1860-1927*. Garden City: Girl Scouts, 1928.

DeVries, Julianne [Julian DeVries]. *The Campfire Girls as Federal Investigators*. New York: World Syndicate, 1935.

Duffield, Elizabeth M. *Lucile, the Torch Bearer*. New York: Sully, 1915.

Foucault, Michel. *Discipline and Punish: The Birth of the Prison*. Trans. Alan Sheridan. New York: Pantheon, 1977.

Frey, Hildegard G. *The Camp Fire Girls Go Motoring*. New York: Burt, 1916.

——. *The Camp Fire Girls on the Open Road; or Glorify Work*. New York: Burt, 1918.

Fussell, Paul. "The Boy Scout Handbook." *The Boy Scout Handbook and Other Observations*. New York: Oxford UP, 1982. 3-8.

Garis, Lilian. *The Girl Scout Pioneers or Winning the First B.C.* New York: Cupples, 1920.

——. *The Girl Scouts at Rocky Ledge or Nora's Real Vacation*. New York: Cupples, 1922.

Girl Scouts of the United States of America *Campward Ho! A Manual for Girl Scout Camps*. New York: Girl Scouts, 1920.

Hoover, Latharo. *The Camp-Fire Boys in the Philippines*. New York: Burt, 1930.

Hornibrook, Isabel. *Girls of the Morning-Glory Camp Fire*. Boston: Lothrop, 1916.

——. *Camp Fire Girls in War and Peace*. Boston: Lothrop, 1919.

Large, Jean Henry. *Nancy Goes Girl Scouting*. New York: Appleton, 1927.

MacDonald, J. Frederick. "'The Foreigner' in Juvenile Series Fiction, 1900-1945." *Journal of Popular Culture* 8.3 (1974): 534-48.

Page, James F. *Socializing for the New Order; or, Educational Values of the Juvenile Organization*. Rock Island, IL: Augustana College, 1919.

Payson, Howard. *The Boy Scouts at the Panama Canal*. New York: Hurst, 1913.

Ralphson, G. Harvey. *Boy Scouts in a Motor Boat or Adventures on the Columbia River*. Chicago: Donohue, 1912.

Roy, Lillian Elizabeth. *Norma: A Garden Scout*. New York: Burt, 1925.

Scouting for Girls: Official Handbook of the Girl Scouts. New York: Girl Scouts, 1920.

Stewart, Jane L. *The Camp Fire Girls in the Mountains; or Bessie King's Strange Adventure*. New York: Saalfield, 1914.

Thurston, I.T. *The Torch Bearer: A Camp Fire Girls' Story*. New York: Revell, 1913.

Vacation Book of the Camp Fire Girls. New York: Camp Fire Girls, 1914.

Vandercook, Margaret. *The Camp Fire Girls by the Blue Lagoon*. Philadelphia: Winston, 1921.

Widdemer, Margaret. *Winona's War Farm*. Philadelphia: Lippincott, 1918.

6

A Companion to History:
Maud Hart Lovelace's Betsy-Tacy Books

Maureen E. Reed

This is one reason I love stories. They allow us a vision of the unknowable. They let us perceive what we cannot prove. They let us see on a slant what we could never confront directly.

—Katherine Paterson[1]

A Confession

I usually end my trips to bookstores with a long stop in the children's section. I search the shelves for books that I read long ago, with the hope of adding them to my growing collection of juvenile fiction, or just losing myself within their pages for a few minutes. My favorite stories are the ones about girls from the American past, who grow up in different eras but find similar happy endings. I feel a little sheepish when I take such books, brimming with illustrated covers and large print, to a cash register. I try to act as if I were buying them for a young relative, rather than planning to read them again myself.

I grew up as a devoted reader of many juvenile authors, but one of my favorites was American author Maud Hart Lovelace, who wrote the Betsy-Tacy series. Written in the 1940s and 50s, the ten novels tell the story of Betsy Ray, a girl growing up in Deep Valley, Minnesota, from the turn of the century until the American entry into World War I. The series became known as the Betsy-Tacy books because it begins when Betsy makes her first friend, Tacy, a character who remains as Betsy's best friend throughout the series. My oldest sister first showed them to me at the library when I was about seven years old, and I read all the books in the series several times as I grew older. Many of the books, however, were out of print and difficult to obtain until recently, when HarperCollins re-issued the entire series in paperback.

Betsy Ray has commanded a following of devoted readers throughout her literary life. An early review of one of the novels highly recommended the books for children, for the same reasons that librarians con-

101

tinue to do so today: "Added to warmth, reality, excellent characterization and dialogue, and very nice writing, the book has a delightful aura of other days which charms its reader" (Cobb 120). Another review suggested that even grown-ups would find the books well-written, enjoyable, and realistic, describing Lovelace's style as one characterized by "the touch of a person who knows that normal love and laughter are just as existent in the world as sordidness and 'complexes,' and far more real" as well as by its skillful "recreation" of the period in which the books are set (Review of *Betsy's Wedding*). The books have remained favorites among children's librarians and female readers since their original publication.

Today, some of the most devoted fans of the Betsy-Tacy books are not children but instead older women who loved them as young girls. A national Betsy-Tacy Society started in Mankato, Minnesota (Lovelace's hometown), in 1990. A convention organized for 1992 received an overwhelming response from long-time fans, who came to Mankato from around the country to share their enthusiasm for the novels. Members of the Betsy-Tacy society number nearly 1,000, with a headquarters in Mankato and local chapters across the United States. There is also a Maud Hart Lovelace Society in Minnesota's Twin Cities. Other evidence of the books' popularity includes a Maud Hart Lovelace biography, *The Betsy-Tacy Companion*, published by Sharla Whalen in 1995, a Betsy-Tacy page on the World Wide Web, and a Maud Hart Lovelace listserv. When I subscribed to the listserv, I received as many as forty messages a day, posted (almost always by women) from all over the country, discussing issues ranging from how to keep the books in print, to recipes for fudge, to which Betsy-Tacy book one should rescue during a fire. I have come across testimonies from women who, like me, not only compare their own lives to Betsy's on a regular basis, but also use Betsy's story as a means for understanding the past and coping with the present. The rallying cry of the fans—"I thought I was the only one!"—reminds me that I am not the only grown-up who indulges in this sort of reading.

Nor is Betsy the only heroine to enjoy this sort of fame. Betsy shares a place in American literary history with characters like Jo March, Laura Ingalls, and Anne Shirley. Jo, of course, came to life in a series of books starting with Louisa May Alcott's *Little Women* (1868-69); Laura was the autobiographical heroine of Laura Ingalls Wilder's Little House books (1932-43); and Anne became popular through Lucy Maud Montgomery's Anne of Green Gables series (1908-39). Beginning with *Betsy-Tacy*, written in 1940, and continuing all the way through *Betsy's Wedding*, written in 1955, Lovelace took part in the American tradition of historical series fiction for girls started in earnest by Alcott.[2] These series resemble each other in many ways: all of the books are set in a definite and not-so-distant period of history; all of the authors relied on autobiographical sources to create the stories, and all of the heroines take part in a determined effort to improve themselves as they grow older—they start out as imaginative girls who get into "scrapes," and grow up to be women who are writers as well as "models of femininity."

It is a genre that lends itself to discussions not only about children's literature, but also about alternative sources of women's and cultural history. For many readers, history begins with stories like Betsy-Tacy. Even as children learn about the past through other mediums, these stories provide a personal link with the past that gradually shapes their understanding of history. We build a sense of the past through a repertoire of facts and chronology, but we come back to the stories to make the past human, to give the facts a face. In their own small way, the Betsy-Tacy books illustrate this story-built relationship between history and individuals, offering a sentimental but realistic reminder that history begins as stories about people, even people who are little girls.

This relationship, however, does not always provide access to the full story of the American past. The history that the Betsy-Tacy books present is a very restricted take on American history, and one that obviously slants towards an optimistic view of the past. Comprehensive accounts of American life between the years of 1897 and 1919 should address issues of racism, labor, sexism, and politics, issues that clearly take a back seat to the sentimental story of Betsy's life in the Betsy-Tacy series. Judged by late-twentieth-century perspectives, Betsy Ray does not seem to represent the average American woman of her era, for she is a white, upper-middle-class, small-town Midwesterner who may take advantage of opportunities for wealth and education without being confronted by the barriers that most Americans face. As a longtime fan of the series, I re-read the Betsy-Tacy books with a sincere love for the familiar stories and the role that they have played in shaping my own identity. But as a cultural historian, I cannot help but notice that this representation of the past is inadequate and misleading.

This essay is comprised of three steps, all taken with this dilemma in mind. First, I will summarize the books and their contributions to the genre of historical fiction for girls as well as to historical education. Second, I will take a step back, and examine the less positive aspects of a series like Betsy-Tacy: in other words, what are the implications of a historical view that ignores major issues, issues that are crucial to understanding our present as well as our past? Finally, I will put forth a possible resolution of my affectionate view of the historical preservation offered by these books with my critical awareness of their historical limitations. In spite of my reservations about the restrictive view of the American past presented by the story of Betsy Ray, I believe it is possible to create a framework within which the Betsy-Tacy books may be read as valuable companions to history, companions with the potential to create essential links between people and the past.

A Different Sort of History Lesson

Elizabeth Warrington Ray Willard, the heroine of the Betsy-Tacy books, is born in 1892 in Deep Valley, Minnesota. The town's first settlers had named their new home Deep Valley because the site was nestled comfortably among rolling hills, along a river winding its way through the town and on to the Twin Cities. Betsy grows up in a happy home, aware of misfortune but protected from it by her loving middle-class family and her own determination to be both a good and a happy person. Betsy shares childhood adventures with her two best friends, Tacy and Tib, inventing schemes for the three of them to carry out, and even including her friends as characters in her stories. Ever since she can remember, Betsy has wanted to be a writer, and as she grows older, she spends more and more time turning her imaginative thoughts into words on paper.

Betsy is sentimental, good-natured and pretty in a down-to-earth way. When she goes to high school, she becomes immersed in good times and friendships. Within this warm environment, Betsy gradually learns how to be herself. She strives towards self-improvement, making lists for activities ranging from beauty regimens to becoming a better daughter, and always planning to devote more time to her writing. After three years of missed opportunities for romance with the handsome Joe Willard, a fellow writer, Betsy and Joe fall in love during their senior year. They both leave Deep Valley after their graduation from high school in 1910; Betsy attends the University of Minnesota, and Joe graduates from Harvard. The course of true love doesn't run smoothly, and Betsy leaves Minnesota for a trip to Europe, intending to forget Joe and to pursue her writing career. A twist of events and some soul-searching leads Betsy back into the arms of Joe. They marry in 1914, and she learns how to be a wife as well as a writer.

Lovelace's story of Betsy Ray portrays the history of an era as well as one girl's growth to maturity. Set against a certain time and place in American cultural history, the Betsy-Tacy books are, at one level, historical documents that chronicle aspects of American life from 1897 to 1917. Lovelace describes Victorian material culture with a keen eye for detail; she includes vivid accounts of architecture, furniture, and fashions. She weaves descriptions of customs, foods, and theatrical performances into the stories with ease. All of the books are dotted by illustrations as well as references to news stories and quotations from song lyrics. The structure of a novel allows Lovelace to tell us how historical details fit into "real life": what someone like Betsy thinks of the latest fashions, which songs she likes to sing, and how she and her friends keep up with the latest slang.

Lovelace's books put a friendly and nostalgic face on one of the most dramatic periods of change in American history, what we often identify now as the last years of an old-fashioned world. The Betsy-Tacy books end when the United States enters World War I, a historical moment that is associated with an "end of innocence" in American culture, a conception reinforced by the sentimental tone of "days gone by" used throughout the series. Though clearly nostalgic, Lovelace does not use this tone to indulge in the notion that life really was simpler then, but, instead, to portray how the world appeared through the eyes of a young woman from a small town in the Midwest.

Lovelace's work as a novelist differs from the task of a historian, for she focuses on one girl's life rather than on one or more of the general trends that make up the American past. Such focus can, however, make room for the individual where the "isms" used by historians simply cannot. Historian Thomas Schlereth, for example, begins *Victorian America: Transformations in Everyday Life, 1876-1915* by emphasizing the study of material goods as a means for understanding a period of fundamental transition. Though Schlereth writes about the same period in which the Betsy-Tacy books are set and describes many of the historical trends that surface in the books, his tendency toward broad generalization, a necessary component of all historical surveys, threatens to rob his work of its sense of human participation even as it aspires to detail everyday life.

Take, for example, Schlereth's introductory description of one of the most significant transformations in Victorian America: a middle-class culture "expanded by increasing bureaucratization, fueled by consumer abundance, promulgated by communications technology and motivated to hold power without property and to maintain hegemony with education and expertise" (xv). Historical fiction can restore the human touch to an era that history texts ultimately must reduce to broad trends, like the "bureaucratization" and "consumer abundance" described by Schlereth. Though restricted by its focus on one character (and her respective region, class, and race), the vivid quality of Lovelace's descriptions allows readers to understand the material and emotional aspects of at least one historic "everyday life." The Betsy-Tacy books, full of objects ranging from parlor furnishings to ladies' clothes, settings ranging from ice cream parlors to German-American farm-houses, and events ranging from a dramatic performance of *Uncle Tom's Cabin* to the first automobile in Deep Valley, bridge the fundamental gap between the individual and historical writing. Stories like Betsy's can provide both an educational and entertaining means of access to the material culture of an era. These books do not achieve the same sort of results that scholarly inquiries into history do, but they do provide a human companion to historical surveys of the period, a way to trace historical facts and trends back to the people from which they emerged.

Using the Betsy-Tacy books as such a companion means subordinating history to the story of one girl's life. Although a vivid sense of historical setting and change emerges from the series, Betsy's character steals the show. Historical observations, like Betsy's decoration of her wall with Gibson Girl drawings, add a nice touch, but the real story is Betsy's growth and development as a character. Lois Banner, a historian of the era, writes that the Gibson Girl was a pictorial representative of the Progressive hope for women's strength and independence, an inspiration for "self-reformation among all" (171). Betsy Ray, on the other hand, can act as a specific example of Banner's conclusion by showing, rather than telling, readers how the Gibson Girl fit into one girl's self-image. Betsy teaches a very particular history lesson, one not far removed from cultural history in content, though certainly distinguished by its form. As both a little girl and a young adult, for example, Betsy thinks consciously about what it means to be a girl, what it means to be religious, and what it means to be American. But Lovelace does not present these sorts of thoughts simply to teach a moral or historical lesson. She is, first and foremost, telling stories about what it was like to be a girl growing up in a specific time and place.

Lovelace knew firsthand what it was like to "live and grow up" in Minnesota at the turn of the century, which undoubtedly accounts for the vividness of the Betsy-Tacy books. The Betsy-Tacy stories began as children's literature in one of its most familiar forms: stories told to a child, shaped by the experiences of the teller, and cultivated by imagination. Maud Hart Lovelace told stories about her own childhood to her little girl, Merian, and found within them the basis for the characters and plots that shape the Betsy-Tacy stories. As Lovelace would write in an autobiographical sketch in 1951:

Children keep asking how much of the stories is true—a question difficult to answer. The background is true, many of the incidents are true—but twisted about . . . almost all of the characters are true, but sometimes two or three people have been combined. . . . ("Maud Hart Lovelace")

Maud Hart was born in 1892 and grew up in a house like Betsy Ray's, which she later described as "a small yellow cottage at the end of a street which, like Betsy's Hill Street, ran straight up into a green hill and stopped" ("Maud Hart Lovelace"). Deep Valley was a fictionalized version of her real hometown: Mankato, Minnesota. Like Betsy, Maud lived in this little town until she went to college at the University of Minnesota. Like Betsy, Maud made a grand tour of Europe before she returned to Minneapolis to marry an aspiring writer, Delos Lovelace. Delos served in World War I as an officer in a machine gun battalion, and later went on to a career in journalism. The couple published two works of historical fiction as collaborative projects, and both wrote adult fiction as well as children's books. But it was Maud Hart Lovelace's Betsy-Tacy books, begun as bedtime stories for their daughter, that brought Maud and Delos their most enduring fame.

According to Suzanne Rahn, a historian of children's literature, historical fiction for children grew in popularity during the twentieth century and "achieved its greatest flowering" in both the United States and Britain in the decades following World War II, the time when most of Lovelace's writing was done (13). Rahn cites the Betsy-Tacy books as an example of the changing nature of the genre. Unlike the focus of much of the historical fiction that preceded the Betsy-Tacy series—for example, the Little House books, which tell of life on the American frontier with an emphasis on detailed description, or Esther Forbes's popular *Johnny Tremain* (1943), about a patriotic boy during the American Revolution—the Betsy-Tacy stories subordinate the historical setting to the development of somewhat ahistorical plots and characterizations. Betsy thinks a lot about history, but in a romantic way; she shows nostalgic concern for the passing of time rather than fascination with progress. Like girls before and after her, she has interests that are quite different from the events that will become known as history, and Lovelace makes a point of showing this discrepancy. Betsy writes in her journal, as she begins her sophomore year of high school, that some things just seem more important: "I don't see why Edison and these people who go around inventing autos and things can't concentrate on something important like how to make a girl's hair stay curled" (*Betsy in Spite* 2). In this deliberate and specific contradiction of what we now consider to be two of the most important technological advances of the time, automobiles and light bulbs, and in her repeated emphasis on small experiences rather than big events, Lovelace achieves what Rahn defines as the aim of historical novelists for children: "They want to bring the culture of some former age to life for a generation with little or no knowledge of it; they are less interested in great historical events and figures than in showing children what it was like to live and grow up then" (3). In short, Lovelace describes history in the way that her readers experience it; she tells a story of "everyday life."

From Deep Valley to the "Great World"

One of the ways in which Lovelace's chronicle mimics our experience of history, and one of the most distinctive characteristics of the Betsy-Tacy series, is the way in which the style of narrative shifts according to the age of the protagonist, growing more complex as Betsy grows older. Lovelace, in other words, is not just turning her memories into stories, but remembering them in a way that corresponds to Betsy's (and the young reader's) development. *Betsy-Tacy* begins with a process of memory—"It was difficult, later, to think of a time when Betsy and Tacy had not been friends" (1)—and from that point on, the memories are presented as Betsy herself would have experienced them. An omniscient narrator guides us through Betsy's life. As Sharla Whalen points out in her biography of Lovelace, since Lovelace writes from her own experience, this narrator's omniscience carries the weight of "testimony" (12). Every so often, we hear a shade of the narrator's perspective, but the story always belongs to Betsy. The series starts when Betsy makes her first friend, an Irish-American girl whose family moves into the house directly across Hill Street from Betsy's home. As Betsy and Tacy grow older, they are joined by Tib, a German-American girl who lives in a "chocolate-colored house" down the street. The cast grows larger as the stories continue, but Betsy remains at the heart of it all.[3]

The series can be divided into four stages. Shifts in writing style correspond not only to the characters' progress in age but also to their geographical progress, as they move further away from home and out into the "Great World." The first stage consists of two books, *Betsy-Tacy* and *Betsy-Tacy, and Tib*, which follow the girls as they are gradually allowed to picnic farther and farther up the big hill that rises behind Betsy's house. Betsy and Tacy expand their circle of friendship to include Tib, and the second stage, made up of *Betsy and Tacy Go Over the Big Hill* and *Betsy and Tacy Go Downtown*, follow the girls as they move up through grammar school, and, as the titles indicate, out into Deep Valley.

In the third stage of the books, the high school stories stage, the girls become young women and move further into the public realm. The nostalgic illustrations of Lois Lenski, featuring simple, angular drawings of the girls and their adventures, change to the more sophisticated and glamorous drawings of Vera Neville. Physical appearance becomes a central issue of the stories: the high-school aged Betsy, the narrator tells us, "worship[s] beauty" (*Betsy Was a Junior* 9). Not only does Betsy keep up on new clothing styles, but she follows the advice of women's magazines religiously. In *Heaven to Betsy, Betsy in Spite of Herself, Betsy Was a Junior,* and *Betsy and Joe,* Betsy learns to combine such impersonal advice with the more realistic words of support that she hears from her friends and family, as well as the wisdom that she gains through her own experiences.

Lovelace wrote that she was inspired to continue the series because she "chanced upon" her own high school diaries about the time that her daughter entered high school, and "was impressed with how similar high school in 1905 was to high school in 1945—fudge, dates, ouija boards, singing around the piano" ("Maud Hart Lovelace"). Once again, Lovelace's memories became stories, and she went on to write a book for each of Betsy's years in high school. Each book sticks closely to themes of adolescence: unrequited love, coming to terms with personal talents and limitations, finding and keeping a diverse group of friends, and pursuing goals amidst heightened pressures and distractions.

Through it all, Betsy makes lists of steps for self-improvement, viewing each year of high school as a chance for a fresh start. She becomes an Episcopalian during her freshman year, and struggles in earnest all through high school to lead a good life. As Lovelace writes in *Betsy in Spite of Herself,* such resolutions are often difficult for Betsy to keep, though she emerges from church with the best of intentions: "Every Sunday morning Betsy resolved dreamily to lead a new life. . . . Usually it didn't last very long. But every Sunday morning she could start one again" (50). Betsy emerges from high school as a heroine who knows her own limitations, and constantly tries to improve herself despite them, in the tradition of American literary figures like Ben Franklin and Jay Gatsby as well as girl characters like Jo March. Betsy's concerns, however, are typically more humorous than these lofty predecessors. Like Ben Franklin (Franklin 95) and Jay Gatsby (Fitzgerald 152-53), she includes frequent bathing and keeping up a good appearance on her list of self-improvement techniques, but she adds "Lavish with bath salts" and "Use only Jockey Club perfume" to her "List of Things I Must Do to be Different" (*Betsy in Spite* 174). The narrator's voice accordingly continues its all-knowing tone of gentle amusement as Betsy finishes her high school years. Lovelace seems to have emerged from her reading of her high school journals with a narrative voice tuned to sentimentality, but wide-ranging enough to laugh at these memories even while indulging in them. Like Ben Franklin, Lovelace uses her "autobiography" as an opportunity to rewrite her personal history with the advantage of hindsight.[4] Although she donated her high school scrapbook to a historical society in Mankato, Lovelace burned her high school journals after she completed the series, thus preventing an exact comparison of Betsy's adventures with Maud's own experiences.[5]

Though the last two books of the series, which take Betsy beyond Deep Valley, are written at a level that even younger girls will understand, they are more complex in content than the previous stories. *Betsy and the Great World* and *Betsy's Wedding* deal with the conflict between independence and romance faced, at some level, by all twentieth-century American women, a conflict that rarely makes its way into the pages of books for young girls. Betsy has grown up to find that the world is not quite as romantic as she thought it would be. Set back by an attack of appendicitis during her freshman year of college, frustrated with her education, and too proud to make up her quarrel with Joe, Betsy sets off to see Europe and to escape her disillusionment, though she finds it difficult to be as brave as she tries to be. In this respect, *Betsy and the Great World* questions the impression of youthful security created in the earlier novels. Betsy's prior sense of completion is undone, and she is faced with challenges that lie beyond Deep Valley.

While in Europe, Betsy does succeed both in coping with homesickness and in publishing the stories that she sends back to American magazines. She regains her confidence and does her best to assume an "indefinable Paris air" (*Betsy and the Great World* 88). After she recovers from an amusing crush on a ship's purser who turns out to be married, Betsy experiences romance in grand form when she receives a proposal from a dashing young Venetian architect. She does not, however, fall into the marriage plot easily. Confused and upset by her unresolved feelings for Joe, she rejects the proposal.

When the Great War starts, and it becomes necessary for Betsy to return to the United States, she is at last reunited with her high school sweetheart. Contrary to romance tradition, in which the wedding *ends* the book, Betsy and Joe's wedding *begins* the novel. The rest of *Betsy's Wedding*, the last book in the series, follows Betsy and Joe through their adjustment to marriage, and their increasing awareness of Betsy's father's cautionary reminder that "marriage isn't all love and kisses" (31). Betsy tries to learn to be "domestic" but finds that she is more comfortable with a pen in her hand than with a broom or a frying pan. When the United States enters the war and Joe goes off to fight, she gives up her pursuit of domesticity in order to take a job in a publicity office. After progressing through the worlds of Hill Street and Deep Valley, and even taking a jaunt out into the "Great World," Betsy at last enters the realm of textbook history. Though she has undoubtedly been affected by history throughout the series, no event causes an impact like that of the war. She offers the reader a human link to the history of World War I; we see it as an event in the life of a character we know well, not just as a series of dates and facts.

Real Women, Real Stories

A familiarity with Betsy's life allows the reader to view a more nuanced account of women's history of the era than non-fiction alone can permit. As often happens in "real life," Betsy's experiences as a woman do not fall easily into categories like "feminism" or "domesticity." Lovelace offers some commentary on these issues throughout these books; as a little girl, Betsy and Tacy wonder why Tib's father tells her that she will be a housewife rather than an architect, though she is as skilled in building a playhouse out of logs as her brother (*Betsy-Tacy, and Tib* 49). In high school, even the boy-crazy Betsy is surprised to meet girls who, unlike her and Tacy and Tib, plan to settle down.

She had been almost appalled, when she started going around with Carney and Bonnie, to discover how fixed and definite their ideas of marriage were. They both had cedar hope chests and took pleasure in embroidering their initials on towels to lay away. . . . When Betsy and Tacy and Tib talked about their future, they planned to be writers, dancers, circus acrobats. (*Heaven to Betsy* 131)

Betsy is hardly a radical feminist, though she tells fellow travelers en route to Europe that she would be marching in suffrage parades if she were back in Minneapolis. One listener doubts her assertion, remarking that Betsy is "pure Victorian" and not at all modern. Betsy responds with her usual naiveté: "Well, I can do the modern dances!" (*Great World* 70).

Betsy's experiences with issues of feminism, though treated subtly, offer a touch of realism that many other girls' stories tend to neglect. The independent and adventure-seeking Nancy Drew, for example, seems shallow in comparison. In her analysis of the "girl sleuth" genre of series fiction for American girls, Bobbie Ann Mason argues that Nancy Drew became a strong but flat heroine for young women: "The indoctrination we have received from the girl detectives has been based on this paradox; they have thrilled us and contented us at the same time" (138). Though late twentieth-century feminism might call Betsy Ray's unquestioning devotion to her husband and future children into question, she does answer Mason's call for more realistic heroines. In the end, Betsy pursues a writing career and a happy marriage at the same time. According to Lovelace biographer Sharla Whalen, Betsy's "undeniable femininity" does not contradict her essentially feminist outlook: "[Betsy] was never militant, precisely because this assumption was so deep-seated;

equality was not something she felt she had to fight for—she took it for granted. Her family treated others, male or female, with respect—and Betsy chose friends who did likewise" (420). In this sense, Betsy's character offers one possible model of feminism during this era.

Betsy's interactions with other women add to the realism of this take on women's history. At one point in *Betsy's Wedding*, Lovelace presents the newlywed Betsy's fear that Tib will face the awful fate of an old maid with gentle irony. In an effort that proves to be futile, Betsy teams up with Tacy, who is now married herself, to find the perfect husband for Tib. Lovelace describes Betsy, a single woman of the world herself not so very long ago, as looking "wise as befitted an old married woman" while she tries to marry off her friend (115). But Tib "likes to paddle her own canoe," and, as she tells Betsy, she wants to wait until she finds a good husband like Betsy's Joe, rather than men who only like her because she is cute and blonde: "He confides in you, listens to your opinions, asks your advice. He thinks your work is important. He thinks *you* are important—as a human being, not just as a girl" (113, 204). Ellen Rothman writes in *Hands and Hearts: A History of Courtship in America* that women of Betsy's era "had long recognized the truth about marriage: that it was perfect in the ideal but flawed in reality, and that it was women for whom the reality was most burdensome" (249). Such recognition did not, however, prevent women from seeking and finding happiness through marriage, as Betsy does, and as her friend Tib hopes to do. By considering the way that Betsy's marriage and Tib's pursuit of marriage are portrayed by Lovelace, we can gain a sense of how women made the negotiations and sacrifices described by Rothman.

Tib finds that "good husband" after all, a soldier freshly returned from fighting Pancho Villa and now preparing for battle in Europe. The book and the series wind to a close with Tib's wedding, which takes place at her parents' "chocolate-colored house" in Deep Valley. When they were little girls, Betsy and Tacy considered the Muller's impressive home to be the "most wonderful house in the whole wide world," and they gazed down upon it in awe from the top of the Big Hill (237). By setting the happy wedding there, Lovelace implies that the house is still wonderful, but for reasons that even imaginative little girls would never have expected. As the women reflect upon their childhood in Deep Valley, the series ends, as it begins, with memories.

Betsy's definition of what makes a good story evolves from youthful fantasy to sentimental realism through the course of the series, much like the changing significance of the "chocolate-colored house." This transition forms a theme within the books that is particularly relevant to their relationship with history. Betsy makes up stories about herself and

Tacy from the time that they first meet, at age five, and it is not long before Betsy starts writing these stories down. By the time she is eleven years old, she works in a writing "office" made by a convenient branch of her back-yard maple tree, composing her stories on notepads from her father's shoe store. The stories that Betsy writes at this age are quite consciously shaped by her reading of dime novels, borrowed from Rena, her family's "hired girl." One story begins like this:

The Repentance of Lady Clinton
by Betsy Warrington Ray
Author of *Her Secret Marriage, The Mystery of the Butternut Tree,
A Tress of Golden Hair, Hardly More than a Child*. Etc. Etc. (*Downtown* 2)

Since Betsy has turned to Rena's dime novels only after finishing all of the books on her parents' shelves, Mr. and Mrs. Ray send her to read the "classics" at the new Carnegie Library when it opens in downtown Deep Valley. Nevertheless, Betsy continues to engage in a flowery style of writing as she grows older, writing about imaginative scenes at the expense of drawing material from her own surroundings. Betsy likes to write the kind of stories that get published in women's magazines, and this means that she invents experiences rather than writing about the world she knows. While on her trip to Europe, she begins to see, for the first time, things that she has been reading and writing about for a long time: "Ladies' maids! She was always putting them in stories. What luck to see some in the flesh!" (*Great World* 30).

Gradually, Betsy begins to see the value of "real" stories, ones that emerge from history or call upon her own experiences. In high school, she looks forward to hearing stories of Deep Valley history told each year at Thanksgiving by a friend's grandmother. They provide a link to an earlier era of American history for the reader as well as for Betsy.

Listening . . . in front of the fire, Betsy saw canoes on the river, the raw log cabins of the earliest settlers straggling along the river bank, the Indian Agency at the top of Agency Hill and the Indians coming to take possession of it. . . . Deep Valley, now so peaceful, had been a perilous frontier. (*Betsy Was a Junior* 126)

When Betsy publishes her first story, during college, it is not a Gothic-style romance but instead a simple tale that she based upon her own trip to California. After her marriage, she finds an unexpected source of stories in Joe's widowed aunt. Aunt Ruth comes to live with the couple for a time during their second year of marriage, and tells Betsy lively tales about farm life in the Minnesota of yesteryear: fires, blizzards, and grasshopper plagues, as well as barn raisings and bobsled parties. "There's a plot in every one, Betsy thought, and started taking notes" (*Betsy's Wedding* 166). Stories like these become Betsy's means of understanding history, as well as her source for new plots. When Joe is accepted for officers' training, and cleans out his desk at the newspaper, Betsy braces herself for sadness by remembering her grandmother's story of her grandfather, a school teacher, going off to fight in the Civil War. She uses the story of a woman from the past to make sense of her own experience, revealing a distinctly gendered response to history as well as an aspect of war that traditional history textbooks do not cover.

Like Grandpa Warrington, Betsy thought, coming across the cornfield with his school books and the big bell sitting on top! '*And the minute Grandma saw it she began to cry.*'

War! Betsy thought, holding back her own tears with all the force of her stubborn will. War! Women never invented it. (*Betsy's Wedding* 228)

Just as Lovelace's heroine discovers "true stories" from history and uses them to come to an understanding of both the present and the past, the young reader of the Betsy-Tacy series can remember Betsy's story when she attempts to comprehend her own place in history. Betsy's realizations invite readers to consider their own heritage as a "true story," and, perhaps, to consider how their past compares or contrasts with Betsy Ray's story.

A Question of Identity

If these books are to be used to build a sense of the American past, the limited nature of Betsy's story necessitates critical comparison on the part of the reader. Though rich and detailed, and even autobiographical, Betsy's experiences of growing up in Deep Valley provide limited information about the past. Betsy is a middle-class white girl living in a small town in the Midwest; many people, events, and perspectives are left outside of her frame of experience. Betsy idealizes the "American pioneer tradition" perpetuated by her family's stories, and turns them into stories of her own. It is not surprising that she does not stop to question the restricted nature of this tradition nor challenge the American institution of white male privilege, but it is an issue worth discussing. Beryle Banfield, a critic of children's literature, discusses similar issues in other authors' works as a type of racism that "has not been generally recognized" in children's literature, a racism that Banfield ascribes not "to a personal aberration on the part of an individual author but a reflection of the institutionalized racism that pervades every facet of US society" (Banfield 37).

Research on the shift from history to historical fiction, especially historical fiction for children, often reveals that fiction about the past does not indicate the extent to which such institutional racism existed. Historian John E. Miller points out that Laura Ingalls Wilder "alluded to anti-Catholic sentiment" in her hometown in an early autobiographical manuscript, but omitted it from her Little House books (78). The confrontations between Native Americans and pioneers like the Ingalls family are described in books like *Little House on the Prairie*, but from an obviously slanted perspective. One must wonder to what extent Lovelace's books "whitewash" the past in order to omit racial conflicts or prejudice.

One must also wonder about the consequences of presenting these books as examples of women's history to little girls who are not Anglo-American. Critics of children's literature have noted the lack of suitable examples of positive, believable, and identifiable heroines in literature written specifically for minority children. Judith Thompson and Gloria Woodard write that the "bulk of that literature which provides identification for black children has so far been confined to the histories, biographies, and autobiographies" (49). One strength of the Betsy-Tacy series is its power to teach through stories; we cannot help but note the need for stories that teach about other identities.

This need is not felt only by those that do not identify with Betsy's race and class, but also those who do share Betsy's world. Even readers who can relate to Betsy do not live in her purely white middle-class America. In a study of the effects of teaching ethnic literature and its relevant historical issues to college students, Thomas Tryzna and Martin Abbott conclude that one of the most effective methods of remedying the "anxiety" faced by students who study minority issues for the first time is to avoid reliance on a single course in multiculturism, and to "reinforce" these issues "elsewhere in the curriculum" (13). The need for education about minority issues well before the college level, perhaps through the medium of children's historical fiction, seems a logical corollary to Tryzna and Abbott's conclusion. If the Betsy-Tacy series contained a more diverse set of characters and outlooks, or if readers of the Betsy-Tacy series also read series of books that were like Betsy's in their strength of characterization, but unlike Betsy's in their choice of characters, they would be familiar with a world of historical fiction that more closely resembled the world they live in. Historical fiction for children could prevent the "anxious" discovery of an unknown past if it portrayed a more accurate and diverse cast of Betsy-like companions to history.

Certainly, Maud Hart Lovelace should not be held accountable for her books' restricted portrayal of history; she wrote the stories much as she had lived them. But she was not completely ignorant of the problematic relationship between the contested concept of American identity and literature for children. During the course of her lifetime, Lovelace became aware of the fact that her stories could not reach many children, on account of their restricted focus, and made a concerted effort to change with the times. In 1964, at the age of seventy-two, Lovelace attended a series of meetings on the civil rights movement in Claremont, California, the town in which she and Delos Lovelace retired (Letter, 21 April 1964). By 1965, she expressed her concern for the state of African-American children's literature, or the lack of it: "It's sad how seldom a Negro child can find a book with Negroes in the illustrations. He shouldn't always have to read about white children" (Letter, 25 July 1965). Lovelace became anxious to write a book featuring an African-American child, and she adapted a story (set in the present) about a new girl at school to the purpose. The story had not, however, originally been written about an African-American child, and her desire was not to write a story about what she alludes to as the "big problem" of racism, but instead to portray a "happy" child. "Only the illustrations will show that the heroine is a Negro," Lovelace wrote of her idea for *The Valentine Box*, which was to be her last book (Letter, 25 July 1965). This decision could be construed as yet another "whitewashing" of historical and contemporary issues, but Lovelace's stated intention indicates her belief in the positive impact of such a project, and her awareness of the desperate need for children's literature that portrayed minority characters positively.

Though Lovelace never gives minorities a predominant role in the Betsy-Tacy series, she does include a few references to people who do not share Betsy, Tacy, and Tib's European-American ethnicity. Two incidents from the series are particularly relevant to a discussion of the issue of identity. The first incident occurs when Betsy, Tacy and Tib are ten years old, in *Betsy and Tacy Go Over the Big Hill*. On one of their trips "over the big hill," the three girls meet a young Syrian girl about their age. Naifi resides in the Syrian immigrant colony on the other side of the hill. Naifi does not become a major character in the novel, but the contact between her and her three new friends becomes a thematic focus of the book. The second time that Betsy, Tacy, and Tib meet Naifi, she is being teased and harassed by a group of boys, led by a rough older boy named Sam in calling "Dago! Dago!" (70). In a display of gender solidarity and open-mindedness, Betsy, Tacy, and Tib join forces to rescue Naifi and the narrator remarks that some of the boys "seemed ashamed" for what they had done (73). Tib ruins her new dress in the heat of battle, and in her account of Tib's mother's response to the incident, Lovelace forges a connection between Tib's German-American heritage and Naifi's Middle-Eastern one.

"It's all right," said Mrs. Muller. "I'm glad Tib stood up for the little Syrian girl. Foreign people should not be treated like that. America is made up of foreign people. Both of Tib's grandmothers came from the other side. Perhaps when they got off the boat they looked a little strange too." (75)

Similarly, Betsy's father gives the girls a lesson in American history when he explains the origin of Deep Valley's "Little Syria" to his daughter and her friends: "A good many of the Christian Syrians are coming to America these days. And they come for much the same reason that our Pilgrim fathers came. They want to be free from oppression and religious persecution. We ought to honor them for it" (147). Lovelace crafts this lesson in American multiculturalism in the voices not only of the parents but also of the girls themselves. After Betsy, Tacy, and Tib make a visit to "Little Syria"—an eye-opening journey that dispels their notions of it as a "dangerous" place—sensible Tib remarks of their Syrian friends that "boys like Sam ought to know more about them" (156).

A more ambiguously narrated incident in the series shows an interaction between Betsy and an African-American. When Betsy is fifteen, she makes her first venture outside of Minnesota in order to visit her friend Tib, who now lives in Milwaukee. She boards the train eagerly, anxious to get her first real travel experience. Soon after the trip begins, the porter, who is described by the narrator as "a colored man in a white jacket," comes along to take her hat and put it in the rack above her (*Betsy in Spite* 115). The porter then temporarily disappears from the narrative. Betsy spends most of the trip looking out the window and imitating the travel customs of her more experienced fellow passengers. By the end of the ride, however, the talkative Betsy chats with a "spinsterish lady" and a "married couple from Waukesha" and tells her three new friends all about Tib. When they start to come into Milwaukee, she awaits her turn to be "brushed" by the porter, who has just come back into the car.

He took her new red hat out of the bag and brushed it and she put it on. She stood up while he brushed the red and green sailor suit and wiped off her shoes. When he had helped her into her coat and furpiece, she gave him fifty cents and he said, "Thank you, miss. I hope you have a good time in Milwaukee with your friend Tib." (115)

The porter's kind comment is strange and surprising given that Betsy never directly tells him about her friend Tib. It is possible that Lovelace merely intends for the reader to note that Betsy talks so enthusiastically about Tib that even the porter, who has disappeared from sight, hears and remembers her words. It is also possible that Lovelace is hinting that a porter who has seemingly "disappeared" from sight plays more of a part in the dynamics of the train car than the casual observer like Betsy would notice. Lovelace's designation of the porter as "a colored man" seems oddly deliberate, both because race is such a non-issue in these books, and because a knowledgeable reader (or participant in train travel in the early twentieth century) would simply assume that the porter was "colored." Perhaps Lovelace, in the detached voice of an omniscient narrator, is subtly trying to draw attention to a race issue that only becomes an issue in Betsy's life when she leaves her sheltered home for the first time. Lovelace may intend for her reader to notice the race of the porter, and to be surprised, as Betsy must be, when he reveals that he knows all about Betsy's trip, despite his seeming invisibility. On the other hand, the description of the anonymous porter and his actions may be just another example of Lovelace's close attention to detail, similar in intention to the "spinsterish lady" and the "married couple from Waukesha." One question, however, remains: why does Lovelace bring the Syrian-American character to life but resign the African-American character to anonymity?

In her critical study of "whiteness and the literary imagination," author Toni Morrison asserts that race functions as a crucial "metaphor for transacting the whole process of Americanization":

Even, and especially, when American texts are not "about" Africanist presences or characters or narrative or idiom, the shadow hovers in implication, in sign, in line of demarcation. It is no accident and no mistake that immigrant populations (and much immigrant literature) understood their "Americanness" as an opposition to the resident black population. (46-47)

In this sense, the porter serves as a "line of demarcation" in the Betsy-Tacy books. His simultaneous presence and invisibility serves as a testament to the institutionalized racism brought out even in the seemingly innocuous medium of children's literature. It is a racism perpetuated historically through a notion of "Americanness" that small-town white Americans, who celebrated their own history of immigration, could apply to some people but not to others. The concept of "Americanness" that Lovelace strives to celebrate in the earlier incident with the Syrian-American girl does not exist without the qualifications revealed by the later incident with the "colored man in a white jacket."

"Delight, not Disappointment"

Critic John Stephens analyzes the issue of cultural perspective with regard to historical fiction for children in *Language and Ideology in Children's Fiction*. He posits that all historical fiction shares a drive towards "authenticity" and attempts not only to create the illusion of an experience of the past, but also to demonstrate the premise that "humans behave and feel in ways that remain constant in different periods" (204-05). Stephens sees most historical fiction as evidence of "secular hagiography" rather than an effective step into the "otherness of the past." In other words, according to Stephens, the language used to create historical fiction for children can only "remake the past in the image of the present" and thus lead the reader to a passive acceptance of the world as it stands (238).

In the case of the Betsy-Tacy books, I agree with Stephens to the extent that I see texts of historical fiction as a limited resource for gaining access to the past. Lovelace's books can serve as a companion to the study of history, but not as a solitary basis for historical understanding. Too much is left out of Lovelace's, or for that matter anyone's, individual perspective. Even with these qualifications in mind, however, Stephens's categorization of historical fiction presents a limited notion of the human mind's ability to engage with and to question a text. According to Stephens, children cannot read books like Betsy-Tacy without swallowing whole an ideological and optimistic take on history and being lulled into complacency. I believe that it is possible to study these texts, as well as their ideological perspectives with the revealing aid of critical questions, seeking an end more productive than blind "hagiographic" acceptance. We do not need to toss out the proverbial baby with the bathwater in order to avoid an overly worshipful or passive view of the past. By using a critical framework that seeks answers even as it recognizes limitations, we can read the Betsy-Tacy books through a filter that allows us to draw conclusions about the past, about why Lovelace chooses to present the past as she does, and, finally, about how such books can shape the way child readers view the present. Toni Morrison enters her project of uncovering the Africanist presence in American literature with "delight, not disappointment . . . about the ways writers transform aspects of their social grounding into aspects of language, and the ways they tell other stories, fight secret wars, limn out all sorts of debates blanketed in their text" (4). Similarly, the reader may meet the limitations of the American identity represented in the Betsy-Tacy books with an anticipation for the discoveries about Americanness made possible by a critical reading. For young readers, such a reading necessitates guidance from parents, teachers, and librarians.

Such a "delightful" critical reading depends first upon an appreciation of the Betsy-Tacy series's important revelations about women's history. In terms of the genre of fiction for young women, the character of Betsy Ray demonstrates important shifts in the notion of what constitutes a proper heroine. In their survey of British and American girls' fiction from 1839 to 1975, Mary Cadogan and Patricia Craig identify Elsie Dinsmore as one of the "first and longest surviving" heroines of American girls' fiction (32). Beginning in 1867 with *Elsie Dinsmore*, schoolteacher Martha Finley wrote twenty-eight volumes about the devout and moral little girl who grows up to be a very proper (and boring) woman. In the first book, young Elsie falls off her piano stool from exhaustion, after several hours of sitting there motionless, rather than agreeing to play music on the Sabbath, because, in Elsie's own pious words, "[I]t says the Sabbath is to be kept holy unto the Lord; that we are not to think our own thoughts, nor speak our own words, nor do our own actions" (225). Louisa May Alcott's *Little Women*, though published in the same year as the first *Elsie Dinsmore* book, provided a more realistic heroine, Jo March. According to children's literature historian Jerry Griswold, Jo enacts Alcott's intention of showing that characters make mistakes but then "mend their ways" (166). It seems that if Jo found herself in Elsie's situation, she would play a thunderous tune on the piano, deliberately shocking an uptight character like her Aunt March, but repent her wrongdoing humbly later in the story.

Betsy Ray, a reader of both *Elsie Dinsmore* books and *Little Women*, takes yet another approach to interpreting rules for the Sabbath. When Betsy visits Tib in Milwaukee, Tib's uncle gives the girls tickets to a play on a Sunday night. Since her family is "not straight-laced, but they wouldn't have dreamed of doing such a thing," Betsy thinks carefully about her choice:

For a moment Betsy wondered wildly whether she should refuse to go. Elsie Dinsmore, she remembered, had refused to play the piano on Sunday. . . . But Betsy had never thought much of Elsie Dinsmore.

"I'm almost sure," Betsy thought, "that Papa would say, 'When in Rome, do as the Romans do!" (*Betsy in Spite* 127)

Betsy goes to the theater, and Elsie Dinsmore goes out of fashion. Unlike Jo March, Betsy's decisions are not played out as personal melodramas, but as processes of independent thought, albeit with the guidance of Papa in mind. In this particular case, Betsy's decision advocates a positive attitude toward cultural difference as much as it shows a girl who knows how to have fun. The Betsy-Tacy series does not present a feminist crusader, and its undistinguished record in calling attention to issues of multiculturalism may make the books seem dated when compared, for example, to the *American Girls* series marketed at children's bookstores today. Nevertheless, the series holds an important place in the history of literary heroines for young American women.

The potential of a series like Betsy-Tacy to contribute to a young reader's awareness of women's history cannot be over-emphasized. When the Betsy-Tacy books were published, they took a new approach to history, making space for a feminine voice largely unheard in history texts. Suzanne Rahn points out that Lovelace and her peers (those who also wrote about girl protagonists) were probably influenced by the early feminist movement, and that "these children's writers established a claim through fiction to a place in history which textbooks were not to recognize for another forty or fifty years" (11). Anne Philips, another critic of children's literature, finds that the Betsy-Tacy series provides a historical example of how woman writers "commonly depict and affirm the community and literature" (145). Though stories about one girl's growth to maturity can't replace the work in women's history done in more recent years, the Betsy-Tacy series' ability to serve as a companion to history textbooks could play a pivotal role in the education of a young person. In a recent article, elementary media specialist Joyce A. Delaney asserts that such companions continue to provide a much-needed remedy to the "noticeable imbalance in the importance given to women's as opposed to men's roles" in American history textbooks. Delaney calls upon educators to "augment" the study of history with "careful selection" of historical fiction that shows "intelligent and independent heroines" (303, 312). In this respect, Lovelace's work serves as both a precursor and a reinforcement of the new women's history.

How, then, can a contemporary reader balance these positive aspects of the books with reservations about their limited coverage of multicultural history, and arrive at the conclusion of "delight, not disappointment" advocated by Toni Morrison? I take heart from the fact that I am not the first cultural critic to undertake a revised reading of a childhood literary favorite. Educator Herbert Kohl asks this question of his beloved elephant *Babar*, featured in Jean de Brunhoff's series of illustrated children's books, in his essay "Should We Burn Babar?" Kohl's return to the books as a teacher and a parent led to his questioning of their appropriateness for children on account of what he sees as the series' inherent racism and sexism. After some deliberation, Kohl concludes that *Babar* offers critical readers, or children guided by critical readers, the challenge of going "beyond the text itself to inquiries abut the author's politics, social class, and family background. . . . In all of these cases, reading becomes dialogue. The text can be reimagined and invested with multiple meanings" (23). Thus, Kohl articulates the dilemma as one of deciding whether or not the advantages of a critical reading of a book outweigh the potential for harm inflicted by an uncritical one, and Babar is spared from the flames.

In the case of the Betsy-Tacy books, I can decide that the "good" outweighs the "bad" with a clear conscience. As both a student of and participant in American culture, I have interrogated the ideologies and identities put forth in Betsy-Tacy as often as I have embraced them—perhaps I have questioned them as much as I have because of my deep-seated connection to Betsy's character. In her introduction to *Little Women*, feminist critic Elaine Showalter argues for a similar perspective on "dated" fiction for young women:

> To read *Little Women* at the end of the twentieth century is thus to engage with contemporary ideas about female authority, critical institutions, and the American literary canon, as well as with nineteenth-century ideas of the relationship between patriarchal culture and women's culture. (viii)

To reject books like the Betsy-Tacy series or *Little Women* as pure ideology, relics from an unusable past, is to dismiss not only our own power to read critically, but also our power to teach children to do the same.

There is yet another reason to read the Betsy-Tacy books: they have the potential to serve as a model for children's literature yet to be written. Like many of the members of the Betsy-Tacy Society, my connection to the books has proven to be strong enough to survive my critical inquiry into the past as well as my growth to a feminist womanhood. It has led me to actively engage with the issues of the past, to wonder what it was like to live then, to think about how the past presented in Betsy-Tacy is different, better or worse, from my own era. Too often, attempts to supplement children's education about the past with historical fiction less restricted in scope than the Betsy-Tacy series have resulted only in stale or unrealistic stories. Judith Thompson and Gloria Woodard describe less successful attempts at African-American children's literature as a "kind of verbal minstrel show—whites in blackface—rather than the expression of a real or imagined experience derived from wearing the shoe" (410). As a young reader, Michael Dorris arrived at a similar conclusion with regard to children's books that portrayed Native Americans:

> I preferred the Hardy brothers, Laura in the "Little House" books (though her mother's unrelenting racism toward Indians did give me pause), or other characters with pluck. . . . Indian kids seemed far too busy making pots out of clay or

being fascinated by myths. . . . They didn't remind me of anyone I knew, especially my cousins on the reservation. (219)

John Stephens's criteria for the genre of historical fiction for children includes the presence of characters that are "credible and invite reader-identification" and the demonstration of commonality between human beings of different time periods (204-05). Stephens sees these criteria as fundamental to an understanding of how this literature unavoidably perpetuates ideologies such as the particular vision of "Americanness" presented by the Betsy-Tacy series. But if the structure and language of historical fiction perpetuates an ideology about an engaging, identity-based vision of the past, why not embrace the genre for minority perspectives that would benefit from a bond with an identity-based past? If Betsy provides readers who share aspects of her identity with a connection to the past, couldn't characters derived from other historical perspectives do the same?

The approach I have advocated here may be perceived as an overly optimistic way of looking at the past, at least from the standpoint of cultural history. The genre of historical fiction for children almost always lends itself to describing positive views of the past, even when it leads to questions about the negative ones. If we supplement the tradition of representing the past through the eyes of characters like Betsy with books that show the perspectives of girls from different race and class backgrounds, we may not end up with anything other than a wide range of "positive pasts" to choose from, and no way to negotiate between these pasts to arrive at an understanding of a history that is less than idyllic. Joyce Appleby, Lynn Hunt, and Margaret Jacob have attempted to point out the necessity of maintaining both "solidarity-building" and critical accounts of history:

Here the pressing question is which human needs should history serve, the yearning for a self-affirming past, even if distortive, or the liberation, however painful, that comes from grappling with a more complex, accurate account? Skepticism offers a way of resolving this tension by rejecting all truths, but . . . it flies in the face of the common experience of knowing. Consider the outrage felt when a remembered experience is misrepresented. (289)

My quest for "positive pasts" emerges from a complex, critical sensibility, not in resistance to it. The alternative to this tension, the skepticism described above, is not an alternative at all, but merely an easy way out. Historical "truth" resides in the continuous negotiation between the past and the present as well as between different perspectives of experience;

the pursuit of it calls upon our identities as readers of stories as well as critics of culture.

Friends Like Betsy

As a child, I did not read books like the Betsy-Tacy stories for a history lesson, but my later history lessons were undoubtedly shaped by them. Before I could quote figures on early-twentieth-century immigration, I could remember that Betsy, Tacy, and Tib got a lesson in multiculturalism when they befriended a girl from the Syrian immigrant colony over the "Big Hill." Before I knew much about the history of the automobile industry, I knew that Betsy's friend Tib got a ride in the first "horseless carriage" in Deep Valley. Long before I learned about the battles of World War I, I read the story of how a panicked Betsy Ray ended her grand tour of Europe when the war began and sailed home to marry her sweetheart, only to watch him march away to war a few years later. I could match these stories with distinct memories of my own family's past: my paternal great-grandparents' immigration from Hungary and their desire to raise their ten children as patriotic "Americans," the day my great-aunt taught my grandmother to drive in their parents' first car, and the letter my maternal great-great-grandfather wrote my great-great-grandmother from a Civil War battlefield, now pressed between the pages of a family bible. Eventually, my history lessons were irrevocably linked to both Betsy's past and my family's own. Despite my embarrassment at the bookstore counter, my penchant for re-reading girls' books like the Betsy-Tacy series enables me to maintain these bonds, re-shaping and strengthening them according to what I continue to learn about the past.

You do not have to be a member of the Betsy-Tacy Society to be inclined to remember historical events through the means of historical fiction. The stories cannot replace the facts, but they can make them more human: they can bring history to life. Betsy is in need of counterparts that will achieve what Betsy has for other perspectives on the American past, perhaps less optimistic views than Betsy's, but no less relevant or truthful. The goal of achieving historical truth through stories about one little girl is, perhaps, an over-ambitious one, but the demonstrated ability of the Betsy-Tacy books to link history and individuals should demand the attention of anyone who hopes to actively engage his or her readers with the issues and the importance of the past.

Notes

1. Katherine Paterson, "Tell All the Truth but Tell It Slant," 52.

2. Two points of clarification: First, as demonstrated by recent scholarship, Wilder's books were the result of a collaborative effort with her daughter, the journalist Rose Wilder Lane. Second, the Anne of Green Gables series is actually a Canadian work, though it continues to enjoy a wide readership among girls in the United States.

3. Lovelace wrote three other books that borrowed characters from the Betsy-Tacy books: *Carney's House Party*, in 1948; *Emily of Deep Valley*, in 1950; and *Winona's Pony Cart*, in 1953. These books will not be considered by this essay.

4. "I should have no objection to go over the same life from its beginning to the end, only asking the advantage authors have of correcting in a second edition some faults of the first. . . . But as this repetition is not to be expected, that which resembles most living one's life over again, seems to be to recall all the circumstances of it; and, to render this remembrance more durable, to record them in writing" (Franklin 16-17).

5. Despite the journals' destruction, Sharla Whalen's *Betsy-Tacy Companion* presents exhaustive research on the subject of the "real-life" people and stories behind the series.

Works Cited

Alcott, Louisa May. *Little Women*. 1868. Ed. Elaine Showalter. New York: Penguin, 1989.

Appleby, Joyce, Lynn Hunt, and Margaret Jacob. *Telling the Truth About History*. New York: Norton, 1994.

Banfield, Beryle. "Racism in Children's Books: An Afro-American Perspective." *The Black American in Books for Children: Readings in Racism*. 2nd ed. Ed. Donnarae MacCann and Gloria Woodard. Metuchen: Scarecrow, 1985. 23-38.

Banner, Lois W. *American Beauty*. New York: Knopf, 1983.

Cadogan, Mary, and Patricia Craig. *You're a Brick, Angela!: A New Look at Girls' Fiction from 1839 to 1975*. London: Gollancz, 1976.

Cobb, Jane. Review of *Betsy and Joe*. *The Atlantic* Nov. 1948: 120.

Delaney, Joyce A. "Voices Not Heard: Women in a History Textbook." *Ways of Knowing: Literature and the Intellectual Life of Children*. Ed. Kay Vandergrift. Lanham: Scarecrow, 1996. 303-19.

Dorris, Michael. "The Way We Weren't." *Against Borders: Promoting Books for a Multicultural World*. Ed. Hazel Rochman. Chicago: ALA, 1993. 219-20.

Finley, Martha. *Elsie Dinsmore*. 1868. New York: Grosset, 1896.

Fitzgerald, F. Scott. *The Great Gatsby*. 1925. New York: Scribner, 1953.

Franklin, Benjamin. *The Autobiography of Benjamin Franklin*. 1771. Ed. L. Jesse Lemisch. Markham, Ontario: Signet, 1961.

Griswold, Jerry. *Audacious Kids: Coming of Age in America's Classic Children's Books*. New York: Oxford UP, 1992.

Kohl, Herbert. "Should We Burn Babar? Questioning Power in Children's Literature." *Should We Burn Babar? Essays on Children's Literature and the Power of Stories*. New York: New Press, 1995. 3-29.

Lovelace, Maud Hart. *Betsy and Joe*. New York: Crowell, 1948.

——. *Betsy and Tacy Go Downtown*. New York: Crowell, 1943.

——. *Betsy and Tacy Go Over the Big Hill*. New York: Crowell, 1942.

——. *Betsy and the Great World*. New York: Crowell, 1952.

——. *Betsy in Spite of Herself*. New York: Crowell, 1946.

——. *Betsy Was a Junior*. New York: Crowell, 1947.

——. *Betsy's Wedding*. New York: Crowell, 1955.

——. *Betsy-Tacy*. New York: Crowell, 1940.

——. *Betsy-Tacy, and Tib*. New York: Crowell, 1941.

——. *Heaven to Betsy*. New York: Crowell, 1945.

——. Letter to R. Lee, 21 April 1964. Quoted in *The Betsy-Tacy Companion: A Biography of Maud Hart Lovelace*. By Sharla Whalen. Whitehall: Portarlington, 1995. 472.

——. Letter to R. Lee, 25 July 1965. Quoted in *The Betsy-Tacy Companion: A Biography of Maud Hart Lovelace*. By Sharla Whalen. Whitehall: Portarlington, 1995. 472.

——. "Maud Hart Lovelace." *The Junior Book of Authors*. Ed. Stanley J. Kunitz and Howard Haycraft. New York: Wilson, 1951. 200.

——. *The Valentine Box*. New York: Crowell, 1966.

Mason, Bobbie Ann. *The Girl Sleuth: A Feminist Guide*. New York: Feminist P, 1975.

Miller, John E. *Laura Ingalls Wilder's Little Town: Where History and Literature Meet*. Lawrence: UP of Kansas, 1994.

Montgomery, Lucy Maud. *Anne of Green Gables*. 1908. New York: Grosset, 1935.

Morrison, Toni. *Playing in the Dark: Whiteness and the Literary Imagination*. Cambridge: Harvard UP, 1992.

Paterson, Katherine. "Tell All the Truth but Tell it Slant." The Zena Sutherland Lecture, May 3, 1985. *The Zena Sutherland Lectures 1983-1992*. Ed. Betsy Hearne. New York: Clarion, 1993. 48-70.

Phillips, Anne. "'Home Itself Put Into Song': Music as Metaphorical Community." *The Lion and the Unicorn* 16.2 (1992): 145-57.

Rahn, Suzanne. "An Evolving Past: The Story of Historical Fiction and Nonfiction for Children." *The Lion and The Unicorn* 15.1 (1991): 1-26.

Review of *Betsy's Wedding*. *The Christian Science Monitor* 23 Nov. 1955: 12.

Rothman, Ellen K. *Hands and Hearts: A History of Courtship in America*. New York: Basic, 1984.

Schlereth, Thomas J. *Victorian America: Transformations in Everyday Life, 1876-1915*. New York: HarperPerennial, 1991.

Showalter, Elaine. Introduction. *Little Women*. By Louisa May Alcott. 1868. Ed. Elaine Showalter. New York: Penguin, 1989. vii-xxviii.

Stephens, John. *Language and Ideology in Children's Fiction*. London: Longman, 1992.

Thompson, Judith, and Gloria Woodard. "Black Perspective in Books for Children." *The Black American in Books for Children: Readings in Racism*. 2nd ed. Ed. Donnarae MacCann and Gloria Woodard. Metuchen: Scarecrow, 1985. 39-51.

Trzyna, Thomas, and Martin Abbott. "Grieving in the Ethnic Literature Classroom." *College Literature* 18.3 (1991): 1-14.

Whalen, Sharla. *The Betsy-Tacy Companion: A Biography of Maud Hart Lovelace*. Whitehall: Portarlington, 1995.

Wilder, Laura Ingalls. *Little House on the Prairie*. 1935. New York: Harper, 1971.

7

"You are needed, desperately needed!": Cherry Ames in World War II

Sally E. Parry

When the role of American women during World War II is discussed at all by historians and social commentators, the focus is usually on the homefront, where women were raising families while their husbands were in service, or doing war work in factories, or serving coffee and doughnuts at the USO canteen.[1] However, many young women wanted to become involved in the war effort in a more direct way. Some women joined the WAVES or the WAAC or the Marine Corps Women's Reserve, some worked with the Red Cross, and some volunteered for the Army or Navy Nurse Corps. Although the majority of women in uniform served either stateside or in zone-of-the-interior billets, about 60,000 women were stationed overseas (Litoff and Smith 81).

Among uniformed women personnel, the greatest demand was for nurses, both civilian and military; thus the government sought to encourage women to consider this line of work as vital for winning the war. Helen Wells, a professional writer of fiction for adolescents, was one of several authors who saw this need for nurses as the impetus for a series that would follow the life of a young woman through her training as a student nurse and then on to the field of battle.[2] The success of the Cherry Ames series far outlasted the war, but its initial popularity was due in part to the way that Wells celebrated nurses' contributions to the war effort. Cherry and her fictional compatriots were usually portrayed as patriotic and self-sacrificing, the sort of young women the government thought worthy of emulation. This passage from *Army Nurse* is an excellent example.

[F]or all the tragic things she saw, there was no horror. . . . [S]he only felt, more strongly than ever before, the glory, the beauty almost, of the service she could give. That heartened her. But something else worried, almost frightened, Cherry. As the war deepened, and there were more and greater battles, more and still more nurses were going to be needed . . . if thousands of men were to be healed and returned to battle . . . *if we were to win*. (193)

129

The Cherry Ames series functions in a cultural context beyond popular fiction for adolescent girls. It emerges from various discourses that sometimes offer conflicting versions of culture. There is the historical discourse, created out of records and letters; the public relations discourse put forth by the government, which creates images but is not always accurate; and the Hollywood film discourse that created narratives to explain events, often in a simplified or melodramatic way. The series is important because it explained to female readers of the 1940s what a nurse does and why this career was an appropriate one for women. As historical documents of the war years, the series shows that the need for nurses was so great that some women were being encouraged to work rather than function primarily as homemakers. In popular culture terms, the series helps to define the war effort to adolescents, especially since it seems to borrow many of the narrative tropes of Hollywood war films of the time. Cherry goes through basic training, has her courage tested, serves in a heroic manner, much like men in combat, and is able to return to civilian life when her job is done. Although she is exposed to some frightening situations, including nursing under fire from the Japanese in the Pacific, she is able to do her job successfully and is rewarded for it by the United States government. This is a somewhat false vision of the war since it shows that she is able to go through a number of serious situations with little ill effect. As Kate Emburg notes, not only Cherry, "but her ENTIRE nursing class, her brother, and both her boyfriends made it through World War Two unscathed" (30).

Of the 150,000 women who actually served in the military during World War II, over a third were army nurses. Because of a shortage of nurses even before the war officially started, registered nurses (RNs) who volunteered for duty were commissioned as second lieutenants, or ensigns if they served in the navy (Blasingame 39). As Joanne Rosenberger has pointed out, Army Nurse Corps recruiting and public relations material tended to show these women as pretty, probably virginal, and usually delicate. This image was promoted because of the uneasiness that the patriarchal culture had with women in uniform and in positions of authority. There was a desire to show that these women were still "girls" who were feminine despite their uniforms.

For a nation just coming to terms with women in such positions as sheet-metal workers and gunnery instructors, nurses were convenient and reassuring "bridge" figures, a model of wartime womanhood at once combat-hardened and nurturing. Also, no matter how dangerous the mission, the girls continue to crack wise [sic] about beauty parlors and high heels, signaling that however harsh the battlefield conditions or masculine the outfits, they still retain the natural instincts of the red-blooded female. ("Girls of War" 7)

Cherry Ames certainly fits this general stereotype. She is pretty; again and again characters comment on her rosy cheeks and black curly hair. She is certainly ladylike. In *Chief Nurse* Cherry comes up with a scheme to cheer up the soldiers on a Pacific island base. "She made a rule that her nurses wear their feminine white uniforms on Sundays and curl their hair and powder their noses, come storms, heat or bombings— and it perked up everybody's morale" (69). Wells may be having some fun at the expense of Cherry's ultrafeminine desires. Cherry's commanding officer tells her to rescind the order because it puts too much of a strain on the laundry staff.

Cherry, like the "red-blooded female" type, is also interested in men, but is most likely virginal. Her first boyfriend is Dr. Lex Upham, an intern she meets while at Spencer Hospital. She remains romantically attracted to him off and on for over a dozen volumes, but there seems to be little more to their relationship than the occasional date and chaste kiss. He does propose marriage to her, but this is during the war when she feels her duty comes first. Later, she realizes that they bicker too much to be compatible. As late as *Country Doctor's Nurse* (1955), Lex is a still a presence in her life who sulks when she seems attracted to someone else. Captain Wade Cooper, an Army Air Force officer she meets in *Flight Nurse*, also proposes to her, but after she saves his life in a boating accident, he rescinds his offer. "I'm going to marry a soft, helpless feminine little girl who'd let me drown," he says (*Veterans' Nurse* 162). Cherry will simply not conform to the helpless woman stereotype that he would like. However, just like Lex, he continues to flirt with Cherry. Throughout her long series, she stays career-minded and never marries, unlike the heroines of other World War II nurse series.

Public relations material also tended to emphasize that nurses were well-behaved young ladies. Implicit in this presentation was that nurses were not allowed to smoke, drink, carry guns, or engage in strenuous physical activity. They were shown providing compassionate care to wounded soldiers, but the rigors of their work were usually understated or trivialized. Although that portrayal was aimed at the home front, the upper echelons in the military did try to force women to conform to certain feminine "norms." Roberta Love Tayloe, a combat nurse who served in North Africa, recalls doing practice drills in full white uniform and receiving a lecture on morals and how to be "perfect young ladies" (12). She and a friend took a "dim view of being treated as children" (12) and expected to fill the role of army officer. Of these three roles—as nurse, perfect young lady, and officer—only the first was really honored by the military.

Historically, Army nurses endured many of the same hardships as combat troops. In July 1943, the Army authorized four weeks of military orientation for newly commissioned nurses including forced marches, gas mask drills, and running an infiltration course under combat conditions (Litoff and Smith 46-49). Nurses also received additional medical training for post-traumatic stress (usually known as shock or combat fatigue), field hospital setup, and aeromedicine. They served overseas in all of the major campaigns in Europe, North Africa, and Asia, although they were usually behind the front lines. Some, for example those who remained on Corregidor when Allied forces surrendered in 1942, were made prisoners of war. Some were killed in action, usually when Japanese or Germans shelled field hospitals.

Nurses also had a symbolic importance that could be considered both flattering and trivializing. As the Chief Surgeon at the 38th Evacuation Hospital told photographer Margaret Bourke-White, "These wounded soldiers are brought in here wondering if they are going to die. Then they see a woman and know that war can't be so bad if women nurses are here. A little of that Eve stuff does a lot of good for those boys when they are brought in from the front" (qtd. in Blasingame 74-75). Although there were some soldiers who did not approve of nurses in combat areas, the nurses' presence boosted morale. Many thought, "[I]f the nurses can take it, so can we" (Blasingame 84).

For the most part, popular culture representations of military nurses tended to minimalize their contribution to the war effort. Hollywood movies made during the war often showed nurses as romantic interests whom soldiers left behind when they went into combat, or as nearly silent, efficient workers who appear in field hospitals after one of the unit is wounded. In *Air Force* (1943), for example, nurses are in the room when one of the crew members dies. In *Dangerously They Live* (1941), *This Above All* (1942), *Thunderbirds* (1942), *Bataan* (1943), and *The Fighting Sullivans* (1944), nurses appear in a scene or two but are practically anonymous. In *God Is My Co-Pilot* (1945), the nurses are literally silenced—they are Chinese and do not speak at all. When authority figures appear, they just giggle and eat rice.

Several B movies during the war moved nurses into the foreground, although usually unrealistically. These films were more common toward the beginning of the war when the novelty of women appearing in uniform and breaking away from traditional domestic drama made good box office sense. Also cooperation from the U.S. military could be obtained if the films helped to get women more involved in the war effort. *Para-

chute Nurse, a 1942 Columbia picture, shows young women flocking to sign up for the adventure as well as the honor of appearing in uniform. *Army Surgeon*, another 1942 film, starred Jane Wyatt as a combat nurse, but still in white uniform and cap despite combat conditions. *Up in Arms*, an early Danny Kaye comedy about life as a hypochondriac recruit, has the star surrounded by army nurses, but the glamour is emphasized. The boyfriend of a combat nurse wrote to her after seeing the film and damned it with faint praise. It is "very good but somewhat misleading as to the grand and glorious life of the Army Nurse Corps" (Wandrey 100).

Three of the five major films that featured combat nurses were inspired by the heroic behavior of army nurses as Allied forces withdrew from Bataan and Corregidor.[3] *So Proudly We Hail*, released by Paramount in September 1943, and starring Claudette Colbert, Paulette Goddard, Veronica Lake, George Reeves, and Sonny Tufts, was certainly the best of these efforts. It was one of Paramount's biggest hits of the year and even ran with a trailer promoting the Army Nurse Corps' need for volunteers (Koppes and Black 104). Although at times melodramatic, the film focused on the hardships the nurses underwent as they were forced to retreat with the Allied forces under Japanese attack. The movie makes clear that conditions were often harrowing as these women tried to care for the wounded and dying and still maintain their dignity as human beings. Most of the film is a flashback as Lieutenant Janet Davidson's nurse friends discuss how to help her as she lies comatose from combat fatigue. They recall how their unit came to be assigned to the Far East, the difficulty of nursing in the caves at Corregidor while under Japanese attack, and the evacuation at the beaches. Several episodes in particular are remembered as contributing to Janet's condition. These include Janet burning her hands while trying to rescue a surgeon, Janet's one-night honeymoon with Lieutenant John Summers before he is sent to another battle site, and the death of fellow nurse Lieutenant Olivia D'arcy. This last event is horrific not only because one of her friends is killed but because Olivia becomes a human bomb, blowing up herself and a squad of Japanese so that the rest of the nurses can escape. Olivia's husband had been killed at Pearl Harbor and her main motivation is to kill some Japanese even if she has to die trying. Some critics saw the film showing that the determination of women is just as great as that of men in trying to defeat the forces of fascism, while others, especially Manny Farber of the *New Republic*, criticized its portrayal of women: "No one would stand for a picture in which male soldiers were so dependent on the opposite sex" (qtd. in Koppes and Black 104).

Released later that same year, *Cry Havoc*, an MGM film with Margaret Sullivan, Ann Sothern, Joan Blondell, and Fay Bainter, also focused on army nurses at Bataan. Based on the play *Proof Thro' the Night* by Allan Kenward, it was predictably compared to *So Proudly We Hail* and praised for its realism in showing "American nurses starving, sweating, and dying in the beleaguered Philippine jungle" (qtd. in Morella, Epstein, and Griggs 161). However, Captain Florence MacDonald, who had been in charge of the Army nurses in the Philippines, felt that there were many gross inaccuracies in the portrayal of nurses. She angrily wrote to Kenward, "You have managed to include horror, war, birth, death, destruction, horror, Lesbianism [*sic*], insanity, hysteria, horror, smut, murder, spies, sex, horror, and even a little nobility. . . . It should bring wonderful box office" (qtd. in Lingeman 208).

Released right after the war ended was *They Were Expendable*, based on the best-selling factual account of the fall of the Philippines by William L. White. Its title came from a discussion White had with a young naval lieutenant who told him, "In a war, anything can be expendable, money or gasoline or equipment or, most usually, men" (qtd. in Morella 234). In this case women were expendable too. Robert Montgomery and John Wayne were featured in this action film, but a telling role was played by Donna Reed as Lieutenant Sandy Davyss. She and John Wayne share a romance as two lonely people, he, a wounded officer, and she, a dedicated nurse. Unlike most Hollywood movies, this romance does not end happily. He must go back into action and she is left behind at the hospital, presumably either killed or captured by the Japanese and interned as a prisoner of war.

Two other films that featured nurses in action were the 1945 *First Yank into Tokyo* and the 1944 *The Story of Dr. Wassell*. Both are unbelievable because of the circumstances in which the nurses find themselves. *First Yank into Tokyo* stars Barbara Hale as a nurse captured by the Japanese and forced to work in a prisoner-of-war camp. The nurse is shown doing the best she can to take care of Allied prisoners with little assistance or supplies from the Japanese. Her fiancé, who has been persuaded by the U.S. government to have his face surgically altered so that he can look Japanese, sneaks into the prison camp to rescue an atomic scientist and Nurse Drake. They escape, but he remains behind so that she will not feel compelled to marry someone who looks like the hated enemy. *The Story of Dr. Wassell*, although based on the true story of a navy doctor in the Far East, did not portray nurses well. Laraine Day stars as a nurse who aids Dr. Wassell (Gary Cooper) and falls in love with him. In reality, the nurse whom Dr. Wassell married did not see service during World War II. The film is an odd combination of drama, romance, and comedy, which was made worse by the overblown direction of Cecil B. De Mille. The film was roundly panned by critics and was one of the least-successful attempts to honor nurses during wartime.

In contrast, the Cherry Ames series used a variety of discourses to present the adventures of an army nurse in a somewhat more accurate and accessible way to an adolescent audience. Wells made clear the amount of training that a nurse had to undergo in the first two books of the series, *Student Nurse* and *Senior Nurse*. Cherry has to learn about nutrition, various branches of nursing, and emergency medical procedures. Three of the books from the series that focus on the war—*Cherry Ames, Army Nurse* (1944), *Cherry Ames, Chief Nurse* (1944), and *Cherry Ames, Flight Nurse* (1945)—are quite authentic in describing the training that a new nurse must undergo before she is sent to help the military overseas. After comparing Cherry's experiences with the memoirs of several combat nurses, I found that the series did a good job of representing certain aspects of military nursing.[4] In *Army Nurse*, Cherry joins the Army Nurse Corps and goes through basic training before being assigned to a military hospital in Panama. *Chief Nurse* finds her serving at a military hospital in the Pacific. And finally, in *Flight Nurse*, she is sent to England to work as a flight nurse, helping transport wounded soldiers from European battlefields back to England. Wells provided great detail on a nurse's life. Her brother recalls that she "was scrupulous about research, and spent a lot of time in hospitals talking with nurses. She even traveled to specialized facilities" ("Wells, Helen" 204).

As with most popular culture of the time for adolescents, the series softened some of the hard edges of reality. Cherry Ames finds romance in almost every volume. One of her friends marries an American soldier in England during *Flight Nurse*, but the rest of the nurses from Spencer Hospital remain single. Cherry and the other nurses do attend their share of dances, although this was true of real nurses in the military. There were so few women and so many men that nurses were always being invited to dinners, dances, and other social events when they were away from the front.

Also, there is not the same amount of drudgery in the series that real nurses endured. There does not seem to be a great shortage of supplies or medical personnel overseas. The shortage of personnel is suggested more in the beginning of the series when the nurses at Spencer are told that they are "needed, desperately needed!" (*Senior Nurse* 215).

To make the plot more interesting for adolescent readers, Wells has Cherry encounter a mystery in every volume. The mystery angle may have been added to allow Cherry Ames a Nancy Drew-like quality, as well as a Drew-like audience. Most of the mysteries, especially early in the series, are related to medicine. In *Army Nurse*, she discovers a man in a deserted house with a mysterious disease that turns out to be a rare form of malaria. Even though he is a civilian, Cherry takes him to a military hospital where the cure for his disease also helps the military. In *Chief Nurse*, the mystery is related to a flier who is in shock and speechless. Cherry figures out that he was wounded by a new type of Japanese weaponry and helps restore him to health.

Later books in the series are less realistic, partly because Wells cannot use the discourses of war to structure the stories. Cherry is peripatetic, having lots of adventures, as a Dude Ranch Nurse, Jungle Nurse, and Ski Resort Nurse. Her personality is shaped during the war, in terms of her being hard-working, cheerful, and always anxious to help, but by 1947 she talks about her past primarily in terms of her nursing school. The series remained popular with readers until Wells's death in 1986, and quite possibly Wells did not want Cherry to age as much as she would have if reference was made to her military career.

Like some of the early war movies, the Cherry Ames series functions not only as entertainment but as patriotic incitement for young women. An example of such patriotism occurs in *Flight Nurse* when Cherry's Chief Nurse tells her, "I wish to goodness more of our young girls would enter nursing. There's the free Cadet Nurse Corps scholarship for them, and all. Student nurses, right at home, could relieve this shortage so much, if they only would come forward to help and release older nurses for overseas duty" (45). The assurance is given that young women could help with the war effort, even if they didn't feel mature enough or adventurous enough to go overseas. They could at least replace experienced nurses on the homefront. This added yet another dimension to stateside work for women in addition to working in factories or doing volunteer work. Bobbie Ann Mason notes that it was "an inspiration to girls to learn that they were needed. War made it possible" (108).

Cherry's relationships with patients, corpsmen, chief nurses, and doctors echo the letters written by real nurses. One Red Cross worker referred to her patients as "'my problem children' right down to the quiet, charming colonel who is their C.O. and one of their greatest pilots" (qtd. in Litoff and Smith 150). At the hospital in Panama where Cherry is serving, the wounded soldiers also are referred to as in a family relationship. They "wanted Cherry to be mother and sister and friend, as well as nurse. She found that half her nursing was kindness. The boys were wonderfully cooperative, heartbreakingly grateful and uncomplaining" (*Army Nurse* 150). Praise for the soldiers and sailors under the nurses' care is reflected in letter after letter. In *Army Nurse*, Cherry notes "Everyone of them was determined to get well quickly, so he could return to his soldier's work. 'We can't win the war lying here,' they said impatiently from their beds" (150). This sentiment is endorsed in a letter written by Lieutenant Frances Slanger, Army Nurse Corps, in 1944 and reprinted in *Stars and Stripes*. "Sure, we rough it, but in comparison to the way you men are taking it, we can't complain. . . . The patience and determination they show, the courage and fortitude they have is sometimes awesome to behold" (qtd. in Litoff and Smith 168-69). Lt. Slanger was killed as a result of enemy action the day after the letter was published.

One way the series is successful is in how it transforms male combat narratives into somewhat comparable questions that women might ask themselves during wartime. The series, like many wartime films, has as a subtext the anxieties and fears that the American people, especially soldiers, faced.[5] Wells uses these concerns that are articulated through male combat narratives and adapts them for the audience of adolescent women who are wondering how they can best contribute to the war effort.

One of the first concerns is bravery. Will I be brave enough to leave home and endure physical hardships including possibly death? Most wartime films that focus on combat have at least one person whose character is tested under fire. In *Bataan*, a young soldier is so anxious to kill the Japanese that he takes unnecessary chances. He is picked off by a sniper. *Destination Tokyo* also has a young soldier who is afraid that he won't be able to do his duty. Unlike the young man in *Bataan*, he is brave enough to dislodge an unexploded bomb that is stuck in the hull of a submarine. Nurses were not usually sent under fire, but they had to be prepared for this eventuality. In *Army Nurse* (1944), Cherry and the group of nurses from Spencer Hospital who joined the Army Nurse Corps go through this basic training course so that they will be ready to work under real combat conditions when necessary:

Cherry lay flat on her stomach, petrified with fear. Then she started to crawl, cautiously, hugging the ground as she had been taught. Bullets sprayed only thirty inches above her. . . . She was quivering and clammy and exhausted and clung flat to the earth, trembling with fright. . . . She had to get to those imaginary wounded soldiers. Every second counted if their lives were to be saved. Cherry crawled, getting her coveralls caught in barbed wire once, once cutting her hand on a stone, but she crawled. After a lifetime of staring at the sun, as nakedly exposed as a fly, she crawled under the final barbed wire. She had made it! (60-61)

Cherry, a nice middle-class girl, who is neither exceptionally strong nor athletic, is able to make it through the obstacle course so that she can learn to help save American lives. The training portrayed is realistic enough, although the possibility of being killed or wounded is downplayed. The message sent is that other ordinary young women are able to endure physical hardship (and probably live through it) for so great a cause.

Related to this idea, that an ordinary person can behave in an extraordinary way if circumstances demand it, is the Hollywood conceit that people from different ethnic and regional backgrounds must be able to work together for the Allied cause. Given a great enough threat, Americans should be able to put aside various biases to fight for a greater good. Many combat narratives seem to have a person from New York City, often Brooklyn, a Southerner, a Texan, and someone from a non-WASP background put together in close quarters. In *Bataan*, for example, an older soldier, a Hispanic from New York, a Filipino, and a kid from Texas all fight together to delay the Japanese advance. The Cherry Ames series uses this conceit as well, with the focus on the group of women with whom Cherry attends nursing school. Her friends represent a wide spectrum: Bertha Larsen, a farmer; Mai Lee, a Chinese-American whose parents' village in China has been destroyed by the Japanese; Vivian Warren, poor and hard-working; and Gwen Jones, a red-headed New Englander. Although they come from different backgrounds, when a recruiter from the Army Nurse Corps who has escaped from Corregidor speaks to their graduating class, they all pledge to enlist together.

Ann had raised her hand. She could hear Ann's quickened breathing. Mai Lee's hand was raised next. The room was filled with tension and breathless silence. . . . Then Bertha Larsen's hand went up; Marie Swift's; Gwen's; Vivian's. Then five more hands shot up, one after another. (*Senior Nurse* 215)

It is as if all of these women are responding to the call of something greater than themselves that they all recognize at the same time. They must volunteer. As the Army recruiter puts it, "All of them are making the greatest offering any woman can" (216). And the implication is that as good American women this is the only way that they can respond to demonstrate unity for the Allied cause.

The second anxiety that is common in combat narratives is worries about leadership. Can the officers who are in charge of so many lives be relied upon? Given the cultural context of wartime writing, the answer would have to be yes. Often in Hollywood films, a hard-nosed veteran is criticized by new soldiers for his insistence on following procedures. But by the end of the film, he is usually shown to be in the right. In *Gung Ho!* (1943), for example, a colonel forces his men to go through a variety of training exercises that many of them are unable to complete. However, by the end of the film, those soldiers who are left alive are grateful for the rigorous training that has helped them to survive. A similar situation occurs in *Wake Island* (1942) when civilian personnel are antagonistic to the idea that they are "subject to military discipline of a routine nature" (qtd. in Dick 127). When the Japanese finally do attack, the civilians realize that military insistence on preparedness and discipline is important. It becomes clear that orders do need to be followed.

Cherry is also faced with several tough commanding officers whose methods she questions. The resolution to the conflicts she encounters is somewhat different from the film narratives. In *Army Nurse* she feels she has been treated harshly by Captain Endicott and Major Wylie. However, Captain Endicott, a new officer, proves to be more interested in advancement than the good of the service, while Major Wylie, although also portrayed as a tough disciplinarian, recognizes when the people under him have performed beyond the call of duty. At the end of *Army Nurse*, Cherry is cited for the important medical victory that has been achieved through her "courage, alertness, and initiative" (208) and she is promoted to chief nurse. Captain Endicott is transferred. There is a certain amount of vindication for Cherry in that the officer with the good of his personnel at heart is the one who also understands why it is important for Cherry to have disobeyed a command. Colonel Pillsbee plays a similar role in *Chief Nurse*, a strict career soldier whose concern for discipline is something that Cherry questions even as she realizes its necessity. This tension surfaces in most combat films as soldiers realize that the good of the many has to outweigh individual hopes and desires.

There are several sets of hierarchies competing in Cherry's narratives. The most obvious is that of the military because rank most often seems to determine who is right. Second, since during the war men tended to outrank women, a male sense of prerogative is valorized. Third, most of the doctors are male and most of the nurses female, which reinforces male authoritarianism. The Cherry Ames series is somewhat subversive in that, although these types of authority are given lip service, when Cherry has to break regulations to help a sick Central American native or to investigate the curious psychological problems of a downed flier, she is usually demonstrated to be in the right. The authorities, be they doctors and/or military officers, sanction what Cherry has done only after the fact. Unlike the movies, where the raw recruit who violates the rules is often picked off by a sniper or blown up, Cherry's innate good sense is rewarded.

The third anxiety that is exhibited in war movies, especially those late in the war, is how the soldier will be received when he returns home.

Will he be able to adjust? Will his family want him back, even if he is injured or maimed? Although it was less likely that women in uniform, even those serving in combat areas, would be gravely wounded, there was still a concern about how they would readjust to civilian life. Women were taking on new roles both in and out of the army and some films expressed the ambivalence that many people felt. *Tender Comrade* (1943) with Ginger Rogers and *Christmas in Connecticut* (1945) with Barbara Stanwyck both show women in nontraditional ways, as a factory worker and as a magazine writer who can't cook. The conclusion of each film tries to create a domestic space for each to inhabit, but neither is altogether convincing. In male narratives, the wounds are usually physical. *Pride of the Marines* (1945) focuses on a soldier who is blinded by a grenade and doubts that anyone will want to marry him. Harold Russell, a double amputee in real life who portrays Homer in *The Best Years of Our Lives* (1946), faces the fear of not being wanted by his long time fiancée because he no longer has hands. Also, Ted Lawson of *Thirty Seconds over Tokyo* (1944) loses a leg and is disfigured in a plane crash. He is reluctant to contact his wife until he can be improved by plastic surgery.

Cherry does not face anything quite so traumatic, nor does she see any of the major battles in North Africa, Europe, or the South Pacific, but her work as a flight nurse is teeming with danger. The planes she travels in cannot be marked with red crosses since the planes carry wounded men one way and supplies the other way.[6] On her flights she is exposed to antiaircraft fire and attack by enemy planes five times. She injures her back, suffers from sleeplessness and tension, and worries about the men she cares for. Eventually she is invalided back to the United States after suffering combat fatigue, but she does receive the United States Air Medal for "professional skill, courage, and high sense of service" (*Flight Nurse* 213).

Although many soldiers worried about returning home, Cherry's transition to civilian life is not as traumatic. She remains feminine despite her uniform and does not seem to be a threat to traditional male roles except in romance, because she never wants to settle down and give up her career. Her adjustment is made easier because of her family's attitude; they have been extremely supportive while she was overseas, sending her letters and packages. Her twin brother Charlie, who is a flier with the Army Air Force, manages to visit her both in the Pacific Theater and the European Theater. Because her brother is aware of the hardships she has undergone, she does not feel alone or particularly misunderstood when she returns home. The postwar world is shown in two books of the series to illustrate Cherry's return to civilian life. These later books do not share the same narrative structure as male combat films and seem to have a more domestic and nurturing focus. In *Veterans' Nurse*, she helps treat men who have received disfiguring wounds including a soldier who needs a prosthetic hand. In *Private Duty Nurse* (1946), after her brother comes home, Cherry feels that she is able to move on to other types of nursing. At times, her readjustment is comic, because Cherry reverts to a persona of a young nurse doubting her abilities to take on new nursing tasks. In *Flight Nurse* she had serious responsibilities, including taking care of soldiers being evacuated from battle. In *Private Duty Nurse* she doubts her ability to nurse one woman suffering from pneumonia. Dr. Joe, her friend and one of the male authority figures in the series, says to reassure her, "There's nothing special to know, child. It's bedside nursing, the same as you've done in Spencer Hospital and in Army hospitals—only this time you nurse the patient in her own home" (9).

Cherry is also reunited with the Spencer nurses with whom she had served overseas. She maintains this affiliation throughout the rest of the series although they usually identify themselves more by their nursing school than by their military service. The fantasy shown here is that things have gone back to normal and that they (and the implication is the rest of the country) can resume their pre-war roles. They become more like the girl chums of countless adolescent series from the Motor Girls to the Babysitters' Club.

Possibly because this series was written for girls in their early adolescence, the series phases out mentions of the war after *Private Duty Nurse*. Given the cultural context for the series, perhaps Wells felt that in 1946 girls reading about Cherry Ames were not as concerned with the sacrifices made, or perhaps she was reflecting the government's attitude about putting the war behind and stressing the new post-war society. In either case, the books after the war do not mention much about sacrifice. Cherry, after some anguish about leaving convalescing soldiers in *Veterans' Nurse*, believes that the best way she can serve peace is out of the Army. "She had no right to be lingering on here in the Army, against the pull of changing times" (212).

The final anxiety that appears in the Hollywood films is: was it worth it? After the fighting and dying and the tremendous changes that society has undergone, can what was done be justified? Perhaps since American society in the post-war books is depicted as so decent and optimistic, the answer to the question about sacrifice is implicit. The only book that tackles the problems of adjustment in the post-war years to any extent is *Veterans' Nurse* where Cherry realizes, "It's an end and a beginning. . . . We'll have to get our wounded veterans cured—start our lives and work all over on a peacetime basis. This war has left us plenty of responsibilities" (4).

The Cherry Ames series, like many male narratives about the war, provides a number of reassurances to its audience. It makes clear that women can play an important role in helping to win the war, that they can be brave enough to stand up to its hardships, that they can endure military discipline (and sometimes subvert it), and that when the war is over they can come home and be welcomed. This vision of war, and the discourses employed, certainly simplified and romanticized the roles that women could play. But the series was important for showing that women, including the adolescent reading audience, could make a difference in the world and be valued for their endeavors.

Notes

1. An interesting contemporary text in this regard is *While You Were Gone*, which has a section on "The Women in the War" written by Margaret Mead. She focuses on how important it is for women to work because they will understand returning servicemen better. Women will know "how hard it is to be responsible for earning for a family" (283). More recent texts on the war often slight women's contributions. See such authors as Fussell, who mentions women primarily in terms of what they lost when rationing was introduced or as wives or sweethearts of servicemen. Weinberg has two paragraphs on American women and the war effort, and the *Oxford Companion to World War II* devotes seven pages out of 1301 to women, plus four sentences for the WAAC, one sentence for the WAAF, and two sentences for the WAVES. Under medicine, women are mentioned only in connection with venereal disease. Ziegler focuses on London rather than America, but still has little to say about women. There are two pages on their role in the war, one page on their smoking, one on their drinking, and several pages on their relationships with American G.I.s. Lingeman's text is one of the few without a specifically feminist focus that discusses women on the homefront and overseas in any great detail.

2. Elizabeth Lansing created two World War II adolescent series about nurses. The Nancy Naylor series had five titles, at least two of which were concerned with the war, *Nancy Naylor, Flight Nurse* (1944) and *Nancy Naylor, Captain of Flight Nurses* (1946). Under the pseudonym Martha Johnson, Lansing created *Ann Bartlett, Navy Nurse* (1941) who appeared in two additional books, *Ann Bartlett at Bataan* (1943) and *Ann Bartlett in the South Pacific* (1944). Penny Marsh, an eight-title series written by a nurse, Dorothy Deming, had at least two war experiences: *Ginger Lee, War Nurse* (1942) and *Penny Marsh and Ginger Lee, Wartime Nurses* (1943). Nurse Blake, created by Marshall McClintock under the pen name William Starret, appeared in three books: *Nurse Blake, USA* (1942); *Nurse Blake Overseas* (1943); and *Nurse Blake at the*

Front (1944). The thirteen-volume Susan Merton series by Louise Logan spanned the years 1941 to 1947. Most of them were concerned with the war including *Nurse Merton—Army Spy* (1942), *Nurse Merton in the Caribbean* (1943), *Nurse Merton, Desert Captive* (1943), *Nurse Merton in the Pacific* (1944), and *Nurse Merton on the Russian Front* (1945). Basil Miller started the Patty Lou nursing series in 1942, but most of her nursing was in the Western Hemisphere, serving as a flying missionary and range nurse among other careers in this fourteen-title series. The two titles related to World War II are *Patty Lou in the Coast Guard* (1944) and *Patty Lou, The Flying Nurse* (1945). In World War I adolescent fiction, the Red Cross Girls by Margaret Vandercook nursed their way through ten titles between 1916 and 1920, the Khaki Girls by Edna Brooks drove with an ambulance corps for four titles between 1918 and 1920, and Ruth Fielding, a Stratemeyer heroine written by "Alice B. Emerson," did some nursing as a Red Cross volunteer in three novels in 1918 and 1919. See *Girls Series Books: A Checklist of Titles Published 1840-1991*, published by the Children's Literature Research Collections, for a complete listing of titles for these series.

3. See Dick, Fyne, Jones and McClure, Koppes and Black, and Lingeman for more information on Hollywood World War II films and their propaganda value.

4. See Litoff and Smith, Tayloe, and Wandrey for examples of combat nurses' writings during World War II. The letters from the nurses often mentioned a lack of supplies, prevalence of bugs and rats, and the safety of others in uniform as major concerns.

5. McLaughlin identified four of these fears of soldiers and how Hollywood narratives about the Doolittle Raid offered resolutions to them.

6. Blasingame (129) confirms the hazards of flight nursing.

Works Cited

Blasingame, Wyatt. *Combat Nurses of World War II*. New York: Random, 1967.

Children's Literature Research Collections. *Girls Series Books: A Checklist of Titles Published 1840-1991*. Minneapolis: U of Minnesota Libraries, 1992.

Dear, I.C.B., ed. *The Oxford Companion to World War II*. Oxford: Oxford UP, 1995.

Dick, Bernard F. *The Star-Spangled Screen: The American World War II Film*. Lexington: UP of Kentucky, 1985.

Emburg, Kate. "Collecting Annuals." *Whispered Watchword* 96.3 (1996): 30-31.

Fussell, Paul. *Wartime: Understanding and Behavior in the Second World War*. New York: Oxford UP, 1989.

Fyne, Robert. *The Hollywood Propaganda of World War II*. Metuchen: Scarecrow, 1994.

"The Girls of War: Rare Combat Classic Gave Women a Fighting Chance." *American Movie Classics Magazine* Sept. 1995: 7.

Jones, Ken D., and Arthur F. McClure. *Hollywood at War: The American Motion Picture and World War II*. New York: Castle, 1973.

Koppes, Clayton R., and Gregory D. Black. *Hollywood Goes to War: How Politics, Profits, and Propaganda Shaped World War II Movies*. Berkeley: U of California P, 1990.

Lingeman, Richard R. *Don't You Know There's a War On?: The American Home Front 1941-1945*. New York: Putnam, 1970.

Litoff, Judy Barrett, and David C. Smith, eds. *We're in This War, Too: World War II Letters from American Women in Uniform*. New York: Oxford UP, 1994.

Mason, Bobbie Ann. *The Girl Sleuth: A Feminist Guide*. Old Westbury: Feminist P, 1975.

McLaughlin, Robert L. "Thirty Seconds over Hollywood: Cultural Representations of the Doolittle Raid." Popular Culture Association/American Culture Association Annual Conference, Philadelphia, PA, April 13, 1995.

Mead, Margaret. "The Women in the War." *While You Were Gone: A Report on Wartime Life in the United States*. Ed. Jack Goodman. New York: Simon, 1946. 274-89.

Morella, Joe, Edward Z. Epstein, and John Griggs. *The Films of World War II: A Pictorial Treasury of Hollywood's War Years*. Secaucus: Citadel, 1975.

Rosenberger, Joanne. "Angels of Mercy in World War II: Media Portrayal vs. Reality." Popular Culture Association/American Culture Association Annual Conference, New Orleans, LA, April 8, 1993.

Tayloe, Roberta Love. *Combat Nurse: A Journal of World War II*. Santa Barbara: Fithian, 1988.

Wandrey, June. *Bedpan Commando: The Story of a Combat Nurse During World War II*. Elmore, OH: Elmore, 1989.

Weinberg, Gerhard L. *A World at Arms: A Global History of World War II*. New York: Cambridge UP, 1994.

Wells, Helen. *Cherry Ames, Army Nurse*. New York: Grosset, 1944.

——. *Cherry Ames, Chief Nurse*. New York: Grosset, 1944.

——. *Cherry Ames, Flight Nurse*. New York: Grosset, 1945.

——. *Cherry Ames, Private Duty Nurse*. New York: Grosset, 1946.

——. *Cherry Ames, Senior Nurse*. New York: Grosset, 1944.

——. *Cherry Ames, Veterans' Nurse*. New York: Grosset, 1946.

"Wells, Helen." *Something about the Author*. Ed. Anne Commire. Vol. 49. Detroit: Gale, 1987. 201-04.

Ziegler, Philip. *London at War, 1939-1945*. New York: Knopf, 1995.

8

The Secret of the Feminist Heroine:
The Search for Values
in Nancy Drew and Judy Bolton

Sally E. Parry

The two adolescent mystery series, Nancy Drew by the pseudonymous Carolyn Keene and Judy Bolton by Margaret Sutton, both provide especially strong role models for young women. Each series features an adolescent female sleuth who is smart, independent, and clever enough to solve mysteries that adults—including male authority figures such as lawyers, police officers, and FBI agents—are unable to figure out. Both young women are amateur detectives, not part of the law enforcement system, but both are nonetheless often more perceptive than their professional counterparts. Unlike adult mysteries, their stories rarely contain murder; rather they involve robbery, blackmail, or missing people or items.

But while both series can be seen, from a feminist point of view, as empowering their women readers via their protagonists, they do so in significantly different ways. Nancy is a proactive person who seeks out mysteries to solve, often ones that her father, lawyer Carson Drew, does not have time for. She seems to work best alone in trying to restore the status quo, with all that implies about ideological, economic, social, and even gender relations. Judy Bolton, on the other hand, becomes caught up in mysteries rather than seeking them out. She is a more collaborative detective, because although she is able to act alone, she is more likely to integrate her family and friends into the mysteries she solves. She is less able to separate her roles as daughter, sister, and wife, from her role as detective. Based on the relationships Judy and Nancy have with friends and family, the classes of people involved, and the kinds of mysteries solved, it seems clear that, although both can be seen as feminist sleuths, Nancy Drew is more likely to uphold the ideological status quo, while Judy Bolton is more likely to restore moral rather than legal order, because her mysteries tend to emphasize human relationships over material possessions.

Although both series were begun around the same time, Nancy Drew in 1930 and Judy Bolton in 1932, the authorship and production is significantly different. Carolyn Keene, the "author" of Nancy Drew, is a pseudonym for a number of writers who are usually not credited with authorship.[1] Nancy, as a character, is created out of collective authorship, with the guidance of the Stratemeyer editors. Her values tend to be somewhat more conservative than Judy's, perhaps because she is representing a corporate consciousness. Judy Bolton was created by one person, Margaret Sutton, who has written a variety of adolescent books in addition to the Bolton series. The series ended in 1967, unlike the Drew series which is stiil going strong.[2] Sutton's philosophy for writing the series was to meet "the real need children have to find a book friend who will appear in story after story. . . . Mine are based on real life experience and each one has a theme or what I call 'reason for being'" ("Sutton, Margaret" 214).[3]

Both of the young detectives assist people who have emotional as well as material problems. Judy and Nancy spend much of their time helping insecure and frightened people find security, sometimes in the form of financial stability through inheritances, legacies, or missing valuables, and sometimes through returning children to a safe family environment.[4] The longer-running and financially more successful Nancy Drew series often features mysteries in which members of the upper class suffer loss. This type of mystery is considered a "classic mystery" because the "emphasis is on . . . the 'thing,' be it a will, a jewel, a map, a clue or a murder weapon" (Winn 35). Since Nancy, especially when she's working for her father, represents an ideological order that privileges material comforts, she helps preserve a value system in which money plays a pivotal role. Nancy's ability to find the clue in the old clock, hidden staircase, or jewel box means that she can solve the mystery, restore the goods to the right person (who usually comes from a "good" family), and then move on to the next case. Madame Alexandra in *The Clue in the Jewel Box* (1943) is a good example of an aristocratic woman with money who is terrorized by a lower-class person claiming to be related to her. He steals her jewels (most likely taken from Russia after the Revolution) and leaves her penniless. Nancy discovers that Madame's true grandson was a person with fine manners who was kidnapped by the impostor. Nancy locates the real grandson, finds the missing jewels, and even helps the grandson meet a nice woman from the old homeland to marry. Nancy sometimes helps people from other classes, as in *The Secret at Red Gate Farm* (1931) and *The Clue in the Diary* (1932), but most often the people she helps are from a "good" background, even if they are not rich.

Judy Bolton is also able to decipher the secrets in the haunted attic, unfinished house, or patchwork quilt, but her triumphs come more from helping families than restoring wealth. She remains connected to the people whose mysteries she solves and many of these characters appear in numerous subsequent books in the series. The millworker Irene Lang, whom she befriends in *The Haunted Attic* (1932), for example, remains a friend throughout the series. After Irene marries, Judy visits her in New York, and in the *Name on the Bracelet* (1940), helps her locate her baby after it is switched with another infant by a nursemaid. In *The Haunted Attic* Judy figures out the parentage of neighbor Peter Dobbs, whom she later marries, and in *The Invisible Chimes* (1932) she deduces that a young woman abandoned by a group of robbers is actually Peter's long lost sister, Honey. Judy succeeds despite the obstacles placed in front of her by a society that wants to limit options for women. With few exceptions, Judy Bolton's mysteries are less glamorous and focus on middle- and lower-middle-class people.

There are certain structural similarities in the Nancy Drew and Judy Bolton series. Nancy and Judy both stumble onto mysteries at home and Nancy also solves mysteries while traveling on seemingly endless vacations. Sometimes a mysterious person appears or a strange occurrence takes place about which they want to know more. At other times something unusual is brought to their attention because of their reputations as famous sleuths. They follow various leads, provided by convenient clues in diaries, letters, pictures, or decorative objects. Sleuthing assistance is occasionally provided by family or friends, although they are more likely to provide companionship or a sounding board for the detective's ruminations rather than real help. Usually there is a coincidence or two that leads to a breakthrough, often accompanied by a chase, sometimes with the sleuths chasing the villains, other times with the villains chasing Nancy or Judy. In nearly every book they face some physical danger. Judy has been locked in trucks (*The Haunted Road*), imprisoned in abandoned sheds (*The Vanishing Shadow*), and kidnapped in a case of mistaken identity (*The Secret of the Musical Tree*). Nancy has been bound and gagged numerous times and hidden in department store stockrooms (*The Clue of the Velvet Mask*), boats (*The Secret of the Wooden Lady*, *The Mystery at Lilac Inn*), and attic crawl spaces (*The Clue of the Tapping Heels*). Both have survived innumerable threats, capsizing boats, and various traffic accidents. Despite the obstacles in their way, however, they are usually able to come up with a solution that restores missing valuables, reunites families, and sends villains to prison. Their success lies in being able to see what others fail to and in combining common sense with observation and intuition.

On the surface, then, the two series greatly resemble each other. However, their differences, in terms of the detectives' relationships with friends and family, their values and way of life, and the types of mysteries they solve, communicate different ideologies. Nancy, despite her traditionally feminine attributes, such as good looks, a variety of clothes for all social occasions, and an awareness of good housekeeping, is often praised for her seeming masculine traits. A banker in *The Sign of the Twisted Candles* says of her that she has "the best ordered mind and keenest ability to put two and two together of any person I ever met" (160). She operates best independently, has the freedom and money to do as she pleases, and outside of a telephone call or two home, seems to live for solving mysteries rather than participating in family life. She is more interested in the public sphere rather than the private or domestic one, and, despite lip service to expectations of women by society, she, like many men, tends to seek "public recognition of . . . achievements" (Evans 2). Newspaper articles frequently feature her, her name seems to be recognized by ordinary people as well as crooks, and she enjoys the sort of deference she receives as a famous detective. For her, "the solution of the mystery is an act of power; the solution confirms her theories" (Zacharias 1035). A glamorous heroine who seems not to have a care in the world except when being attacked by villains, Nancy is able to succeed within the "official" ideological systems and often seeks to restore the status quo in terms of gender and class roles.

Judy Bolton has the same keen intelligence as Nancy Drew but must solve her mysteries in a problematic world where women are often patronized and poor people are looked down upon. Because she must attend school and later work, she does not have the same freedom to travel that Nancy does. Since she does not own a sporty roadster, she is often dependent on her brother or husband for transportation. Judy is in many ways an ordinary young woman in a male-dominated society who is expected to be a dutiful daughter and wife. Her mother expects her to do housework (because there is no live-in housekeeper like the Drews'), but Judy has little enthusiasm for it.[5] In *The Invisible Chimes* (1932) Mrs. Bolton tells Judy that her visiting friend Honey is "like having another daughter and, if you'll forgive me for saying it, Judy, she helps me more than you ever did" (67). Most of her mysteries are related to the problems of her family and friends rather than to rich, mysterious strangers. While Nancy has been criticized for being "achievement-rather than affiliation-oriented" (Wertheimer and Sands 1134), Judy tends to be connected to others, caught in the web of relationships even within her mysteries, in a way that Carol Gilligan has defined as more likely to be part of a woman's experience (49).

Some of Nancy's attributes can be seen as traditionally masculine and understood in relation to her role model and father, noted lawyer Carson Drew. She is in many ways the son he never had. He shows respect and affection for her and provides her with everything she needs, from money to transportation to information that he can obtain from his contacts in law enforcement. Nancy patterns herself after him, asking probing questions of potential clients (his as well as hers), springing into action at a moment's notice, and daring physical harm if it will help solve the case. She often refers to herself as her father's partner and asks to investigate cases he does not have time for. As Patricia Meyer Spacks has noted of young women Nancy's age,

[a] woman on the brink of adulthood evokes special complexity—particularly about her power. Lacking the wifehood that would assign her comprehensible, measurable status by virtue of her association with a more or less powerful man, she may partake of her father's status. . . . A sexual being yet unpossessed, she wields a power independent of social position. (19)

It is understandable why critic Betsy Caprio has compared the structure of the Nancy Drew series to an archetypal male quest myth. Nancy, although young (16 in earlier novels, 18 in later ones), takes the initiative to solve some sort of injustice, undergoes many trials, and is threatened by death, but she perseveres so that order is restored and is praised and then receives some sort of reward for her efforts (Caprio 131-53).

Although Nancy is heroic, she does not always operate alone. She frequently arranges to have companions with her, most often cousins Bess Marvin and George Fayne. These two can be seen as representing the female and male sides of Nancy's personality. Bess has many "feminine" traits such as a weakness for fattening food (and a concomitant concern about her weight), a desire for frilly dresses, and a great interest in boyfriends. George is a tomboy, often described as having short hair, an athletic build, and tailored clothes. In the early volumes they have steady boyfriends, Dave Evans for Bess and Burt Eddleton for George. Bess and George are usually glad to accompany Nancy on her travels, but they sometimes place eating, shopping, or going out on dates as a higher priority than solving a mystery, thus limiting their effectiveness in aiding Nancy.

Nancy also has a boyfriend, the long-suffering Ned Nickerson. They meet in *The Clue in the Diary* (1932) and maintain a relationship off and on for most of the series.[6] He accompanies her to dances, organizes barbecues in her honor, and helps provide "muscle" to open locked rooms and lift heavy objects. He envisions a more romantic relationship than she wants to grant, which often causes frustration on his part. In a *Seventeen* magazine article Joanne Furtak wrote, "After her first date with handsome Ned Nickerson, Nancy went to bed dreaming of clues, not kisses. She was a feminist's dream before the dream became fashionable, a Gloria Steinem without an air of defiance" (qtd. in Plunkett-Powell 103). Although at times Nancy seems to care for Ned, often she uses him as a convenient man to aid her in her detective work.

Nancy Drew is a good feminist hero in that her role in these mysteries is a strong and active one. She often serves as a protector for orphaned children, helpless older women, or poverty-stricken older men. She is sometimes extraordinary, capable of driving automobiles, airplanes, and boats, as well as riding horses, playing golf, and swimming and diving in an expert manner. Francis FitzGerald believes that Nancy's car "gives her total mobility and, while she's driving it, a physical equality with men" (qtd. in Felder 32). In the earlier novels, although she is too ladylike to fight, she can trip up villains and chase them to their hideout. She sometimes convinces Ned to accompany her on sleuthing trips, but more often than not he's conveniently away—at college, at camp, at work. The responsibility for solving the mystery is Nancy's. When physical effort is required, such as knocking out a villain in *The Clue of the Tapping Heels* (1939) or sailing a ship in *The Secret of the Wooden Lady* (1950), Ned and sometimes his friends Dave and Burt will appear, but Nancy usually needs little real help.

Nancy also seems to need no female role model. She is independent enough to know what she wants, and because her father is well-to-do, she is not tied to domestic chores like Judy. Because her mother died when she was young, her only maternal figure is housekeeper Hannah Gruen who, especially in the earlier novels, is treated more as a servant than as a friend or mother substitute.[7] Nancy does have a nurturing side, which she seems to come by instinctively. In *The Clue of the Broken Locket* (1934), for example, Nancy tries to find the parents of two abandoned children and at the same time shows "mothering" instincts that the children's adoptive mother does not share.

In her mysteries, Judy Bolton does less independent investigation. She relies more on family and friends, who both help her investigations and mark the social relations by which she defines herself: daughter, wife, and friend. Unlike Nancy, she is part of a "traditional" family with a mother, a father, a younger brother Horace, and a family pet: Blackberry the cat. Her father, like Nancy's, is a professional man but without a national reputation. His doctor's office is even part of the family home. While Nancy remains a perpetual adolescent, Judy ages from fifteen to twenty-two during the course of the series, maturing as a young woman.

Although she often follows up clues by herself, she is much more willing than Nancy to work in a collaborative manner with others including her husband, Peter Dobbs. She is able to deduce the significance of a number of mysterious explosions in *The Rainbow Riddle* (1946) by visiting certain inns while on her honeymoon. This work leads Peter to a breakthrough for the FBI in closing down an illegal munitions ring. Brother Horace attributes his job on the Farringdon newspaper to Judy's investigative work on the substandard building materials that caused the Roulsville flood. Even rich Lorraine Lee admires her empathy for the less fortunate and skill at helping others, almost leading to a catastrophe in *The Riddle of the Double Ring* (1937), where Lorraine is mistaken for Judy by fur thieves and kidnapped. The chronology of the series, as the relationships of characters grow and change, contributes to a better understanding of Judy Bolton and her family.

More ordinary than Nancy Drew, Judy has fewer fantastic abilities. She also recognizes flaws about herself—her temper, her inability to sing, her impatience. She is quick to give others credit for their part in solving mysteries and eager to help her friends from various walks of life appreciate each other. Nancy Drew is happy in her current niche in society, but sometimes Judy feels constrained by the expectations of a male-dominated system. In *The Vanishing Shadow*, for example, Judy says, "Sometimes I wish I were a boy. . . . A detective, . . . A great one who goes into all kinds of dangers" (53).[8] For her, detective work is an avocation, while for Nancy it is a profession, if usually an unpaid one. Judy is more often defined in the series through affiliation as Dr. Bolton's daughter or Peter Dobbs's wife. She is proud of her intelligence but feels limited by her options. Her friend Pauline Faulkner tells her, "College is a bore, unless you're planning a career" (*The Yellow Phantom* 5). Realizing she probably cannot be a detective, Judy attends secretarial school after high school and works for the lawyer she eventually marries. Her later triumphs come as she helps Peter (who has become an FBI agent) solve cases involving kidnapping, interstate robbery, and weapons smuggling.

Judy and Peter share a strong relationship because they complement each other. They work as equal partners, except when he is constrained from talking about his FBI cases. She is more intuitive about people and their motives than he is, while he is adept at creating a liaison with official agencies, testing her theories, and, most important, believing her reasons for taking action. "Through all of the books, Judy and Peter are friends sharing the details of the mystery at hand" (Russell 40) as well as husband and wife. For example, her curiosity about a little boy who is abandoned by his parents leads to the solution of a federal crime the FBI is investigating in *The Discovery at Dragon's Mouth* (1960). Because the patriarchal system valorizes men in official positions, the credit she receives is mostly from friends and family. She does not receive the public attention that Nancy does, possibly because Nancy is sanctioned by the establishment through her father's position. As Bobbie Ann Mason notes, "Judy is both protected and challenged by the male world with which she manages to cope, and against which she jousts—with wits, not Wonder Girl advantages" (84). Judy is torn between traditional and nontraditional roles, hoping for marriage and a family at the same time she wants independence and respect for her detective skills.

Although both series have as an ultimate goal the sense that order must be restored, authority figures are often subverted. This is due in large part to the fact that the young women are shown to be more clever than male police officers, detectives, and lawyers. Despite being the best lawyer in the state, Carson Drew never beats Nancy to the solution of a mystery (Deane 83). In the revised Nancy Drew series some attention is paid to the importance of the law; in the original books, contempt is often shown for the police by Nancy and her father (Jones 709-10).[9] In *The Clue of the Broken Locket* a detective is even shown as corrupt, stealing a diamond locket and running off with a servant. One would think that the Drews would support the legal system, but instead they display the superiority felt by the upper class toward public servants. Thus Nancy feels she can go beyond the rules for ordinary people. In *The Password to Larkspur Lane* (1933) the narrator states, "Many a problem which had baffled professional mystery-solvers had been cleared up by her keen mind" (13). Nancy displays elements of an Old West hero who is above the law when necessary in order to right wrongs. Even as late as 1993 in *Choosing Sides* Nancy picks a lock because she needs to find out some information.[10]

Judy subverts the patriarchal system but superficially seems to defer to authority. She is almost always on good terms with the police chief of Farringdon. He respects her judgment, but only after she earns his respect through a series of several books, starting with *The Haunted Attic*. She is often able to work through clues in connection with a crime or mystery much more quickly than male authority figures, but because of her less aggressive style and her collaborative methods, she seems less threatening to the patriarchy and not as quick to be believed. Often, not until the last minute will the FBI believe the deductions that Judy has made, such as in *The Whispered Watchword* (1961) where congressional actions are being compromised.

Material success and, concomitantly, class consciousness, are much more important for Nancy Drew than for Judy Bolton. Nancy is obviously upper-middle class and prefers to associate with the well-to-do who embody the dominant value system. She aligns her sense of good with wealth, believing, like the Puritans, that those who succeed in a material sense are inherently better people. She approves of the Aborns in *The Bungalow Mystery* (1930) because she hears that they are "very acceptable people" (Keene 43). She judges by appearance, often disapproving of the nouveau riche, like the Blairs in *The Clue of the Broken Locket*, for their crude behavior and ostentatious display of possessions: "Kitty Blair was over-rouged and over-dressed. Her bearing was proud and haughty, her gestures dramatic. Her voice had a hard, metallic ring, except when she tried to be particularly agreeable. It was clear to Nancy that the actress considered herself very important" (7). She even prefers poor people who come from good families, like Mr. March in *The Secret in the Old Attic* (1944) or Laura Pendleton in *The Bungalow Mystery* (1930), who at least have appropriate pedigrees. Her world is one in which every respectable family ought to have at least a housekeeper or maid. In *The Mystery at Lilac Inn* (1930), for example, much of Nancy's time is taken up with trying to locate a replacement for Hannah Gruen, who has to leave the Drews because of family problems. Lower-class people tend either to be docile, like Millie Burden in *The Mystery of Red Gate Farm* who knows her place in the world and accepts it, or angry and prone to criminal behavior, like Stumpy Dowd in *The Bungalow Mystery* or Ralph Snecker in *The Clue in the Velvet Mask* (1953). Such characters tend to live in obviously lower-class areas with class-specific names like Milltown or Dockville, which Nancy describes as "row upon row of tenement houses, all alike and of a dingy and uninviting appearance" (*Mystery at Lilac Inn* 93). In a typical example Nancy trails a young woman of questionable character; her reputation is soiled when Nancy traces her to a dilapidated building: "Surely, she wouldn't live in a place like this unless she were reduced to the lowest sort of poverty, and her clothing doesn't indicate that" (*Lilac Inn* 97).

Judy Bolton's family is more obviously middle class than Nancy's and her concern for and identification with people in lower socioeconomic classes is much greater. She maintains an ambivalent view about the way the social hierarchy is organized. At the start of the series, her family suffers from a tragedy that makes Judy sympathetic to people from lower economic classes. Her family's home is washed away in a flood, and they are forced to relocate to Farringdon. Because they have few possessions and little money left, they are loaned a run-down house in one of the poorer sections of town. Near their home, a row of houses, all exactly alike and all painted yellow, stood on a high bank and flight after flight of rickety steps led up to them. In almost every front yard clothes lines full of clothes, some white and some not so white, fluttered in the breeze. Judy set her lips tight together. She had not realized what it meant to be poor in a small city. (*Haunted Attic* 21)

The description is similar to Nancy's, as above, but the condescending tone of the Keene novel is obvious.

Although the Bolton family fortunes eventually improve, Judy tries to be friends with people of various social classes. When told by one of the richest girls in town that she should not associate with factory workers, Judy retorts, "[D]o you mean to tell me that just because I treat a few poor girls like human beings, all your crowd will turn me down?" (*Haunted Attic* 37). Judy tries to treat everyone in the same way, manifesting an implicit desire to subvert social norms and destroy the existing hierarchy that valorizes people in existing positions of power. She shares this feeling with her father, for "the kind-hearted doctor numbered his patients among rich and poor alike and his daughter, although considered one of the select 'down town' crowd, had broken the invisible barrier and succeeded in making friends among the mill workers too" (*Seven Strange Clues* 11).

In order to compare the detecting styles of Nancy Drew and Judy Bolton, it may be useful to compare one book from each series with similar titles and plots. The Nancy Drew book *The Secret in the Old Attic* (1944) concerns a poverty-stricken older man, Mr. March, whose son and daughter-in-law have died, leaving him custody of their only child. March's son, Fipp, had written music, which March hopes to locate and sell so that he can make a good home for his granddaughter. However, weird noises in the attic and several break-ins almost prevent March's dream from coming true. Judy Bolton, in *The Haunted Attic*, faces a similar dilemma, with an attic that has strange noises emanating from it as well as a connection to a crime family that her family fears will return. The difference in the detective styles used by Nancy and Judy is indicative of the way they function in the world. Mr. March originally asks Carson Drew to help him locate the music of his dead son. Nancy, because of sympathy for the older man and curiosity about why some of Fipp's music is currently being heard on the radio, takes charge of the case, with her father's encouragement. From then on, she occasionally asks for Mr. Drew's advice, but it is her mystery to solve. Nancy plays a dominant role, not only removing primary responsibility for the case from her father but also trying to control the lives of Mr. March and his granddaughter. She hires a maid for the Marches, brings in groceries, and sells valuable objects she finds in their attic so they can afford various homely comforts. One reason for Nancy's interest in Mr. March may be that he comes from an old family that has made a significant economic contribution to the region. His family estate is so large that it once had slaves and a stable of race horses. As Mr. March explains, "The Marches have been proud, well-to-do people—several generations of us in River Heights. I'm not going to be the one to ask for charity" (5). Nancy seems to have an implicit desire to restore the status quo and, indirectly, the official ideological system by helping the March family. Locating the music fulfills her need to solve mysteries and also brings those with social position back to their accustomed places in society. Nancy shows a more traditional feminine side through her nurturing of Susan, Mr. March's granddaughter, making sure that Susan is happy and has enough to eat. There is also a subplot about whether Ned will ask Nancy to a big dance at Emerson College. These aspects of the text pale in comparison to Nancy's heroic actions, which include chasing prowlers, escaping from a locked factory, and not only finding the music but solving a case of industrial espionage as well. Her ostensible reward is an evening gown, emblematic of something prized by a traditional woman, but her true reward is increased fame and satisfaction that order and social hierarchy have been restored.

Judy Bolton's mystery in *The Haunted Attic* is much more related to her family life. Rather than aggressively seeking a case to solve, like Nancy, Judy is drawn into a mystery when she investigates strange rapping noises in the house her family has moved into after the flood. Although she has curiosity about the sounds, her desire to solve the mystery is primarily for her family's comfort. She is also happy to direct her energy away from the trauma caused by the trouble adjusting to a new school and the social cliques there. Because her father is a doctor, well-to-do girls Lois Farringdon-Pett, Lorraine Lee, and Kay Vincent consider being her friends, but they are hesitant since the Bolton house is not in a "good" section of town. Judy is not impressed by the status quo and would rather break down the rigid hierarchies of Farringdon. She tells Peter Dobbs, one of her few sympathetic friends, that she is planning a Halloween party to bring together people from her school and the neighbors who work in the factories. While planning the party, she and her brother Horace discover several reasons why there are noises in the attic, all stemming from some stolen property that had been hidden there by earlier tenants. The discoveries are announced by Horace at the party, but they are the result of a collaboration among Horace, Judy, and several of her friends. However, the stolen jewels are less important to the novel than finding out the parentage of Peter Dobbs. In *The Haunted Attic* family relations are prized above material possessions.

Judy Bolton and Nancy Drew can both function as role models for young women within the world of adolescent series fiction because they are strong, intelligent women who can solve problems. However, readers should be aware that Nancy Drew, although a talented and independent young woman, tends to restore order to the official ideological systems of her society. Judy Bolton, in contrast, works in a collaborative way that subverts dominant values. Although both detectives can stand as feminist heroines, Judy Bolton's life is more expressive of the tension that exists when a woman tries to succeed in a nexus of systems—political, economic, ethnic, and gender—that define society.

Notes

1. Edward Stratemeyer, creator of the Stratemeyer syndicate, has been credited with starting the Nancy Drew series. However, the syndicate tended to send outlines of various adolescent titles to a stable of writers who would compose the actual text. The real authors were required to sign a contract pledging not to disclose their contribution to the series. His daughter, Harriet Stratemeyer Adams, claimed for years that she was Carolyn Keene. In 1980 the real authors of the Drew series were made public following a trial that focused on which publisher had the right to reprint old titles in the series. See Plunkett-Powell (23-40) and Benson for more information.

2. Nancy Drew as a character appears not only in the Nancy Drew mystery stories, but also in the more violent and sophisticated Nancy Drew Files, which started in 1986. Nancy Drew joins forces with the Hardy Boys for a number of Supermysteries, starting in 1988. Nancy Drew on Campus, where Nancy, Bess, and George all finally become college students, started in 1995. There is a Nancy Drew series for younger readers which also started in 1995. The heroine is eight-year-old Nancy who solves mysteries such as stolen birthday party invitations.

3. Janet Ghent, in an article in the *Oakland Tribune* on May 25, 1987, asserted that Sutton felt pressured by Grosset & Dunlap to phase out Judy Bolton in favor of Nancy Drew (qtd. in Caprio 182).

4. The need for young people to feel secure about themselves and their place in society is reflected by the very fact that they read series novels. As John Cawelti wrote about formula fiction in general, "Audiences find satisfaction and a basic emotional security in a familiar form; in addition, the audience's past experience with a formula gives it a sense of what to expect in individual new examples" (9). Although teachers and school librarians over the years have dismissed series fiction as "trash," Paul Deane notes that "one of their basic charms is familiarity. . . . Children come to know the characters in a series as they do actual friends and acquaintances" (52). Adolescent mystery series pro-

vide several different types of security for the reader, an anticipated structure, familiar characters, and as is true of many good mysteries, reassurance that "there is order in chaos, and that in a disorderly world, justice can triumph" (Moran and Steinfirst 116).

5. Judy develops some domestic skills once she marries and occasionally is shown cooking dinner. However, her nurturing skills are more developed, especially in the group of books featuring the supposed orphan Roberta who is introduced in *The Secret of the Barred Window* (1943) and reunited with her real parents in *The Clue of the Stone Lantern* (1950).

6. In the Nancy Drew on Campus series, Nancy breaks off with Ned because he seems too controlling.

7. Jones cites the revised edition of *The Hidden Staircase* as proof that the relationship between Nancy and Hannah Gruen has changed. "Hannah had become like a second mother to Nancy. There was a deep affection between the two, and Nancy confided all her secrets to the understanding housekeeper" (rev. ed. *Hidden Staircase* 10).

8. Craig and Cadogan note that "Nancy has never had to waste time wishing she were a boy; for all practical purposes she *is*. . . . She drives a blue roadster, knows how to handle a speed-boat and an aeroplane, round up steers, keep control of an unruly mount and stun a would-be kidnapper with a single blow" (150).

9. Carolyn Keene (Harriet Stratemeyer Adams in this instance) noted in 1978 that Captain McGinnis, the police chief of River Heights is "one of her best friends" ("Nancy Drew" 84) and that "Nancy has no illusions about the superiority of the police over her work as an amateur" (84), but there is much evidence to belie that.

10. In the new (1995) syndicated Nancy Drew television series, Nancy maintains this superior attitude towards the law. In one episode focusing on arranged marriages by Indian immigrants, Nancy cuts the wires of a home security system so that she can break into the suspected villain's house to obtain some information.

Works Cited

Benson, Mildred Wirt. "The Nancy I Knew." *The Mystery at Lilac Inn*. By Carolyn Keene. Bedford, MA: Applewood, 1994. n.p.

Caprio, Betsy. *The Mystery of Nancy Drew: Girl Sleuth on the Couch*. Trabuco Canyon, CA: Source, 1992.

Cawelti, John G. *Adventure, Mystery, and Romance: Formula Stories as Art and Popular Culture*. Chicago: U of Chicago P, 1976.

Craig, Patricia, and Mary Cadogan. *The Lady Investigates: Women Detectives and Spies in Fiction*. New York: St. Martin's, 1981.

Deane, Paul. *Mirrors of American Culture: Children's Fiction Series in the Twentieth Century.* Metuchen: Scarecrow, 1991.

Evans, Sara M. *Born for Liberty: A History of Women in America.* New York: Free, 1989.

Felder, Deborah. "Nancy Drew: Then and Now." *Publishers Weekly* 30 May 1986: 30-34.

Gilligan, Carol. *In A Different Voice: Psychological Theory and Women's Development.* Cambridge: Harvard UP, 1982.

Jones, James P. "Nancy Drew, WASP Super Girl of the 1930's." *Journal of Popular Culture* 6.4 (1973): 707-17.

Keene, Carolyn. *The Bungalow Mystery.* 1930. Rev. ed. New York: Grosset, 1960.

——. *The Clue of the Broken Locket.* New York: Grosset, 1934.

——. *The Hidden Staircase.* 1930. Rev. ed. New York: Grosset, 1959.

——. *The Mystery at Lilac Inn.* New York: Grosset, 1930.

——. "Nancy Drew." *The Great Detectives.* Ed. Otto Penzler. Boston: Little, 1978. 79-86.

——. *The Password to Larkspur Lane.* New York: Grosset, 1933.

——. *The Secret in the Old Attic.* New York: Grosset, 1944.

——. *The Sign of the Twisted Candles.* New York: Grosset, 1933.

Mason, Bobbie Ann. *The Girl Sleuth: A Feminist Guide.* Old Westbury: Feminist P, 1975.

Moran, Barbara B., and Susan Steinfirst. "Why Johnny (and Jane) Read Whodunits in Series." *School Library Journal* 31.7 (1985): 113-17.

Plunkett-Powell, Karen. *The Nancy Drew Scrapbook.* New York: St. Martin's, 1993.

Russell, Luana. "A Judy Bolton Mystery—'Blacklisted Classics.'" *Clues* 2.1 (1981): 35-44.

Spacks, Patricia Meyer. *The Adolescent Idea: Myths of Youth and the Adult Imagination.* New York: Basic, 1981.

Sutton, Margaret. *The Haunted Attic.* New York: Grosset, 1932.

——. *The Invisible Chimes.* New York: Grosset, 1932.

——. *Seven Strange Clues.* New York: Grosset, 1932.

——. *The Vanishing Shadow.* New York: Grosset, 1932.

——. *The Yellow Phantom.* New York: Grosset, 1933.

"Sutton, Margaret." *Something about the Author.* Ed. Anne Commire. Vol. 1. Detroit: Gale, 1987. 213-14.

Wertheimer, Barbara S., and Carol Sands. "Nancy Drew Revisited." *Language Arts* 52.8 (1975): 1131+.

Winn, Dilys. *Murderess Ink: The Better Half of the Mystery.* New York: Workman, 1979.

Zacharias, Lee. "Nancy Drew, Ballbuster." *Journal of Popular Culture* 9.4 (1976): 1027-38.

9

Nancy Drew As New Girl Wonder: Solving It All for the 1930s

Deborah L. Siegel

The New York Public Library's Rare Books Division recently welcomed a new addition: Alongside Thomas Jefferson's handwritten copy of the Declaration of Independence, patrons will soon be able to read the manuscripts of such other treasured documents as *Nancy Drew: The Mystery at Lilac Inn*.[1] Once classified and dismissed as "unacceptable" fiction by youth services librarians, the cultural guardians of an earlier era, Nancy Drew has since secured a place for herself on the shelves of one of the nation's prominent historical repositories. Indeed, Nancy has enjoyed a remarkably long shelf life, with new volumes produced annually to date. According to Karen Plunkett-Powell, author of *The Nancy Drew Scrapbook: Sixty Years of America's Favorite Teenage Sleuth*, the series is the best-known, longest-running girls' detective series in publishing history.[2] Since her arrival in 1930, Nancy has appeared in a variety of cultural forms, ranging from the series book to a cookbook and from a ballet to a rock group. In April 1993 (Nancy's official birthday month), the sleuth was the focus of an academic conference at the University of Iowa devoted to the feminist endeavor of "Rediscovering Nancy Drew." In 1995, Nancy celebrated her sixty-fifth year as America's eternally teen-aged amateur detective.

A resurgence of Drew-mania in recent decades, sparked, perhaps, by the publication of a new and updated line of Nancy Drew mysteries in 1986, has resulted in a significant amount of scholarship locating Nancy in the story of her production. As critics have noted, the character has evolved to keep up with the times. Nancy has worn the fashions and hairstyles of each decade, and her age has changed from sixteen to eighteen so as to allow her to drive legally in every state. She now sports designer jeans and spends time at the mall, and, perhaps most significantly, her famous blue roadster has become a blue Mustang GT convertible.[3] Whereas Nancy's concern was once limited to restoring stolen inheritances to deserving orphans who crossed her path in River Heights (her fictional midwestern hometown), she now chases international jewel thieves around the globe. Needless to say, the cultural and ideological currency of the figure of the girl sleuth has adapted to changing circumstances. Yet, Nancy is most often remembered as the multitalented superteen cruising the social landscape for clues that neither man nor boy can discern; the motherless daughter of a famous father, who frequently breaks the law in order to solve mysteries that baffle both father and the police; the self-appointed sleuth in a sports dress engaged in the serious business of restoring order to a chaotic and corrupt world. A number of feminist critics have commented on what the experience of reading Nancy Drew has meant for constructions of American girlhood across the decades. Interestingly, few have ventured beyond a cursory examination of the significance of Nancy Drew for the 1930s.[4]

What is frequently overlooked in critical analysis is that Nancy first captured the American imagination—or at the very least the imaginations of a critical mass of eight- to twelve-year-old girls—ten years after women had secured the right to vote and one year into the Great Depression. Given that a bold young female sleuth arrived to restore the financially downtrodden to their rightful state of ownership during a historical moment in which the financial order was radically and unexplainably upset, the question of what Nancy Drew emerged as a figure for becomes of increasing interest. For indeed, she arrived on the heels of the era that witnessed the rise of the revolutionary demographic and political phenomenon known as the New Woman—the social, economic, and political advancement of single, highly educated, economically autonomous bourgeois women who fought for professional visibility, eschewed marriage, espoused economic and social reform, and wielded real political power.[5] With the rise of the New Woman, Victorian constructions of femininity underwent drastic reconfiguration. In 1930 and beyond, the nation was still in the process of assimilating women's new sociopolitical status, as well as reorienting to the ever-shifting ideological construct of "the feminine." Images of "womanhood"—and with it "girlhood"—figured varyingly in the nation's popular imagination. In an effort to explore the politics of Nancy Drew for the 1930s, and thereby begin to fill a gap in Drew scholarship, I will discuss the early volumes of the series in relation to various discourses concerning class, gender, and American girlhood in circulation at that time. My approach combines close textual readings of these volumes with a consideration of various other materials, ranging from parents' guides to children's reading and advertisements for the series to contemporary scholarship on images of the New Woman and the Modern Girl. Contextualizing these early volumes with an analysis of sociological, political, and industrial concerns centered around the mass production and consumption of the fantasy that was Nancy Drew, this essay will interrogate the resonance of that fantasy for girls in the 1930s.

As media critics and other recent scholars of popular culture contend, mass art functions in a highly contradictory manner. Rather than assume that artifacts of popular culture function merely as transmitters of dominant ideology from "the culture industry" down to "the masses," the reading offered here assumes that popular fictional forms most often articulate conflicting discourses, and that the space of popular fiction engages an ideological economy that is far more complex, contradictory, and ambivalent than the orthodox Marxist position might imply. The work of feminist scholars such as Susan Bernstein, Tania Modleski, and Janice Radway has been particularly helpful in understanding how popular formulaic genres such as mid-nineteenth-century sensation fiction and late twentieth-century romance can be simultaneously reaffirming and subversive of traditional values, can both stimulate and allay social anxieties.[6] In light of the ever-growing interest in the complex relations between popular fiction and ideology, it has come time to apply such methods to a consideration of the consumption of girls' series fiction by the girls who read them first. It is my hope that the following study will serve as an early foray into a cultural history of a series that has had a profound effect upon subsequent generations of American women.

Quintessential Drewness

Given the character's various permutations over the years, how might one locate the "real" Nancy Drew? As Nancy Pickard writes in an introduction to the re-issued edition of the original *The Hidden Staircase* (1930), "The real Nancy Drew mystery may be the Mystery of the Appeal of Nancy Drew herself, and of her phenomenal attraction to successive generations of American girls" (n.p.). Even as Nancy's character has undergone multiple transformations, critics, readers, and publicists alike continue to point to the timeless quality of the "series-heroine-turned-superhero" figure. Of the attempts to pinpoint those aspects of Nancy's character that have sustained an avid readership over the years, almost all emphasize Nancy's ability to transcend history. An advertisement for the Nancy Drew Files (an updated series) reads:

Nancy Drew is back, transcending the decades to land in the 1980s. While the details have been updated . . . the essential Nancy is the same level-headed, good-girl heroine earlier generations of readers loved and admired. In retrospect, Nancy was always an independent, take-charge young woman long before it was fashionable to be one. She still is today. Returning in a new era and likely to be as popular as ever, Nancy Drew is proving herself a girl for all seasons as well as all readers. (n.p.)

The image this promotional description sells is that of ephemeral feminist Nancy Drew. This is the Nancy that feminist scholar and mystery writer Carolyn Heilbrun/Amanda Cross celebrates as "a moment in the history of feminism" (11) and about whom romance writer Eileen Goudge Zuckerman similarly testifies in *Publisher's Weekly,* addressing Nancy directly: "[L]et's be honest. It wasn't Ned Nickerson or even your father, Mr. Drew, who solved all those mysteries, was it. Long before *The Female Eunuch* and *The Women's Room,* you were my first feminist role model" (74).[7] It is this Nancy, too, who has inspired numerous women mystery writers—including Margaret Maron, Sara Paretsky, Nancy Pickard, and Amanda Cross—to go on to create their own adult versions of the female sleuth. The editors of the reissued originals released by Applewood Books in 1991 underscore this feminist answer to the mystery of Nancy's appeal, for each Applewood edition features an introduction by one of the aforementioned authors. Taken together, these introductions function as evidence of the contemporary construction of Nancy Drew as a feminist superheroine and testimony to the breadth of her influence.

Whether her admirers are girls who grew up to be feminist scholars/women mystery writers, intent upon reconstructing a lineage of headstrong, rebellious heroines who venture beyond the domestic sphere and challenge existing power structures or whether they are nostalgia buffs interested in reconstructing the "richness" and "simplicity" of a bygone era, as the dust jackets of the Applewood editions suggest, Nancy's notoriety is rooted in her status as a mythic figure. Many of the grown-up readers who construct a narrative of the series history for the popular press and for scholarly journals alike generally concern themselves with the task of pinpointing the exact qualities that constitute "Drewness." Whether Drewness translates as the chutzpah of a protofeminist or the clarity of vision assumed to represent the *zeitgeist* of an earlier season, Nancy's appeal across the decades—her very ability to transcend time—paradoxically makes her all the more "real" in the eyes of her celebrants. Among the most telling of the various attempts to get at that transcendent real of Nancy Drew is an excerpt from the "Series Bible" for the television series that premiered in the fall of 1995. The guide, which is used by the production staff, describes the show's characters, themes, and tone; the section below is titled "Style":

Nancy has a unique ability to make clear choices. She lives in a moral universe that is simple and straightforward. When we are in her world, those values will be reflected. It is something she cannot escape from, nor would she want to—it is her quintessential "Drewness." This quality is expressed in her wardrobe. She chooses clear, saturated colors that reflect her moral certainty. When Nancy wears green, it's not olive or sea foam or celadon. It's *green*. And the design is always deceptively simple, regardless of how au courant the particular outfit may be. Even at her young age, Nancy brings order to chaos. The objects in her apartment radiate a feeling of security; they have a timeless quality that is impossible to date. This creates a sense of heightened reality: a sofa is a *sofa*, not art deco or faux country or Seventies chrome and leather. It has a pure design that reflects a sofa's essence, its *truth*. Visually, Nancy's world will make sense. ("Nancy Drew's" 28)

The stereotype of Drewness recounted above suggests that Nancy functions as a signifier of that which stands outside the real of a world in flux; she exists as a fantasy of purity and stability in an increasingly complex universe. The green-ness of the green she wears, the sofa-ness of the sofa upon which she sits are markers of the world she inhabits, signs of a universe governed by Truth, Sense, and Certainty. In contrast to the feminist interpretation of Drewness as forward-looking and hence radical, then, the impulse of Drewness, as constructed in the "Series Bible," is conservative. Rather than making trouble, Nancy Drew makes order. This reactionary construction is assimilated by publicists for the Applewood editions, as well as through promotional packaging. A blurb on the dust jacket for *The Mystery at Lilac Inn* bears the following comment from a self-identified Drew fan: "In the space of the first three Nancy Drew books I returned to a world I thought long lost; an innocent and enchanted place where I have never felt so secure again."

In addition to radical and conservative constructions of Drewness, the escapist appeal of the series has also been foregrounded. Arthur Prager, author of *Rascal at Large or The Clue in the Old Nostalgia*, solves the mystery by attempting to name the fantasy that Nancy's ethereal universe provided readers in the 1930s. He locates the world of River Heights outside of history, noting that

[t]he books have an odd, timeless quality. . . . Like the land of Oz, Nancy Drew Country is in another time dimension, untouched by the outside world. The Depression came and went, followed by three wars, but they were passed unnoticed in Midwestern, suburban River Heights, where Nancy and her chums and their well-to-do country-clubbing parents live. Teen-agers all have new cars there. They buy unlimited pretty clothes, and they summer at fashionable resorts. They give lovely parties. . . . There was always plenty of gasoline for [Nancy's] convertible. Hungry kids, shattered by the announcement of bubblegum rationing, drowned their sorrows in Nancy's world. (76)

Prager and others drawn to the mystery of the Drew phenomenon attribute her success to the allure of the fantasy such readily available fiction promised a Depression-era audience. The Nancy that emerges from such descriptions is an aristocratic ideal—"untouched" by the shortages suffered by most during the early 1930s, "unlimited" by material restraints, unrestrained in the pursuit of leisure, and, above all, "lovely." In this respect, bourgeois Nancy embodied an ideal that might have been unavailable to some of her literally and figuratively hungry readers. Publicists for the earlier Grosset & Dunlap line join Prager in associating the initial success with the escapist pleasure such fantasies offered children of the Depression. Notes Nancy Axelrod, an editor and writer with the Syndicate from 1965 to 1984, "Nancy Drew grew out of the Depression and out of wanting to give children something to think about other than problems at home" (qtd. in Felder 30). According to these various accounts, Drewness, at the moment of its inception, was virtually removed from the material reality that most likely shaped the lives of a large portion of Nancy's readership.[8] The appeal and the allure of Drewness thus lay in its extreme ahistoricity.

While, on the one hand, these varied stereotypes of that which Drewness signifies—ephemeral feminist, transcendent morality, aristocratic ideal—are true, there is also a very real sense in which the original Nancy Drew Mystery Stories directly engaged the historical moment out of which they emerged. Unlike Dorothy or Alice, whose adventures are altogether otherworldly, Nancy exists as a daughter of the 1930s and, as we learn in the initial volume, as "a true daughter of the Middle West" (*The Secret of the Old Clock* 26).[9] Indeed, the social landscape Nancy inhabits bears literal references both to the region and to the time. Nancy functions as a historical figure on a number of different levels. As I shall argue, both the composite image of girlhood that Nancy embodies and the particular nature of the mysteries she solves function as the ideological markers of the era that was the 1930s.

Nancy Drew in the 1930s

Though she was neither the first nor the last of the girls series' heroines, Nancy Drew has been one of the few to achieve such mythic status. How and why did the myth originate? Nancy Drew first hopped behind the wheel of her shiny blue roadster and dashed onto the scene of American juvenile fiction in 1930 with the publication of *The Secret of the Old Clock*. The title was the first in a long line of Nancy Drew Mystery Stories written by a string of ghostwriters published under the shared pseudonym of "Carolyn Keene." The series was an immediate commercial success, and its heroine's rapid rise baffled even the publishing establishment that engineered her creation.[10] Nancy was the brainchild of the man known as the Henry Ford of the children's series mass market, Edward Stratemeyer. Founder of the Stratemeyer Syndicate, a highly successful fiction factory established in 1903, Stratemeyer created and produced dozens of different series, including the Hardy Boys, the Bobbsey Twins, and the Tom Swift series.[11] Nancy Drew was Stratemeyer's first female sleuth and his final creation before his death. Though Stratemeyer completed outlines for the first three Nancy titles, which he then farmed out to ghostwriters, he did not live to see the publication of the inaugural volume. Upon his death in 1930, his daughter Harriet Stratemeyer Adams took over and ran the Syndicate, with sister Edna's help, for the next fifty years. Though Adams introduced many of the elements that contemporary readers associate with Nancy Drew—including Nancy's loyal boyfriend Ned Nickerson and her two girlfriends, dainty Bess Marvin and tomboy George Fayne—the books continued to follow a formulaic plot informed by the stalwart combination of adventure and mystery.

In stark contrast to the girls' mystery series published contemporaneously with the Nancy books, most of which were set firmly within the domestic world of the school and home, the Nancy Drew Mystery Stories were mystery stories first and foremost. Among Nancy's contemporaries, the Dana Girls series (1934-1979) combined girl detective fiction with boarding school story, a genre fading in popularity by the 1930s. In the Kay Tracey series (1934-1942), Kay's authority was undercut by her clear identification as a school girl.[12] The Melody Lane mysteries (1933-1940), also published by Grosset & Dunlap, followed a formula similar in many aspects to that of Nancy Drew. Yet in contrast to the figure of the competent and confident girl sleuth, this series featured whining girls who met with disparagement from boys in every direction. In this series, men solved the problems that baffled women and girls. Other rivals outside of the Stratemeyer Syndicate included the Judy Bolton series (1932-1967) by Margaret Sutton. As Anne Scott MacLeod notes, though also a sleuth, Judy's stories were as much schoolgirl stories as detective yarns. As Judy's involvement with love-interest Peter Dobbs developed, the series became romance as much as mystery.

Celebrated for her remarkable independence, Nancy is never identified as a "mere" school girl, nor is romance placed at the center of the early narratives. The stories conveniently take place during the summer, which Nancy spends pursuing her calling as an amateur sleuth. Rather than reinforcing her status as a young girl subject to institutional authority and constraint, references to her affiliation with school serve to further our understanding of her extraordinary mental prowess: "Nancy had

studied psychology in school and was familiar with the power of suggestion and association" (*The Secret of the Old Clock* 88). Above all, Nancy
is identified as an adventurer. This psychologically attuned heroine not
only has "a natural talent for unearthing interesting stories" but soon
gains a "reputation for 'making things happen'" (*The Secret of the Old
Clock* 32; *The Clue in the Diary* 10). Though her readiness to initiate
adventures is frequently credited to her "pluck," Nancy's power is
unique. Her mobility, signaled by the infallible roadster that takes her
anywhere and everywhere she wants to go, is legendary. She occasionally travels in a pack, yet Nancy essentially operates alone, the primary
thinker and actor in her detecting adventures (MacLeod 314).

The name of the villain and the nature of the adventure change from
one volume to the next, but the basic formula of a typical early Nancy
Drew Mystery Story is as follows: Nancy befriends a poor unfortunate.
She soon learns that her new acquaintance has been robbed, cheated, or
manipulated into the loss of his or her fortune. Nancy single-handedly
takes on the "case," occasionally turning to her father, the well-known
lawyer Carson Drew, for assistance in legal matters. (In later volumes,
Bess and George come along for the ride, and Ned makes some rather
timely appearances.) After performing a slew of amazing feats for a girl
her age—she repairs motorboats, falls down a staircase without sustain-
ing head injuries, administers first aid, and offers correct psychological
diagnoses all in the first few installments, as various critics note—Nancy
hunts down the criminals and turns them over to the police. Danger is a
given. When wrong is righted and wealth restored, her father, the police,
and her beneficiaries gather round Nancy in awe. Someone usually
exclaims "We owe it all to you, Nancy Drew!" Nancy never accepts cash
for her services, but she does accept souvenirs. By Christmas of 1934,
the formula had proved a tremendous commercial success, for the Nancy
Drew Mystery Stories were outselling every other juvenile title on the
shelves.[13]

While a fair number of girls in books including the Dana Girls and
Judy Bolton joined Nancy in venturing beyond the home and actively
pursuing adventures of their own, perceptions of girlhood, as articulated
by members of the children's book publishing industry, varied from one
review to the next. In an era marked by changes in women's status and
shifting constructions of femininity, publishers' conjectures about what
modern girls wanted were full of contradictions. While some lauded
what they saw as images of more active and adventurous girls in books,
others complained about the relative dearth of satisfying story lines. In
an essay entitled "Girls in Books" (1934), Helen Forbes celebrated the
fact that young heroines were becoming thoroughly "modern":

This year girls in books are hard at work. Whether their background is town or country they are aware of the problems of today and although they dream and hope and love clothes and romance as much as any girls in stories ever delighted in those joys of life, they spend most of their waking hours in good solid work. They no longer putter about, contented with "helping," but look squarely at the future as boys are supposed to do.

Without sentimentality they seem to have decided that honest labor bears a lovely face. It must be admitted that they also expect that it will get its just reward, although they all are not so sure of that as they were in the days when *The Five Little Peppers* were being written. Today they want recognition of their abilities, not special dispensations because they are girls. (370)

The rhetoric of equality employed here to describe the needs and desires of girls in books resonates strongly with that of the suffrage movement of a decade earlier. The construction of the Modern Girl as she who labors in the world, who demands recognition of her competency rather than protection for her difference, who "looks squarely at the future as boys are supposed to do" yet who is "not so sure" of the benefits she will reap as a result of her new status bespeaks an anxiety about the long-term effects of the changing sociopolitical status of grown women and raises questions about the aspirations and expectations of a generation of women-in-training.

Calling attention to the needs of such a generation, Mary Graham Bonner, author of a 1926 parent's guide to children's literature, spoke out against the paucity of satisfying fiction geared toward an audience of modern adolescent girls. Bonner suggested that girls—and their fictional counterparts—continued to be held to a double standard:

Perhaps the main reason why there are not better books for girls between the ages of 13 and 18 is because of a fear on the part of both publishers and authors. Boys can have books of adventure. They can be made interesting. But girls aren't even supposed to have these to the same degree, even in these pro-feminine days. (109)

Book dealer Polly Ann Scott reiterated this critique in an article for *Publisher's Weekly* in 1930 (the year of Nancy's debut). If Bonner bemoaned the lack of "interesting" heroines for girls in the face of an emergent feminism and chided book publishers for their lack of imagination, Scott firmly located the problem in industry politics. Wrote Scott, "There seems to be more time, energy and money devoted to the betterment of *boys'* books" (3150). Moreover, she argued, mystery, as a sub-genre of adventure, was off-limits to girls. For Scott noted that while a boy in his teens "demands" mystery stories, "[m]ost girls like a good mystery story, but the average mother will not purchase them" (3148).

Regardless of what might have been construed by genteel mothers as a transgressive purchase, girls in the 1930s were consuming Nancy Drew Mystery Stories in droves. In order to read the series as a fantasy born of that era, it is crucial to understand the material conditions under which such a fantasy circulated. What was the status of the Nancy Drew series? How might an understanding of the status of the children's series book genre further an understanding of the politics of Nancy Drew for the 1930s? For in stark contrast to the latter-day celebration of the mass-produced fantasy of Drewness, librarians and other reviewers of children's literature in the 1930s castigated the series book, along with other works of popular fiction, as utterly "unacceptable" reading material. While bookstores eagerly lined their shelves with Stratemeyer Syndicate titles throughout the 1930s, the Nancy Drew Mystery Stories were emphatically banned from those of the nation's public libraries.[14]

The unacceptability of the genre was supported by various rationales. To begin with, mass-produced fiction betrayed a Victorian ideal held dear to the children's librarian. The librarian's role was to mediate the sacred connection between author and child. The very concept of the modern fiction factory undercut the romantic notion of authorship. Through the production and consumption of series books, then, the special relationship between the author and the child, a relationship that librarians in the early decades of the twentieth century worked hard to help cultivate, was obliterated. Moreover, series books were of questionable literary merit. Marked by the predictable formulas, the wooden characters, the poor quality of the writing, the coincidence-ridden plots, series books fell into the category of nonliterature. In the 1934 essay entitled "Girls in Books," Helen Forbes lamented, "It seems sad that [authors of sets and series do] not think it worthwhile to give modern girls pictures of life that they can recognize as authentic" (371). "Sad" is a mild word for the outpouring of outrage leveled by librarians against the inauthenticity of series books. More often, criticism of the "false" view of life portrayed in the average series book was couched in a rhetoric of moral indignation. The construction of the series book as outrageously false and inauthentic often went hand in hand with a critique of series books as "sensational."[15]

Nancy and her Syndicate siblings were notably absent from children's selection lists and prestigious annual awards, and the Nancy mysteries were not reviewed in highbrow journals of children's literature such as *Horn Book*. Writes Esther Green Bierbaum in her discussion of the relationship between librarians and series books,

As far as librarians and their bibliographic power structure were concerned, such books did not exist. Certainly, they were not to be given shelf room. They were, moreover, not discussed in children's literature textbooks. The H.W. Wilson Company did not print catalogue cards for them. They were nonbooks. (94)

Not content with simply excluding the series books from the shelves, librarians publicly spoke out against the threat such books posed to young minds. As library historian Christine Jenkins points out in her study of the regulatory function of the nation's librarians, the youth services librarian from the late nineteenth century through the 1930s defined her role as protector of public morals in print, a literary mother, guardian of the well-being of the child's intellect.[16] Bad selection habits developed early on were understood to jeopardize a child's future health. Librarians serving young readers thus condemned popular mass market children's series books in a rhetoric of alarm: the series book was condemned as "unhealthy," "unwise," and even "guaranteed to blow boys' brains out" (West 137). Critics of popular juvenile fiction urged parents to join in the effort to counter the temptation of such mass-market trash with a steady diet of life-sustaining classics.

In her parent's guide to children's reading, for instance, Bonner warns "serious" readers of the temptations of popular fiction, which she refers to as "that cheap kind of book pastry" masquerading as solid fare (113). The literary value of children's fiction, and of fiction in general, was often appreciated through food analogies; the series book, of course, was poison, an addiction that, once indulged, required the administration of a remedy. Bonner reflects upon her own illicit childhood experience of reading "the terrible little book" with the "amazingly lurid and daring title" (111). She tells of a clandestine meeting between herself and a girlfriend during which they had agreed to "do something [they] had never done before" (111). Having "smuggled" the contraband into her room, she and her unsuspecting girlfriend read and read on until they could read no more. Much to her chagrin, Bonner found the writing to be "dull, flat, endlessly stupid." When the experience became "more than [they] could endure," she and her friend "almost automatically . . . reached for [her] copy of 'Nicholas Nickelby' and read it, late into the night—the little yellow book and its ilk banished voluntarily and forever from [their] reading hours" (111-12). Bonner's confession provides an apt summary of the threat of—and the proposed solution to—the series book phenomenon as perceived by its critics in the 1930s. Designed to lure young readers with its sensational albeit poorly written tales, mass-produced fiction was not worth the pulp upon which it was printed. Nothing could manage the menace of poorly written fiction like a good dose of Dickens. Good children would naturally resist the temptation, or, if tempted, would instinctively know to temper the bad fare with books far more suitable, sanctioned, and accepted.

The menace—and its critique—finds its antecedent in the nineteenth-century dime novel. Dime novels and weekly magazines appeared after 1860, first as western adventures and increasingly as detective stories by the 1880s and 1890s.[17] As Catherine Sheldrick Ross argues in her historical overview of the hostility librarians harbored against popular fiction at the turn of the century, the rise of the dime novel stimulated anxieties about "uncultivated readers with low tastes reading too many books, enjoying it too much, and acquiring false views of life" (210). Such fears about the reading practices of low people with low tastes betray both a class bias on the part of genteel critics and a general anxiety about the excessive pleasure involved in the act of mass cultural consumption.[18] By the turn of the century the era of the dime novel was almost over, but the fiction factory methods carried over in the production of series books. The same rhetoric that was used to dismiss dime novels in the 1880s was applied to the Stratemeyer Syndicate series books throughout the first half of the twentieth century. If anxiety about excessive consumption of mass fiction dulling the mind and weakening the spirit bore a particular urgency during the era that first witnessed the proliferation of mass culture, this anxiety was heightened for regulators of children's reading material. For according to the critical construction of juvenile "trash," the baseness lay not merely in the quality of the writing but in the ideological effects that the act of reading series books worked upon the young, impressionable mind.

If the taint of mass culture imbued the Nancy Drew Mystery Stories with the status of "forbidden" reading in the 1930s, we must, of course, examine the politics of the story the mysteries tell. As a generic rule, of course, the early Nancy Drew books tell the same story over and over again. What kept hungry Depression-era readers coming back for literally more of the same? If the formulaic narrative of popular generic forms provides a cultural realm in which competing value systems exist in a state of sustained dissonance and in which social conflict is ultimately and repeatedly worked out, as Thomas Schatz argues in *Hollywood Genres: Formulas, Filmmaking, and the Studio System* (29), what then was the conflict that the Nancy Drew Mystery Stories engaged? What, specifically, was the cultural work of the story that is repeated in the early series volumes? What was the real mystery that Nancy was called upon to solve?

Nancy Drew and Constructions of Girlhood

To answer this question, let us consider the characterization of the girl heroine. While Nancy, as a detective, restored order to the disorderly world around her, the appeal of Nancy Drew also lay in the character's ability to transcend paradox. During a time when competing codes of feminine conduct raised questions about standards of behavior for women-in-training, an adolescent heroine—half woman, half girl— cruised gracefully onto the scene and offered an ideal of girlhood that resolved all contradiction. Nancy functioned historically—and politically—as a liminal figure. Suspended at the threshold of childhood and adulthood, marrying the Victorian and the modern, Nancy's character bridged many worlds. Interestingly, there has been little attempt to locate this contradictory characterization—what might indeed be Nancy's quintessential Drewness—within a historical framework.[19] Turning to a discussion of verbal and visual portraits, motif, and narrative strategy, I argue that Nancy Drew in the 1930s "solved" the contradiction of competing discourses about American womanhood by entertaining them all.

Martha Banta's wide-ranging analysis *Imaging American Women: Ideas and Ideals in Cultural History* provides a useful model for interpreting the resonance of images of femininity as they appear in popular cultural forms. In her study of iconographic images of America and American womanhood beginning in 1876, Banta delineates three symbolic forms—the Beautiful Charmer, the Outdoors Girl, and the New England Woman—through which the "meaning" of femininity was constructed at various moments in American history. While Banta's concern ends with the year 1918, these forms and their corresponding implications for representations of femininity mobilized in and by the popular imagination carried over well into the culture of the 1920s and beyond. Banta argues that these three types were distinct yet overlapping:

If each type stands opposed at times to the other two (the Charmer charms, the New England Woman thinks, the Outdoors Girl cavorts), there are points at which the three begin to overlap and even to merge. The particular mark of the times becomes apparent when the images of the Beautiful Charmer, the New England Woman, and the Outdoors Girl evolve into yet another type—the New Woman. (47-48)

This notion of intersecting and merging images of femininity is useful in generating a reading of the verbal portraits and visual iconography of the early Nancy Drew. For although only an adolescent, the early Nancy is indeed an amalgamation of the three types that Banta identifies here. At the tender age of sixteen, Nancy amalgamates not quite into the New Woman but rather, perhaps, into the New Girl.

Nancy is Outdoors Girl, Beautiful Charmer, and New England Woman all in one. According to Banta's reading, the image of the Outdoors Girl bore various meanings. On the one hand, she could signal the vigor of determined young women making real changes in American society, or on the other, she could stand for the fun-loving girls who offer no direct threat to the status quo (Banta 88). In the case of Nancy Drew, athletic ability—and mechanical aptitude as well—functions as a sign of the heroine's infallibility. There is nothing this girl cannot or will not do. As critics like to point out, Nancy fixes motorboats in darkness, changes tires in thunderstorms, rides horses, and sleeps outside. She spends her leisure time living dangerously. Nancy's yen for physical activity and physical adventure is presented as more a need than a whim. She never loses an athletic contest; her physical prowess is a hallmark of her character. Nancy walks faster, endures inclement weather better, and carries heavier loads than any of her less physically fit companions. Her physical strength imbues her with confidence. When her chums would run the other way, Nancy remains strong, reassuring them that "[t]hree capable, muscular, brainy girls such as we are shouldn't need any help" (*The Clue in the Diary* 174). Her physical endurance signals her utter fearlessness, her resolve, and above all her boundless capacity to go out into the world and "make things happen."

Nancy is the girl of superb bodily health (Outdoors Girl), yet she simultaneously is the girl with the pretty face (Beautiful Charmer). While the early books are filled with the comments of passersby who remark upon Nancy's extraordinary physique and remarkable energy, readers are just as often reminded that Nancy's appearance conforms to standards of classical, angelic female beauty. She is introduced as "an unusually pretty girl, fair of skin with friendly blue eyes and golden curly hair" (*The Hidden Staircase* 11). Her father, Carson Drew, is repeatedly charmed by his angelic daughter, as in the following passage narrated from his point of view: "Now, as he gave her his respectful attention, he was not particularly concerned with the [case] but rather with the rich glow of the lamp upon Nancy's curly golden bob. Not at all the sort of head which one expected to indulge in serious thoughts, he told himself" (*The Secret of the Old Clock* 2). Carson is characterized as an indulgent father, and his weakness, it appears, is often triggered by Nancy's attractive exterior.

Above all, however, Nancy's beautiful head does indeed indulge in serious thoughts (New England Woman). For next to her excellent driving abilities (references to her "skillful" handling of the roadster abound), her mind is her superpower, the mechanism through which she makes order out of chaos where others have sorely failed. At the turning point of each of the early narratives, Nancy assesses the situation and accesses her powers of ratiocination: "As Nancy gazed at the disorder about her, she searched her mind for an explanation. What could it mean?" (*The Secret of the Old Clock* 123). A descendent of the scientific male detective of the nineteenth century—a teenage, female Sherlock Holmes—Nancy bears little resemblance to the sensational heroines of crime stories created by nineteenth-century women writers who, as critics note, infused elements of romance, sentimentalism, sensationalism, and domesticity into the mystery genre. Instead, there is a constant emphasis on Nancy's rational detection method, and each story becomes a showcase for Nancy's clear thinking, remarkable competence, and steady nature. Even while under incredible emotional duress, as during an episode in which she is locked in the air-tight closet of an abandoned house and left to starve, Nancy remarkably keeps her cool: "I'm only wasting my strength this way," she tells herself. "I must try to think logically. If I don't, I'm lost" (*The Secret of the Old Clock* 135). Nancy privileges logical reasoning; rarely does the reader see Nancy acting upon hunches, notions, or (feminine) intuition. Through successive demonstrations of the sheer force of her mental brawn, Nancy repeatedly wins the admiration and respect of the police. She becomes an authority to whom adult male authorities pay homage.

The only child of Carson Drew, "a noted criminal and mystery-case lawyer known far and wide for his work as a former district attorney" (*The Secret of the Old Clock* 1), Nancy is in every respect her father's daughter. Though she depends upon her mind to get her through a tight situation, in the early volumes Nancy occasionally carries her father's revolver. Armed with this appendage, Nancy is often *more* effective than the police. While she may carry a gun and act like a boy, her "feminine" identity is never in question. Lest she be mistaken for the mannish Lesbian type, another caricature of womanhood in circulation at the time, readers are never quite allowed to forget that she is a girl. Nancy is occasionally required to perform her femininity, letting out her "longest and loudest feminine scream" in one instance to convince a potential ally that she is no "robber boy" impersonating a "lady," as is feared (*The Secret of the Old Clock* 138). As an amalgamation of Outdoors Girl, Beautiful Charmer, and New England Woman, Nancy transcends the paradox of changing and competing scripts of feminine conduct by playing them all. Following on the heels of the New Woman, Nancy represents a composite type that spoke to the paradoxes of changing expectations for feminine behavior in the 1930s, an era in which women's recently reconfigured sociopolitical status was still being absorbed.

If Nancy's character is an amalgamation of various types, her visual repertoire is similarly diverse. When considered as a whole, the early dust jackets and interior illustrations of the Nancy Drew Mystery Stories paint a portrait of the title character as a sophisticated and genteel woman/girl.[20] While Nancy has the same physical features in the first seven volumes (blond hair, blue eyes), the details of her overall visual representation vary greatly from one illustration to the next. In the first volume alone there are at least two contradictory images, or forms, for the figure of the teenage sleuth. The illustration that graces the cover of *The Secret of the Old Clock* cuts a rather cartoonish figure of Nancy as New Woman (New Girl): dressed in a three-quarter-length skirt, strapped stiletto heels and a Flapper-like cap, New Woman Nancy is on the move. She is painted here in midflight, running, no doubt, for her very life. Yet the expression on her face exudes that hallmark self-confidence. In stark contrast, an interior illustration included in the same volume portrays Nancy as a Victorian waif; designed to showcase Nancy in a dangerous situation, this portrait constructs Nancy as a helpless young innocent. Fearful and small before the older, taller man who threatens her, and whose body stands between Nancy and the viewer, Nancy literally blends into the scenery, one hand clutching her throat, the other braced for support upon the half-open door behind her. Whereas most of the early cover illustrations suggest that Nancy is more woman than girl, in this particular drawing, as in others that suggest her vulnerability, her identification as a girl outshines the image of the independent woman. The juxtaposition is typical of the portraiture contained in the early volumes.

Once again, we see that Nancy "solves" the contradiction of competing discourses of femininity—whether the opposition be girl/woman or Victorian/Modern—by striking a composite pose. Yet even as the character oscillates between the prescribed roles of New Woman/Girl and Victorian Waif, perhaps the greatest constant in the early characterization is her ability to transcend gendered expectations altogether. Young and unmarried, Nancy rejects social conventions, especially those imposed upon women. In the early volumes, Nancy is not interested in Ned Nickerson's tentative overtures; she has more "important" things to do—like solve crime and save her hometown from immanent corruption. Nancy echews domesticity and with it the attendant scripts dictating stereotypical "feminine" behavior. On the one hand, she does not tend to domestic chores because, as the only daughter of a well-to-do father, she does not have to; domestic duties at the Drew household are conveniently managed by the elderly housekeeper Hannah Gruen. Yet, on the other hand, Nancy's license to engage in extra-domestic activity and participate in the conventionally male universe of mystery and adventure serves to liberate her from restrictive codes of female conduct. With no mother around to instruct her in the social codes of "proper" womanly conduct, Nancy Drew is free to literally and figuratively inherit her father's business.

While Nancy herself is at home in a stereotypically masculine economy, those with whom she comes into contact often express discomfort in the face of Nancy's gendered transgressions. Villains are naturally dumbfounded when they learn that they have been outwitted by a girl. Nancy's stereotypically "unfeminine" behavior—which ranges from infiltrating a counterfeiting ring to changing tires in the rain—is attributed, in part, to her father's progressive parenting. "And you've often said you wanted me to grow up self-reliant and brave," Nancy reminds Carson Drew when he hesitates before granting her permission to spend a night in a haunted mansion (*The Hidden Staircase* 53). When Carson worries about his daughter's safety, Nancy retorts, "You really wouldn't want me to be sedate and prim, would you, Daddy?" (*The Secret of Red Gate Farm* 206). At times, however, Nancy surprises even her father with her unconventional demands, as evident in the following exchange:

"Now what?" her father asked, smiling as she burst in upon him. "Is it a new dress you want?"

Nancy's cheeks were flushed and her eyes danced with excitement. "Don't try to tease me," she protested. "I've stumbled onto something important, and I want information!" (*The Secret of the Old Clock* 62)

Such good-natured exchange, a recurrent narrative device, serves both to foreground Nancy's difference and to manage, through humor, the threat such transgressions ultimately pose to a patriarchal order that depends upon the maintenance of rigid binaries. Though he may occasionally tease his daughter, suturing her into the "proper" female role of consumer and negating her attempt to fashion herself as a consumer of knowledge, Carson Drew most often stands behind his female progeny's forays into a typically male realm of danger, adventure, and "information." Indeed, he provides emotional, financial, and legal backup at the bat of Nancy's golden eyelashes.

In many respects, Nancy Drew exists as a wish fulfillment. As critics have noted, in a time when girls her age had mothers, curfews, and at least some domestic duties, Nancy was free to go out into the world and have adventures. Yet rather than an ahistorical fantasy, the character of Nancy Drew was very much a product of the 1930s. Beautiful *and* active; endowed with physical *and* mental prowess; Outdoors Girl, Beautiful Charmer, New England Woman condensed into one New Girl; Nancy embodied a composite image, one that united conflicting codes of

Victorian and Modern femininity. Unbounded by domestic responsibility and graced with remarkable mobility, she was able to indulge, volume after volume, in noble yet unconventional pursuits. This brings us, in conclusion, to the question of what Nancy initially pursued. What, on another level, was the ideological work of the mystery early Nancy Drew was repeatedly called upon to solve?

"Not to Be Administered unto but to Administer"

As a New Girl, and as a member of the genteel class, Nancy goes out into the world and performs a social service. A true daughter of Wellesley graduate Harriet Stratemeyer Adams—who was herself a New Woman in many respects—Nancy lives by the motto of her creator's college: Non Ministrari Sed Ministrare (Not to Be Administered unto but to Administer). Indeed, Adams is said to have given Nancy Wellesley's motto. Unlike her predecessors of the Progressive Era who sought to ameliorate social ills conditioned by forces of industrialization and urbanization through social reform, Nancy performs a civic service of a slightly different nature and on a slightly grander scale. A New Girl transposed to the 1930s, Nancy Drew undoes the work of the Great Depression.

The narrative pattern of the early volumes follows a formula in which Nancy emerges as a kind of Robin Hood for the 1930s, one who restores wealth and property to the temporarily disenfranchised. In the initial volumes, the narrative is set into motion when Nancy takes pity on a newly destitute acquaintance. In *The Clue in the Diary*, Nancy happens upon a poor little girl at the local fair and muses, "Somehow, I can't bear to think of that little girl without the things she needs. I mean to visit the family one of these days and see just how they are getting along" (4). Her beneficiaries are never by nature members of the disenfranchised class. Rather, it is clear that conditions of economic depression have brought on hard times. Whether through explicit references to economic hardship or through the narrative device of a sudden reversal of fortune, it becomes evident that the Depression has been the cause of her new friend's great misfortune.

By narrative's end, Nancy single-handedly has restored riches to the deserving poor, has punished the undeserving and greedy nouveau riche, and in so doing has restored the American Dream to those "rightfully" entitled to it.[21] By the closing chapters, the run-down farmhouses where her less fortunate friends have been forced to live are given fresh coats of white paint. Her beneficiary's parents and grandparents purchase new clothes and new cars. All are eternally grateful and shower Nancy with praise: "I was completely discouraged before [Nancy] came," says Millie Burden's grandmother in *The Secret of Red Gate Farm*. "Now everything is changed" (204). The early Nancy Drew formula thus functions as a totalizing narrative, a fantasy of resolution during an era that struggled to find resolution to the unsolvable crime of economic depression. Just as the figure of Nancy herself can be interpreted as a historical construct, so too the ideology informing the formulaic narrative can be understood to be historically contingent.

The initial volumes of the Nancy Drew series, then, directly engaged the Depression by offering a fantasy of resolution, rather than an escape. Drew Country exists not as a retreat from history, but as a site at which historical conflict, however displaced, is nonetheless played out through the novel's formulaic narrative. Whereas the ahistorical readings of "Drewness" offer a solution to the mystery of Nancy's mythic appeal, Nancy's composite image, her particular brand of morality, and her status as a genteel ideal are all in fact historical constructs rooted in the sociopolitical culture of the early 1930s. While other series heroines might have shared some of Nancy's traits, no other girls' series spoke to the conditions of the 1930s in quite the same way. Indeed, the fantasy of this particular girl sleuth presented young female readers of the early 1930s with an ideal of girlhood and a solution to the Depression that was not to be found elsewhere. In the final analysis, Nancy Drew emerged not merely an ahistoric fantasy—a girl wonder—but as a New Girl wonder who would leave an indelible mark upon the imaginations of generations of American women to come.

Notes

1. Paramount Publishing, owner of the Stratemeyer Syndicate, donated its collection of 7,000 volumes and 150 cartons of arcana to the library in 1993. The collection should be catalogued and made accessible to patrons by 1996. See Douglas Century, "Herman Melville . . . T. S. Eliot . . . Franklin W. Dixon?"

2. By 1982, over 60 million of the Nancy books had been sold worldwide, in hardcover and paperback, including translations (Felder 32).

3. Betsy Caprio, in *The Mystery of Nancy Drew: Girl Sleuth on the Couch*, identifies five different Nancys within the first 107 volumes of the Nancy Drew Mystery Stories, each shaped by changing ghostwriters and/or publishers' demands. Caprio's categories are as follows: "Classic Nancy," "Transitional Nancy," "Two-Dimensional Nancy," "Watered-Down Nancy," and "Shape-Shifting Nancy."

4. For readings of Nancy Drew as a product of the 1930s, see Deidre Johnson, "Nancy Drew—A Modern Elsie Dinsmore?" and James P. Jones, "Nancy Drew: WASP Supergirl of the 1930s."

5. For an extended discussion of the New Woman, see Carroll Smith-Rosenberg, *Disorderly Conduct: Visions of Gender in Victorian America* 245.

6. See Susan David Bernstein, "Dirty Reading: Sensation Fiction, Women, and Primitivism"; Janice Radway, *Reading the Romance: Women, Patriarchy, and Popular Literature*; and Tania Modleski, *Loving with a Vengeance: Mass-Produced Fantasies for Women.*

7. In recent decades, *Ms.* has featured a number of articles discussing the impact of Nancy Drew as a feminist role model. See for instance Jane Ginsburg, "And Then There is Good Old Nancy Drew" (1974); "Nancy Drew, Yuppie Detective" (1986); and Jackie Vivelo, "The Mystery of Nancy Drew" (1992). For a sample of feminist criticism that reads the girl sleuth as proto-feminist, see Ellen Brown, "In Search of Nancy Drew, the Snow Queen, and Room Nineteen: Cruising for Feminist Discourse;" Bobbie Ann Mason, *The Girl Sleuth: A Feminist Guide*; and Carolyn Stewart Dyer and Nancy Tillman Romalov, *Rediscovering Nancy Drew.*

8. While to my knowledge there has been no empirical research specifically documenting the demographic and economic makeup of the readership of the Nancy Drew series in the 1930s, reports from the Civilian Conservation Corps (CCC) and the National Youth Administration (NYA), two federal agencies established in 1933 and 1935 respectively in response to the plight of young people during the Depression, suggest that a large portion of the nation's youth was directly affected by the economic crisis. Lester V. Chandler, author of *America's Greatest Depression, 1929-1941*, estimates that the number of young people unemployed at the nadir of the Depression was at least four million and notes that "the heavy impact of unemployment on the young, their lack of opportunity to develop skills, rising unhappiness and dissent among them, and the large number of young nomads roaming the country" contributed to a general mood of frustration among a large percentage of the nation's youth (203).

9. The fictional metropolis of River Heights is often assumed to be located somewhere in Iowa. Iowa was home to Mildred Wirt Benson, one of the early and most talked-about Carolyn Keenes. For a discussion of the social landscape of River Heights, see Susan Brooker-Gross, "Landscape and Social Values in Popular Children's Literature."

10. The first hardcovers hit the stores in late March 1930 and quickly sold out. As a *Fortune* analyst wrote in 1934, "Nancy is the greatest phenomenon among all the fifty-centers. She is a best seller. How she crashed a Valhalla that had been rigidly restricted to the male of her species is a mystery even to her publishers" ("For It Was Indeed He" 87).

11. Most Stratemeyer series books were published by Grosset and Dunlap, a publishing establishment that marketed itself throughout the 1930s as "the bread-and-butter line" of the book business (Grosset & Dunlap 1152). The concept of a book-packaging house was not a new idea in publishing, but Strate-

meyer capitalized on it with unprecedented success. The master plan for series production was both innovative and cost effective: Stratemeyer created the basic concept for a series and constructed plot outlines for the initial volumes, which he would then farm out to free-lance ghostwriters to whom he paid a paltry fee. All proceeds from book sales went to the Syndicate.

12. For a more detailed account of the Nancy Drew spinoffs, see Anne Scott MacLeod, "Nancy Drew and Her Rivals: No Contest." As MacLeod points out, both the Dana Girls and Kay Tracey were Stratemeyer products designed to capitalize on the Nancy Drew phenomenon, yet neither approached the record sales of their originator.

13. As MacLeod notes, the formula of a middle-class girl sleuth, one parent (a father), two chums, one boyfriend, and a car became a standard pattern in series fiction after Nancy Drew, yet again none enjoyed the success of their originator (315).

14. The stigma of the series book endured, for it was not until the mid 1970s that the New York Public Library system carried the Nancy Drew Mystery Stories.

15. For instance, in an essay published in the 1935 issue of the *Ontario Library Review*, entitled "The Menace of the Series Book," Lucy Kinloch called the series book "worthless, sordid, sensational, trashy and harmful books" and "*the* menace to good reading" (74, 75; qtd. in Bierbaum).

16. In 1930, 91.4% of the nation's librarians were female (Jenkins 604). Librarian Mary E.S. Root was one of the many to include Stratemeyer titles in "Not to be Circulated" lists.

17. Edward Stratemeyer himself wrote twenty-two episodes of the Nick Carter weekly dime detective stories in the 1890s, and it was from there that he went on to create mystery series explicitly for juveniles. For an extended analysis of the dime novel, see Michael Denning, *Mechanical Accents: Dime Novels and Working-Class Culture in America*.

18. With the confluence of increasing rates of literacy among the working classes and advances in the printing industry making cheap pulp fiction readily available, genteel critics were anxious about the detrimental effects of the excessive consumption of bad fare upon the newly literate and otherwise "impressionable" consumer. Instead of extensively reading a few sanctioned and largely religious texts for the purposes of moral edification, such as the Bible and *Pilgrim's Progress*, "impressionable" readers—code for women, children, and members of the working class—were now indiscriminately consuming vast quantities of the cheap secular materials pouring from the presses (Ross 210).

19. For a discussion of Nancy's liminal status as an adolescent, see Kathleen Chamberlain, "The Secrets of Nancy Drew: Having Their Cake and Eating It Too." See also Deidre Johnson, "Nancy Drew—A Modern Elsie Dinsmore?"

20. Illustrator Russell H. Tandy was responsible for the early dust jackets, glossy frontispieces, and interior line drawings. Beginning in 1937, the interior drawings were dropped from the books. According to Plunkett-Powell, the inspiration for the original Nancy was a professional New York model named Grace Horton. Yet Nancy does not begin to resemble this model until the 1940s, whereafter her image proceeds to take on recognizable traits of movie stars, including Carole Lombard.

21. Blaming the Depression on the greed of immoral individuals was a common interpretation in circulation during the era. In 1932, the editors of *Horn Book*, a quarterly children's journal comprised largely of reviews of "serious" children's literature (the "healthy" kind) published by the Women's Educational and Industrial Union since 1926, asked Joseph L. Snider, an associate professor of Business Statistics of the Harvard Graduate School of Business Administration, to explain to young people "why the United States and the world in general are having such a hard time; what has caused 'the depression;' and what can be done about it" (Snider 151). In an essay entitled "Can We Solve Our Problems?" the first of a series of three short articles carried by the journal in August 1932, November 1932, and May 1933, Snider argues that one of the causes of the development of this "dangerous situation" was "unwise action on the part of individual people" (153). He goes on to suggest in the third article, "Greed is perhaps the outstanding element in the moral breakdowns which carry us into unwholesome business and speculative excesses and then precipitate us into the depths of economic depression" (62). The Nancy Drew Mystery Stories play into this interpretation, for the early narratives blame the Depression on greed and punish the culprits, thus eradicating the evil responsible for the economic catastrophe. The villains are often caricatures of greed, nouveau riches with bad taste and, as Jones suggests, no class.

Works Cited

Banta, Martha. *Imaging American Women: Ideas and Ideals in Cultural History.* New York: Columbia UP, 1987.

Bernstein, Susan D. "Dirty Reading: Sensation Fiction, Women, and Primitivism." *Criticism* 36.2 (1994): 213-41.

Bierbaum, Esther Green. "Bad Books in Series: Nancy Drew and the Public Library." *Lion and the Unicorn: A Journal of Children's Literature* 18.1 (1994): 92-102.

Bonner, Mary Graham. *A Parent's Guide to Children's Reading.* New York: Funk, 1926.

Brooker-Gross, Susan R. "Landscape and Social Values in Popular Children's Literature." *Journal of Geography* 80.2 (1981): 59-64.

Brown, Ellen. "In Search of Nancy Drew, the Snow Queen and Room Nineteen: Cruising for Feminist Discourse." *Frontiers: A Journal of Women's Studies* 13.2 (1993): 1-25.

Caprio, Betsy. *The Mystery of Nancy Drew: Girl Sleuth on the Couch.* Trabuco Canyon: Source, 1992.

Century, Douglas. "Herman Melville . . . T. S. Eliot . . . Franklin W. Dixon?" *New York* 6 Sept. 1993: 23.

Chamberlain, Kathleen. "The Secrets of Nancy Drew: Having Their Cake and Eating It Too." *Lion and the Unicorn: A Journal of Children's Literature* 18.1 (1994): 1-12.

Chandler, Lester V. *America's Greatest Depression: 1929-1941.* New York: Harper, 1970.

Denning, Michael. *Mechanic Accents: Dime Novels and Working-Class Culture in America.* London: Verso, 1987.

Dyer, Carolyn Stewart, and Nancy Tillman Romalov, eds. *Rediscovering Nancy Drew.* Iowa City: U of Iowa P, 1995.

Felder, Deborah. "Nancy Drew: Then and Now." *Publisher's Weekly* 30 May 1986: 30-34.

Forbes, Helen. "Girls in Books." *Horn Book Magazine* Nov. 1934: 370-73.

"For It Was Indeed He." *Fortune* Apr. 1934: 86-89.

Ginsburg, Jane. "And Then There Is Good Old Nancy Drew." *Ms.* Jan. 1974: 93.

Grosset & Dunlap. Advertisement. *Publisher's Weekly* 20 Sept. 1930: 1152.

Heilbrun, Carolyn. "Nancy Drew: A Moment in Feminist History." *Rediscovering Nancy Drew.* Iowa City: U of Iowa P, 1995. 11-21.

Jenkins, Christine A. "'The Strength of the Inconspicuous': Youth Services Librarians, the American Library Association, and Intellectual Freedom for the Young, 1939-1955." Diss. University of Wisconsin-Madison, 1995.

Johnson, Deidre. "Nancy Drew—A Modern Elsie Dinsmore?" *Lion and the Unicorn: A Journal of Children's Literature* 18.1 (1994): 13-24.

Jones, James P. "Nancy Drew: WASP Supergirl of the 1930s." *Journal of Popular Culture* 6.4 (1973): 707-17.

Keene, Carolyn. *The Secret of the Old Clock.* New York: Grosset, 1930.

——. *The Hidden Staircase.* Facsimile ed. Simon, 1930. Reprinted by Applewood Books, 1991.

——. *The Mystery at Lilac Inn.* Facsimile ed. Simon, 1930. Reprinted by Applewood Books, 1994.

——. *The Secret at Shadow Ranch.* Facsimile ed. Simon, 1931. Reprinted by Applewood Books, 1994.

——. *The Secret of Red Gate Farm.* Facsimile ed. Simon, 1931. Reprinted by Applewood Books, 1994.

——. *The Clue in the Diary.* Facsimile ed. Simon, 1932. Reprinted by Applewood Books, 1994.

Kinloch, Lucy M. "The Menace of the Series Book." *Ontario Library Review* 19.2 (1935): 74-76.

MacLeod, Anne Scott. "Nancy Drew and Her Rivals: No Contest." *Horn Book Magazine* May-June 1987: 314-22.

Mason, Bobbie Ann. *The Girl Sleuth: A Feminist Guide.* New York: Feminist P, 1975.

Modleski, Tania. *Loving with a Vengeance: Mass-Produced Fantasies for Women.* New York: Methuen, 1982.

The Nancy Drew Files. Advertisement. The Cooperative Children's Book Collection, University of Wisconsin-Madison. March 1988.

"Nancy Drew's Moral Universe." From the Series Bible for the syndicated television program, "Nancy Drew." *Harper's Magazine* Nov. 1995: 28.

Pickard, Nancy. "I Owe It All to Nancy Drew." Introduction to *The Hidden Staircase.* Facsimile ed. Simon, 1930. Reprinted by Applewood Books, 1991.

Plunkett-Powell, Karen. *The Nancy Drew Scrapbook.* New York: St. Martin's, 1993.

Prager, Arthur. *Rascals at Large; or, The Clue in the Old Nostalgia.* New York: Doubleday, 1971.

Radway, Janice. *Reading the Romance: Women, Patriarchy, and Popular Literature.* Chapel Hill: U of North Carolina P, 1984.

Robbins, Louise. Personal interview. 17 Nov. 1995.

Ross, Catherine Sheldrick. "If They Read Nancy Drew, So What?" *Library and Information Science Research* 17.3 (1995): 201-36.

Schatz, Thomas. *Hollywood Genres: Formulas, Filmmaking, and the Studio System.* Philadelphia: Temple UP, 1981.

Scott, Polly Ann. "Children's Books through the Eyes of the Dealer." *Publisher's Weekly* 28 June 1930: 3147-50.

Smith-Rosenberg, Carroll. *Disorderly Conduct: Visions of Gender in Victorian America.* New York: Oxford UP, 1985.

Snider, Joseph L. "Can We Solve Our Problems?" *Horn Book Magazine* Aug. 1932: 151-53.

Vivelo, Jackie. "The Mystery of Nancy Drew." *Ms.* Nov.-Dec. 1992: 76-77.

Wartik, Nancy. "Nancy Drew, Yuppie Detective." *Ms.* Sept. 1986: 29.

West, Mark I. "Not to Be Circulated: The Response of Children's Librarians to Dime Store Novels and Series Books." *Children's Literature Association Quarterly* 10.3 (1985): 137-39.

Zuckerman, Eileen Goudge. "Nancy Drew vs. Serious Fiction." *Publisher's Weekly* 30 May 1986: 74.

Contributors

Kathleen Chamberlain is associate professor of English and Women's Studies at Emory & Henry College. A long-time collector and student of juvenile series fiction, she has published articles and reviews on Nancy Drew, on series about the American West, on girls' career series, and on dime-novel representations of the Lizzie Borden case. She currently serves as a member of the governing board of the American Culture Association and is working on a book-length study of American girls' school stories.

Sherrie A. Inness is assistant professor of English at Miami University. Her research interests include children's literature, nineteenth- and twentieth-century American literature, popular culture, and gender studies. She has published articles on these topics in a number of journals, including *American Literary Realism, Edith Wharton Review, Journal of American Culture, Journal of Popular Culture, NWSA Journal, Studies in Scottish Literature, Studies in Short Fiction, Transformations*, and *Women's Studies*, as well as in four anthologies. She is also the author of *Intimate Communities: Representation and Social Transformation in Women's College Fiction, 1895-1910* (Popular Press, 1995).

Deidre A. Johnson is associate professor of English at West Chester University. She serves as area chair of the Dime Novels/Pulps/Juvenile Series Books division of the Popular Culture Association and as assistant editor of *Dime Novel Round-Up*. Her articles about series books, dime novels, and the Stratemeyer Syndicate have appeared in a variety of publications, including *The Lion and the Unicorn* and *Rediscovering Nancy Drew* (University of Iowa Press, 1995); she has presented papers on these topics as an invited speaker at several national conferences. She is also the author of *Stratemeyer Pseudonyms and Series Books* (Greenwood Press, 1982) and *Edward Stratemeyer and the Stratemeyer Syndicate* (Twayne, 1993).

Sally E. Parry is assistant professor of English and assistant to the chairperson of the Department of English at Illinois State University.

Two years ago she was awarded the Herb Sanders Award for Outstanding Academic Advisement and last year received a national Certificate of Merit from the National Academic Advising Association. Her published work includes articles on adolescent fiction, Sinclair Lewis, Marjorie Kinnan Rawlings, Margaret Atwood, and Upton Sinclair, and chapters in three books: *Visions of War: World War II in Popular Literature and Culture, Germany and German Thought in Contemporary American Literature and Cultural Criticism*, and *Sinclair Lewis at 100*. She is executive director and former president of the Sinclair Lewis Society. She also served as assistant to the executive director of the Modern Language Association.

K. L. Poe is a doctoral student in English literature at Loyola University Chicago. Her research interests include gender studies, culture studies and children's literature, specifically the works of L. M. Montgomery, Lenora Mattingly Weber, Maud Hart Lovelace, and Lois Lenski. Her research on these authors has resulted in articles which have appeared in several publications and have been presented at national conferences. She is actively involved in the promotion of children's literature, both in programs encouraging children to read and in the recovery of out-of-print texts.

Maureen E. Reed is a Ph.D. student in the program in American Civilization at the University of Texas at Austin. Her research interests include women's studies, nineteenth- and twentieth-century American literature and painting, the American Southwest, and alternative formats for teaching American cultural history. Before attending graduate school, she worked in museum education at the Bayou Bend Collection in Houston and the Metropolitan Museum of Art, and taught U.S. history at the Woodberry Forest School in Virginia.

Nancy Tillman Romalov is currently teaching at Drake University, after receiving her Ph.D. in American Studies from the University of Iowa. She has taught courses in children's and adolescent literature, as well as in women's studies and German, at the University of Iowa, Pacific Lutheran University, and the University of Montana. She is co-editor of the recently published anthology *Rediscovering Nancy Drew* (University of Iowa Press, 1995) and is also co-editor of the forthcoming collection, *Reading Nancy Drew* (University of Iowa Press). She has published articles in a variety of journals, including *The Lion and the Unicorn, Children's Literature Association Quarterly*, and *The Journal of Popular Culture*.

Deborah L. Siegel is a doctoral candidate in the Ph.D. program in English and American Literature at the University of Wisconsin, Madison. Her research interests include nineteenth- and twentieth-century American women's narrative, autobiography, and popular culture. She has recently published articles on the interconnections between young women and feminism. Before entering graduate school, she worked as a Research Associate at the National Council for Research on Women, where she investigated reports on issues including sexual harassment, women and philanthropy, and "political correctness."

Index

Abbott, Jacob, 3-4

Abbott, Martin, 115

Alcott, Louisa May, 4, 120

Alpine Path: The Story of My Career, The (Montgomery), 18

Anne of Avonlea (Montgomery), 23, 24, 66

Anne of Green Gables (Montgomery), 2, 12, 17-18, 20-22, 23, 24, 25, 32, 63, 125n.2

Anne of Ingleside (Montgomery), 19, 26, 29

Anne of the Island (Montgomery), 24, 25

"Anne Shirley: The Heroine Shines and Fades" (Atwell), 71n.6

Anne of Windy Poplars (Montgomery), 19, 20, 27

Anne's House of Dreams (Montgomery), 27-28, 30

Appleby, Joyce, 123

Army Surgeon, 133

Ashmun, Margaret Eliza, 37, 40, 41, 42, 45, 46-48, 50, 51

Atwell, Mary, 71n.6

Audacious Kids: Coming of Age in America's Classic Children's Books (Griswold), 2

Auerbach, Nina, 15

Avery, Gillian, 16

Aviator Girls, 84

Axelrod, Nancy, 164

Baden-Powell, Lord, 91

Baldwin, Douglas, 17

Banfield, Beryle, 114-15

Banner, Lois, 106

Banta, Martha, 171, 172

Berg, Temma F., 23

Betsy and Tacy Go Over the Big Hill (Lovelace), 116-17

Betsy and the Great Wall (Lovelace), 101

Betsy in Spite of Herself (Lovelace), 109

Betsy-Tacy Companion, The (Whalen), 102

Betsy-Tacy series, 101-02, 104
  as a model, 122
  feminist views, 121
  reviews of, 102
  stages of, 108-09
  women's history, 120, 121

Betsy's Wedding (Lovelace), 110, 112

Billman, Carol, 86n.4

Blanchard, Amy, 92-93

Blumin, Stuart, 38-39, 54

Bierbaum, Esther Green, 168-69

Bildungsroman, 22

Bonner, Mary Graham, 167, 168

"Boy Scout Handbook, The" (Fussell), 89, 90

Boy Scout series, 98n.3

Boy Scouting, 91, 94

Boys' adventure series, 4

Cadogan, Mary, 63, 66, 67, 68, 120, 157n.8

Campbell, Marie C., 30

Camp-Fire Boys in the Philippines, The (Hoover), 95

187

Hoover, Latharo, 95
Hornibrook, Isabel, 93
Hope, Laura Lee, 79, 81
House in Good Taste, The (DeWolfe), 51
Hunt, Lynn, 123
Hunt, Peter, 11n.2,
Huse, Nancy, 31

Imaging American Women: Ideas and Ideals in Cultural History (Banta), 171, 172
In Camp with the Muskoday Camp Fire Girls (Blanchard), 92-93
Inglis, Fred, 17, 32
Inness, Sherrie A., 7
Invisible Chimes, The (Suton), 147
Isabel Carleton at Home (Ashmun), 45
Isabel Carleton books, 46,
    class and boundaries, 45-46, 53
    class and gender, 37-38, 40
    and domesticity, 49-50
    and ethnicity, 54
    plot in, 45
    the series, 42
Isabel Carleton in the West (Ashmun), 44, 52, 54
Isabel Carleton's Friends (Ashmun), 44
Isabel Carleton's Year (Ashmun), 43

Jackson, Susan, 22
Jacob, Margaret, 123
Jenkins, Christine, 169
Johnson, Deidre, 6-7, 177n.4
Jones, James P., 152
"Josephine Lawrence: The Voice of the People" (Guilfoil), 60
Judy Bolton, 145-46, 147, 165
    class, 153, 154
    as compared to Nancy Drew's

detective style, 154
connection to others, 148
as a role model, 156
traditional family life, 150

Keene, Carolyn, 145-46, 153, 157n.9
Kohl, Herbert, 121-122
Kolodny, Annette, 70
Kornfeld, Eve, 22

Langland, Elizabeth, 37, 39-40, 56n.2
Language and Ideology in Children's Fiction (Stephens), 119
Lansing, Elizabeth, 142-43n.2
Large, Jean, 96
Lawrence, Josephine, 59-60, 62, 70
Lears, T. J. Jackson, 86n.5
Lerner, Gerda, 32
Linda Lane Experiments (Lawrence), 71n.7
Linda Lane series, 59, 60, 70-71
    characteristics of, 65-66
    depiction of the orphan, 59, 61
    summary of stories, 61
    women in, 62
Linda Lane's Big Sister (Lawrence), 70
Linda Lane's Problems (Lawrence), 72n.10
Little Kingdom of Home, The (Sangster), 50
Little Women (Alcott), 4, 120
Lovelace, Maud Hart, 101, 106-07, 109, 112, 116-18, 125n.3
Lucile, the Torch Bearer (Duffield), 93

MacLeod, Anne Scott, 4, 165, 179n.12
MacLulich, T. D., 25
Majority Finds Its Past: Placing Women in History, The (Lerner), 32
Matthews, Glenna, 49